ST. MA...BRARY

S0-BBR-327

Presented To

St. Mary's
College of Maryland
Library

By William Aleck Loker

Date 12-68

NIXON

A POLITICAL PORTRAIT

Earl Mazo and Stephen Hess

NIXON

A POLITICAL PORTRAIT

1817

HARPER & ROW, PUBLISHERS

NEW YORK, EVANSTON, AND LONDON

For Mac

Chapter 1 is adapted from *The Republican Establishment*. Copyright © 1967 Stephen Hess and David S. Broder.

NIXON: A POLITICAL PORTRAIT. *Copyright © 1968 by Earl Mazo and Stephen Hess. Copyright © 1959 by Earl Mazo. Printed in the United States of America. All rights reserved. No part of this book may be used or reproduced in any manner whatsoever without written permission except in the case of brief quotations embodied in critical articles and reviews. For information address Harper & Row, Publishers, Incorporated, 49 East 33rd Street, New York, N.Y. 10016.*

FIRST EDITION

LIBRARY OF CONGRESS CATALOG CARD NUMBER: 68-31363

G-S

28428

Contents

Authors' Note   vii

1. INTRODUCTION   1
2. EARLY YEARS, 1913–1937   9
3. WHITTIER LAWYER, 1937–1942   24
4. CONGRESSIONAL CAMPAIGN, 1946   34
5. HISS CASE, 1948   44
6. SENATORIAL CAMPAIGN, 1950   64
7. IKE'S RUNNING MATE, 1952   76
8. THE FUND, 1952   91
9. CHECKERS SPEECH, 1952   111
10. COMMUNISM AND MCCARTHY, 1950–1954   126
11. "DUMP NIXON" MOVEMENT, 1956   144
12. IKE'S ILLNESSES, 1955–1957   158
13. LATIN AMERICAN MISSION, 1958   165
14. MOSCOW MISSION, 1959   188
15. HOME WORK, 1953–1961   207
16. PRESIDENTIAL CAMPAIGN, 1960   220
17. PRIVATE CITIZEN, 1961   251
18. GUBERNATORIAL CAMPAIGN, 1962   264
19. WALL STREET LAWYER, 1963–1968   283
20. POLITICS, 1963–1968   293

Appendix: Nixon Speaks, 1968   309

Index   317

Authors' Note

WE think that in at least one respect this book is a unique undertaking: it is a book based on a book. Or, in architectural terms, it might be considered a new building raised on an existing foundation.

In 1959 Harper & Brothers published *Richard Nixon: A Political and Personal Portrait,* by Earl Mazo. It was thought "determinedly fair [and] well-balanced" (by the Washington *Post*), while the *New York Times* said that "historians would be fortunate if it set a new pattern for political biography." Yet much has happened in the decade since it was researched and written. Not only has Richard Nixon continued his active career in public life, but new sources have appeared to help explain his earlier activities, notably his own memoirs, *Six Crises* (Doubleday, 1962). Moreover, a somewhat longer historical perspective has given new shape or meaning to past events. (Harold Stassen's attempt to deny Nixon renomination for Vice-President in 1956 seems less important to our story in 1968 than it was in 1958, for instance.) Therefore, although we have built on a sturdy foundation, this is designed as a new book, rather than a revised edition.

The introductory chapter is adapted in part from *The Republican Establishment,* by Stephen Hess and David S. Broder, published by Harper & Row in 1967. We are grateful to our friend and colleague, Dave Broder, for allowing us to benefit by his research and insight.

Much helpful information on Nixon's legal career in New York comes from an unpublished manuscript by William M. Treadwell, Assistant Professor of Law at Gonzaga University, Spokane, and Joel M. Fisher, Assistant Professor of Political Science at California State College, Fullerton. We acknowledge our debt to these learned gentlemen.

Among others who have given us help and encouragement are Christine Buckley, Walter de Vries, Irving Ferman, Leonard Garment, Vera Glaser, Herbert Klein, Victor and Patricia Lasky, Leroy Sandquist, Sherman Unger, Anne Volz, W. Allen Wallis, John C. Whitaker, Rose Mary Woods, Nancy Lyons, and Nicole MacInnes.

EARL MAZO
Washington, D.C.

STEPHEN HESS
Cambridge, Massachusetts

May 31, 1968

NIXON

A POLITICAL PORTRAIT

1 ✵ *Introduction*

EARLY in November of 1961 arid southern California experienced a disastrous series of brush fires, which played an eerie game of leapfrog from house to house in the fashionable Bel Air and Brentwood sections of Los Angeles. Richard M. Nixon, at the time, was renting a movie director's English Tudor house on North Bundy Drive. Across the street flames destroyed the residence of actor Joe E. Brown. And, as the first press photographer reached the scene, the former Vice-President was hosing down a small fire. "He got a true action photo," a Nixon aide later commented. But true to the code of the *paparazzi*, the photographer insisted that Nixon re-enter his house and pose at the door with a suitcase. The next day almost every newspaper in the country showed Nixon with suitcase instead of Nixon with hose. For the real Nixon looked posed and the posed Nixon looked real.

The search for "the real Nixon" now has been a popular pastime since 1948. He has been written off as finished, *kaput*, done for, washed up and all through in national politics more often by more people and more erroneously than anyone else in American life. In 1948, his closest friends thought he was signing his political death warrant by taking up Whittaker Chambers' charges against Alger Hiss. In 1952, when the "Nixon fund" story broke, Thomas Dewey and other top Eisenhower advisers told him bluntly to get off the national ticket. In 1960, having survived a minor challenge to his nomination, he proceeded to lose a presidential campaign which most Republican politicians thought he should have won, and by a margin so close that the second-guessers had a field day at his expense.

In 1962, incredibly even to himself, he lost the governorship of California to Democratic incumbent Edmund G. Brown. "And the morning after the election," as *Time* reported, "Nixon wrote his own political obituary" with his bitter attack on the press. "Barring a miracle," said the magazine on November 16, 1962, "his political career ended last week."

But he was alive again in 1964. Alive enough for his backers to run him in three of the presidential primaries and even for Nixon himself to consider a bid to be Vice-President. All failed, and in January, 1966, Nixon told William Lawrence of ABC News, "As a practical political realist, I do not expect to be a nominee again."

Yet 14 months later, in March, 1967, a group of reputable and well-financed Republican professionals announced the formation of a Nixon for President committee, whose chairman asserted with confidence, "When the time is right, we will have a candidate." And sure enough, on January 31, 1968, Nixon declared, "America needs new leadership . . . and I believe I have found some answers. I have decided, therefore, to enter the Republican presidential primary in New Hampshire."

What kind of man pushes himself this way?

The same kind of introverted, self-contained, driven man who, as a student, worked uncomplainingly one hot North Carolina summer for a law professor at Duke, handcranking an inky mimeograph machine eight hours a day in an airless cubicle. Nixon did this drudgery during the Depression because it paid well and he needed the money to complete law school. Then and thereafter, the end justified the means.

For Richard Nixon, the end is power—specifically the incomparable power of the presidency. He moved toward it in a spectacular, meteoric career. Congressman at 33. Important congressman at 35. Senator at 37. Vice-President at 39. Only two-term Republican Vice-President at 43.

So often the prize seemed close. In 1955, the serious heart attack of President Eisenhower made Nixon, in effect, the acting President. A year later, Eisenhower contemplated retiring, a step that undoubtedly would have led to Nixon's nomination and very probably to his election. Through other illnesses in Eisenhower's second term, Nixon was forced to prepare himself mentally for the task of national leadership that could at any moment have been thrust on him.

And then in 1960 came his chance, his shining chance. He campaigned flat-out for nine weeks, sparing himself nothing, trying to manage every detail of the race. He charged from Baltimore to Indianapolis to Dallas to San Francisco the first day, and rarely slackened the pace thereafter. He drove himself, his staff and his wife, who went every step of the way with him, to the edge of exhaustion, sustaining himself through the endless, weary days of parades and speeches and crowds in the only way a presidential candidate can survive the ordeal of the campaign—by knowing the value of the prize at the end of the road.

And then he lost. Lost by an eyelash—118,574 votes—less than one vote per precinct, two-tenths of one percent of a total vote of nearly 69 million.

He lost honorably. He debated his less-well-known opponent, although he knew it was not the politically expedient thing to do. He firmly dampened the religious issue among his own adherents, while Catholics were swinging over decisively to his opponent. He refused to challenge the results in Illinois and Texas, where there was substantial suspicion of vote fraud and where a shift would have given him the election.

In almost two centuries of the American Republic, as Richard Nixon, amateur historian, knows, no man defeated for the presidency and denied renomination in the subsequent election has later been able to recover sufficient political strength to achieve election. The man whose career most parallels Nixon's is the long-forgotten John C. Breckinridge of Kentucky. As presiding officers of the Senate, Vice-Presidents Breckinridge and Nixon—exactly 100 years apart—officially announced their own presidential defeats, the only two men to officiate at their own political wakes.

But unlike Breckinridge, who faded to obscurity after losing to Lincoln, Nixon may still prove to be a political Lazarus. Though Richard Rovere dismisses him as a "connoisseur of defeat," each time Dr. Gallup takes the pulse of the nation Nixon is right there on the "most admired" list. Above all else, Richard M. Nixon is durable.

This durability may, in a strange way, be related to the eternal puzzling over what makes Nixon tick. It is hard to avoid concluding that the "mystery of Nixon" has added years to his political life. Who, after all, still wonders about "the real Harold Stassen"? After dishonor, the worst thing a public figure can do is bore. And in a celebrity culture where the sway of an author is measured in weeks, of a pop singer in months and of an athlete in years, Nixon's is measured in decades.

Washington editor Meg Greenfield wrote in the spring of 1967 a savagely funny lament for herself and the 9,534,000 others who turned 21 in time to cast their first presidential vote in 1952—the members of what she called the Nixon Generation:

> At regular intervals now, ever since that first vote in 1952, my generation has either been supporting or opposing Richard Nixon. The psychological implications of this fact are staggering: half of us have lived our whole adult life as a series of dashed hopes and disappointments, while the other half have passed the same period in a condition of perpetual anxiety over the prospect that he would succeed. . . . What distinguishes us as a group from those who came before and those who have come after is that we are too young to remember a time when Richard Nixon was not on the political scene, and too old reasonably to expect that we shall live to see one.

If Americans as a whole have long been almost equally divided between the fans and the critics of Richard Nixon, there is one subgroup in the society—the intellectuals—whose verdict has been a nearly unanimous vote of no confidence. As New York writer Victor S. Navasky said, "You can't have voted for Richard Nixon and be a member of the New York intellectual establishment."

Ironically, Nixon fancies himself as an intellectual. He told Jules Witcover of the Newhouse newspapers in a 1966 interview: "I wish I had more time to read and write. I'm known as an activist and an organizer, but some people have said I'm sort of an egghead in the Republican party. I don't write as well as [Adlai] Stevenson, but I work at it. If I had my druthers, I'd like to write two or three books a year, go to one of the fine schools—Oxford for instance—just teach, read and write. I'd like to do that better than what I'm doing now." One of the few commentators who saw this side of Nixon was Stewart Alsop, who, in a 1960 book, noted that there was "an oddly academic flavor to much of Nixon's conversation" and credited him with having an "inquiring, absorptive mind" and being "a rather judicial-minded fellow, a bit academic in manner."

Probably in the true sense, Nixon is an intellect but not an intellectual, at least if one accepts the distinction of R. H. S. Crossman, the Labourite Member of Parliament, that "what distinguishes the intellectual from other politicians is his application of theoretical arguments to the solution of practical problems." For Nixon, like most politicians, has little interest in general and abstract theory. He probably would agree with novelist Saul Bellow, who told a startled group of Communist writers in Poland, "Ideology is a drag."

Yet Nixon is an intellectual to the extent that he thrives on the play of the mind. It is the part of politics that he enjoys most and at which he is best. Even in his agitated state during the so-called "last press conference," he reminded the reporters, "I have welcomed the opportunity to test wits with you."

He also has a claim to the respect of intellectuals on much of his record. His attitude has been firmly internationalist, including early and consistent advocacy of large-scale foreign aid, a position that was hardly designed to win him votes. On civil rights, Nixon had the solidest record of any man in the Eisenhower administration—and before that, a voting record in Congress that matched John F. Kennedy's and surpassed that of Lyndon B. Johnson. Moreover, he was one of the first Republicans in the country to take on the John Birch Society, again a stand that was hardly calculated to win him votes.

Nixon uses well the intellectual's own key tools—language and logic. His syntax is generally orderly, his arguments are systematically arranged and he even has the ability to turn

a phrase. The essay he submitted to meet the admission requirements for the New York bar was described as the finest
of the thousands that have come in through the years.

Why then the breach between Nixon and the intellectuals?
The antagonism for many goes back to the Hiss case and the
McCarthy era. Clearly no young politician could have more
thoroughly damned himself from the start than the freshman
congressman, lowliest member of the House Committee on
Un-American Activities, when his persistence and constant
probing led to the conviction of Alger Hiss. "My name, my
career," Nixon was later to write, "were ever to be linked
with the decisions I made and the actions I took in that case."
The accusation against Hiss was a challenge to all that
liberalism had represented for over 20 years. Most intellectuals, feeling deeply threatened, reacted with righteous indignation. Many whom the public would recognize as the "best
people" rallied instinctively to Hiss's cause; the President of
the United States called the investigation a red herring. When
Hiss was finally convicted, some of the intellectuals saw in
the conviction elaborate conspiracy theories—"forgery by
typewriter," homosexuality, counterespionage. Wrote sociol-
ogist E. Digby Baltzell, "Many [intellectuals] refused to face
the evidence, and most never forgave Richard Nixon for his
part in the case."

Nor did they forgive him for his equivocal relationship to
the junior Senator from Wisconsin, Joseph R. McCarthy, and
the style of politics that bore his name. Nixon, like most
Republicans, found no reason to denounce McCarthy publicly
until McCarthy turned his guns on the Republican administration of which Nixon was a part. Meantime, Nixon's own
speeches in the 1954 Congressional campaign were tinged
at times with the McCarthy hallmark.

Politicians are not averse to hyperbole. Some get away
with it; others do not. Early in his political career Nixon was
one of the latter. For example, his unsophisticated manipula-
tion of the word "traitor" while campaigning for the Republican Congressional candidates more than a dozen years ago
hardened the bitter enmity of President Truman, House
Speaker Sam Rayburn and other major Democratic figures
whose dislike for Nixon stemmed originally from his aggres-

sive investigation of Alger Hiss. The "traitor" episode occurred in 1954, while Nixon was stumping solidly Democratic
Texas in behalf of Republican candidates. In bidding for the
votes of grass-roots Democrats he charged that "real Democrats are outraged by the Truman-Acheson-Stevenson gang's
defense of Communism in high places" and Truman, Stevenson and Acheson were "traitors to the high principles in which
many of the nation's Democrats believed." Was that nothing
more than an appeal for the votes of "real Democrats," as
the Republicans insist? Or was it slick juggling, meant to
highlight "traitor" and "Communism in high places"?

But the intellectuals' dislike of Nixon goes beyond these
questions of substance. It involves something else on which
they place great emphasis—style.

Nixon's public style is that of the college debater. He debates well, controlling his material and his environment as a
good debater must. Like most good debaters, he learned the
technique young, and its habits are almost impossible to
shake. The debater strives for points, not images. Not surprisingly, Nixon's speeches are loaded with "my three-point
program," "a seven-point plan." In an age of television, debater Nixon is geared to the big hall, not the living room.

The debater oversimplifies. Confined to a few minutes, his
technique is to hit and run. It is quick and graphic to label
Senator Fulbright and his supporters as the "appeasement
wing" of the Democratic party. The equation appeasement =
Munich = sellout may not be lost on the audience, although
Nixon could claim that the dictionary definition is not pejora-
tive. Over the years Nixon has made an art of the almost-in-
nuendo, an art for which Democrats from Lyndon Johnson
on down will not forgive him.

What upsets the intellectuals even more is Nixon's tone,
perhaps best recalled by the famous "Checkers speech" of
1952 in which he invoked his wife's "respectable Republican
cloth coat" and his daughters' "little cocker spaniel dog" in
defense of an $18,000 fund which a group of wealthy Cali-
fornians had raised for Nixon's use in politicking between
campaigns. While this sort of thing may be a bit unctuous, the
Checkers speech undoubtedly saved Nixon's political career.
But while Nixon may be a dirty word in the intellectual cor-

ridor from Cambridge to Washington, he has proved his capacity to thrill millions of other Americans, especially in the Middle West, South and Rocky Mountain regions.

Ultimately what may disturb Nixonphobes the most is a belief that he is putting them on. They may shake their heads sadly at a "true believer" like Governor George Romney of Michigan, but Richard Nixon they quickly accuse of just saying the things he thinks the electorate wants to hear.

David S. Broder, the chief political correspondent of the Washington *Post,* in an April, 1968, column examining the harsh attacks on President Johnson by Robert Kennedy and Eugene McCarthy, wrote that the Democratic Senators' "charge of fomenting civil war and the implication of un-Americanism are unjustified, even by the loose standards of political rhetoric." Added the writer: "Had Richard M. Nixon uttered those words, it would have been taken by many as proof that 'the old Nixon' had returned to American politics. Why a more lenient standard should apply to McCarthy's or Kennedy's words than to Nixon's is not clear to me." Indeed, Nixon is one of the few politicians whose *motives* are always questioned.

2 ❋ Early Years, 1913–1937

NIXON has managed to stand out in one way or another for a good part of his life. He was the first child born in Yorba Linda, a farming village 30 miles inland from Los Angeles. (Next day there was a partial eclipse of the sun.) Nixon's father, whose wide-ranging talents included carpentry, built the family homestead alone, except for the fireplace.[1] The small frame house, perched on a knoll above a deep irrigation ditch bordering the lemon grove from which the elder Nixon tried to coax a livelihood, was difficult to heat. Hot wind blasts from the California desert normally scorched Yorba Linda by day. But its nights were often cold, particularly in January and February. When the town was cold, the Nixon house was very, very cold. The family dressed in the kitchen, huddled around the cooking stove, and the children played close to the living-room fireplace. But on the night of January 9, 1913, the whole house was warm and comfortable, especially the tiny alcove that served as master bedroom. Francis A. (Frank) Nixon had a collection of stoves operating in tandem with the fireplace, and he pulled aside the curtains that separated the alcove from the living room so the heat would flow into the room where his second son, Richard, was to be born. Mrs. Henrietta Shockney, a practical nurse who helped with the delivery, still marvels at the "even temperature." The Nixons were a pleasant family, easy to work with, she says. The father harnessed his excitement that night by fussing around with the stoves. Harold, the baby's four-year-old brother,

[1] The townspeople and school board dedicated the house as a "historic site" on Nixon's forty-sixth birthday, January 9, 1959.

9

carefully avoided getting in anyone's way, and Mrs. Elmira Milhous, the grandmother, fulfilled her role as matriarch without pestering doctor or nurse.

Nurse Shockney recalls Richard as a "roly-poly, good-natured" infant with brown eyes and brown hair. The first characteristic that impressed Mrs. Nixon was her new son's "decided voice." To Grandmother Milhous the resonant "yowl" meant the boy would be a preacher or a lawyer.

Richard took his spankings without a whimper. He was a willing helper around the house when the chores were "men's work." But before submitting to tasks associated with girls, like washing the dishes, he would draw the blinds tight to shut the world out from his humiliation. Richard was unlike his contemporaries around Yorba Linda only in that he was an avid newspaper reader when they were starting with picture books, and he preferred daydreams to anything else on earth. The great joy of his early boyhood centered on a spurline of the Santa Fe Railroad. There were toughness, vigor and unbendable firmness in the smooth steel tracks that stretched beyond sight in both directions and at one point were just across an irrigation ditch and a roadway from the Nixon house. Long freight trains rumbled past at all hours. The Nixon homestead shook and the throbbing stirred in Richard visions of faraway places. In his fantasies the ugly, noisy freighters were spotless passenger mainliners with the sure hand of Engineer Nixon on the throttle. "The train whistle was the sweetest music I ever heard," he recalls.

Naturally he aimed to become a railroad man. His determination was reinforced by the practical prospect of making money and achieving social status. "The best-off man in town was an engineer who ran the Santa Fe train from Los Angeles to Needles," Nixon says. "Every time I saw him or heard his name I thought that being a railroad engineer was an awfully good job to have."

Nixon stuck by his railroading dreams until he was practically in high school. His mother hoped he would become a musician or, if not that, a preacher. He had never seen a real live lawyer when he switched ambitions. From his newspaper reading he developed a fascination for the law. Lawyers seemed to be involved in all the intriguing doings of government. In elementary school he became a star debater and orator and once or twice overheard an adult say, "Dick is a born lawyer." There was also his tenth birthday present from Aunt Edith—a large volume on American history, which he read and reread and practically memorized. The book glorified nonmilitary heroes, all of whom appeared to be lawyers.

Finally, there was the Teapot Dome Scandal. Nixon's father, who might have been an oil millionaire with better luck,[2] became increasingly livid over each new disclosure in the sensational theft of government oil reserves through the connivance of principles in President Harding's administration. His diatribes against "crooked politicians" and "crooked lawyers" dominated the family conversation for weeks and provoked 12-year-old Richard to abandon the romance of railroading for a more idealized road to greatness.

His mother was the first to be told of the decision. She recalls that the boy declared, "I will be an old-fashioned kind of lawyer, a lawyer who can't be bought." Donald, the third Nixon boy and Richard's junior by two years, believes his brother "made up his mind to political life then and there, whether he realized it or not."

"Dick was always reserved," Donald says. "He was the studious one of the bunch, always doing more reading while the rest of us were out having more fun." In 18 years as a student he ran for many offices and lost only one election. It was the first and last time he ever underestimated the opposition. At stake was the student body presidency of Whittier High School. For years the contest for the position had been between the political machines of the junior and senior classes, controlled by their respective faculty advisers. Though he had just transferred from Fullerton High School,

[2] The elder Nixon tried his hand at running a trolley car, working as a carpenter and operating an orange and then a lemon ranch before settling down with a gasoline station in 1922. Two good sites for the station were available to him. They were two miles apart. After much deliberation he chose the East Whittier site over one at Santa Fe Springs. A year later oil was discovered on the Santa Fe property. The very first well was a 25-barrel-a-day gusher. It has been difficult for the Nixons to forget altogether how close they had been to becoming rich.

the senior class organization nominated Nixon; the junior class group nominated a friend, Roy Newsome. The campaign was progressing according to form when a venturesome boy named Robert Logue defied tradition by entering the race as an independent. On top of that, while Nixon and Newsome stuck by the practice of relying on their respective "machines," Logue made a vigorous personal campaign. He electioneered at recess, shook all the student hands he could reach and produced banners and literature urging one and all to "Stop, Think and Vote for Bob Logue."

Logue won. "He had something new," says Nixon. "He deserved to win. There were no hard feelings."

In the storied format of poor but honest folks, Nixon's parents gave their five boys each a name, a religion, a political identification and the basis for a way of life. "Allowances" and "spending money" were unheard of. The honorableness of hard work was emphasized as a matter of necessity. Richard began to earn his way as soon as he was big enough to hire himself out as a part-time farm laborer. He was ten or 11 and picking beans was his first specialty. ("It was awfully hard work, I can tell you.") Over the years the boy's main work was in the general store his father opened after the lemon grove failed. He pumped gasoline, culled rotten potatoes and apples, delivered groceries, and on entering college he became manager of the vegetable department and bookkeeper. There were many outside jobs to supplement the income. One, as handyman and sweeper in a packing house, caused young Nixon 16 weeks of misery. The boy tended to motion sickness, even in automobiles, and the whirling, churning and hammering of the packing house machinery nauseated him.

A season as janitor at a public swimming pool was more pleasant, as were two stints of three weeks each as barker for the wheel of chance at the "Slippery Gulch Rodeo" in Prescott, Arizona. Nixon barked for the legal front of the concession, where the prizes were hams and sides of bacon, which was a "come on" for a back room featuring poker and dice. Pay was based on total concession earnings, front and back. Nixon earned a dollar an hour the first year, quite a windfall for a 14-year-old. The next was a depression year, and his pay fell to 50 cents. What with jobs, school and studies,

16-hour workdays were commonplace for Nixon before he was 16 years old.

A buggy accident in which he was almost killed happened near his home in Yorba Linda. "We had taken my aunt to the train at Placentia," his mother recalled. "I held Donald, the baby, in my lap and drove the buggy. I couldn't handle both boys because Richard, then three, was too lively. So a little neighbor girl came along to hold him."

As the buggy rounded a steep curve along the bank of the irrigation ditch, Richard outsquirmed his young guardian and fell into the road. The heavy wheel grazed his scalp before Mrs. Nixon could stop the horse. Blood spurted from a gash that stretched clear across the top of his head, a little to the left of center. The nearest hospital was 25 miles away, too far for a dash by buggy. The Quigley family owned the only automobile in town. It was nearby and available; the doctor told Nixon's mother later that Richard reached the hospital emergency room just in time to save his life. The ugly scar is still there—from above the forehead to the neck—hidden by hair always parted on the right.

Nixon has been susceptible to illnesses of one kind or another since that childhood experience. When he was four he nearly died of pneumonia. During his senior year at high school he had a severe attack of undulant fever. His temperature rose to 104 degrees every day for over a week. He was absent much of that school year, but he managed to graduate with honors, maintain his four-year "A" average in Latin and win the oratorical contests and debates he entered, and also to take the Harvard Club of California Prize awarded annually to the school's outstanding all-around student. The prize was a biography of Dean Briggs. "I thought he was remarkable then and I still do, and I got a great opinion of Harvard from that book," Nixon says.

Nixon's ancestry dates back almost as far as one can in North America. A kinsman of his mother came to Delaware from Wales in 1690. The first Milhous, a Quaker, left County Kildare, in Ireland, for the religious freedom of Chester County, Pennsylvania, in 1729. His father's line on this continent began when James Nixon landed at Brandywine Hundred, Delaware, from Ireland in 1753. The family's roots and branches spread through the nation's history. One forefather crossed the Delaware with General Washington and survived a dozen battles of the Revolution. Another is buried on the Civil War battlefield at Gettysburg. The Nixons and the Milhouses followed the frontier—to western Pennsylvania—to Ohio—to Indiana—and then to California. Generation after generation they were mostly farmers. Also among them were preachers, teachers and a few merchants. None before Richard became known outside his community, but quite a few achieved local prominence.

On his father's side, Nixon's forebears were tough, straitlaced, Bible-pounding Methodists. His mother's family were devout and gentle Quakers. They tolerated violence only to save bodies and souls—mainly those of runaway slaves. Grant Smith, an aged resident of Columbus, Indiana, says the countryside where he lives is filled with descendants of slaves rescued by one of the most effective underground railroad operations in the nation. It was run, at their peril, by the Milhouses and fellow Quakers in southern Indiana.

Nixon's father and his mother's parents emigrated to southern California for reasons of health. But the family is unusually long-lived. The ancestor who landed in 1690 passed away at age 105. Nixon's great-grandmother Milhous lived to 96, Grandmother Milhous to 94, and his mother died in 1967 at 82.

Whittier, California, was the first among the places that markedly affected Nixon. It was a tranquil town of orange and avocado groves, unostentatious homes and Quaker purity when the Nixons moved there from nearby Yorba Linda in 1922. The very reason for Frank Nixon's choice of Whittier foretold for it a much less tranquil future, however. The elder Nixon sought to open a gasoline station. He felt the area's biggest build-up of auto traffic would be along East Whittier Boulevard, so he set his family and his gasoline pumps up on one of its barren corners.

A leader of the Society of Friends had chosen the Whittier townsite because it was the least likely place in southern California to attract mainline railroads and the noise and bustle of industry and commerce that would spring up at a maddening pace in the wake of good transportation facilities. But that was in 1887. The broad meadow abutting the Puente Hills, with a view of the Pacific in the distance, epitomized the tranquillity of Quaker living. Los Angeles was a safe 13 miles away. How was the founder of the new Quaker mecca in California to know that someday there would be automobiles?

Nixon's mother, Hannah Milhous, came in an early wave of emigrants from Butlerville, Indiana. In the family caravan were her parents, grandmother, eight brothers and sisters, the cows and horses, and a freight car of lumber, doors, windows and miscellaneous building material that her father feared would not be available in the California "wilderness."

Nixon's father happened upon Whittier much later. It was after the turn of the century, in fact, and he was searching for sunshine and warmth to ease a gnawing pain in his feet. The severe frostbite he suffered while running an open-vestibule trolley in Columbus, Ohio, had gone, but the agony remained.

Frank Nixon was motorman of a trolley in frost-free southern California when he met Hannah Milhous in February, 1908. They were married four months later, and Frank became a Quaker. Their first son, Harold, was born in 1909. Then came Richard, in 1913; Donald, in 1914; Arthur, in 1918 and Edward, in 1930. Harold and Arthur have died.

Several men and women influenced Nixon's early development. Lewis Cox, his seventh-grade teacher, impressed on him more forcefully than anyone else, for instance, "the importance of fighting hard all the time and working hard all the time." Fundamentally, however, his family intimates see Richard Nixon as a composite of his father, mother and grandmother.

Nixon recalls that his grandmother "had a big house on the boulevard and every year at Christmas and usually once during the summer we had a family reunion. She kept the family together through the years. She was a prolific letter writer. On birthdays she composed rhymes and couplets and sent them to us. She used the plain speech [thee and thou] exclusively. My mother used the plain speech in talking with her and her sisters, but never with the children. So with us, the children, we don't use it at all.

"My grandmother set the standards for the whole family. Honesty, hard work, do your best at all times—humanitarian ideals. She was always taking care of every tramp that came along the road, just like my own mother, too. She had strong feelings about pacifism and very strong feelings on civil liberties. She probably affected me in that respect. At her house no servant ever ate at a separate table. They always ate with the family. There were Negroes, Indians and people from Mexico —she always was taking somebody in."

The jutting jaw, thick eyebrows, tendency to jowls and up-swept nose that caricaturists have made Nixon's trademark are actually the Milhous family imprint. The former Vice-President's brothers have the same no-nonsense look, and Hannah Nixon was a small, dainty, gray-haired replica of her sons.

To his mother the former Vice-President was "Richard," not "Dick." "We named him Richard, and he just seems like Richard to me, just as Donald is Donald, and Edward is Edward," she said. Furthermore, she recalled in 1958, Richard's standout qualification among the brothers was as a potato masher. "He never left any lumps. He used the whipping motion to make them smooth instead of going up and down the way the other boys did."

Hannah Nixon worked endless hours to help lift her family from its early poverty. When the boys were young, her day would begin before dawn, when she would get up to bake pies for sale that day in the store. Always the family would sit down to breakfast together. "That permitted us to say our prayers and Bible verses together each morning," she recalled. When the oldest boy, Harold, contracted tuberculosis, Mrs. Nixon took him to Arizona in the desperate hope that his lungs would heal in a drier climate. For two years she stayed at the nursing home with her ill son, and paid the board by scrubbing, cooking, tending the furnace and doing whatever else needed to be done there. Frank Nixon met the huge medical bill by selling half of the acre of land on which his store stood. It was a period of extreme hardship for the whole family. In

Whittier the father, Richard and the other boys took turns preparing the meals—usually canned chili, spaghetti, pork and beans, soup, and at least half the menus consisted of either hamburgers or fried eggs. "Odd as it may seem, I still like all of those things," Nixon admits. "There were many mornings when I ate nothing for breakfast but a candy bar."

Meanwhile Arthur, the fourth son, became seriously ill, and a week or so later died of tubercular meningitis. He was seven. "It is difficult at times to understand the ways of our Lord," Mrs. Nixon confided to a neighbor after the funeral, "but we know that there is a plan and the best happens for each individual."

The long stay in Arizona did not cure Harold of tuberculosis, and he and his mother had to return to Whittier. Harold was given the downstairs bedroom, the one his parents had occupied. One morning he asked Richard to drive him into town so he could buy a birthday present for his mother. He selected an early-model electric mixer, and smiled at the thought of all the elbow bending it would save her when she baked angel food cake. Richard took Harold back to the house, then headed for school, 15 minutes away. A message awaited him in the classroom. "Come home," it said. "Your brother has died."

Much of Richard Nixon's early life centered at the East Whittier Friends Meeting House—the Quaker church—where he and his family attended one form of service or another four times on Sunday and several times during the week. Richard played the organ at the meetinghouse and taught Sunday school. His high-school principal says he was "a self-starter . . . a fighting Quaker." Dr. Albert Upton, professor of English and drama at Whittier College, says, "The Dick I knew so well in college was not what I would call a militant Quaker. He was just a typical American Quaker." Merton G. Wray, a schoolmate of Nixon's in high school and college and now a Municipal Court judge in Whittier, says, "I cannot reconcile his massive retaliation policy in politics and as a public official with what I understand of the Quaker philosophy and of their fellowship of reconciliation." Wray, who was often an opponent of Nixon's in speaking contests during their school days, adds, "Since high school Nixon has had an uncommon ability to take advantage of a situation before and after it develops. . . . His success is due to knowing what to do and when to do it, perfect timing in everything."

Nixon's brother Donald recalls that "Dick always planned things out. He didn't do things accidentally. . . . He had more of Mother's traits than the rest of us. He wouldn't argue much with me, for instance, but once, when he had had just about as much of me as he could take, he cut loose and kept at it for a half to three quarters of an hour. He went back a year or two listing things I had done. He didn't leave out a thing. I was only eight, and he was ten, but I've had a lot of respect ever since for the way he can keep things in his mind."

Nixon was 17 when he entered Whittier College, a small Quaker institution with exacting standards. Within a month he was part of a cabal that formed a new student fraternity, the Orthagonians, or Square Shooters, to compete with the Franklins, a long-established group that had a reputation for being highbrow and favoring the town's wealthier families. Franklins always wore black ties to school functions and when posing for photographers. The Orthagonians, most of whom could not afford evening clothes, adopted slouch sweaters and open, tieless collars as their trademark. Nixon composed the club song. He collaborated in writing its first play, a shocker entitled *The Trysting Place,* and was its director and male lead. Needless to say, he was elected first president of the Orthagonians, his freshman status notwithstanding. Furthermore, he was elected president of the freshman class almost unanimously, and won a place on the college Joint Council of Control, all during that first, flashy month as a college student.

During his sophomore year Nixon represented Whittier in more than 50 debates, winning the bulk of them, including a match with the national champions. The topic was Free Trade. Nixon was for it. Debating and oratory were Nixon's specialties. But he worked much harder—and with considerably less success—at trying to make the football team. A classmate recalled that "Dick had two left feet. He couldn't coordinate. But boy, was he an inspiration. He was always talking it up. That's why the chief [the coach] let him hang around, I guess.

He was one of the inspirational guys." Another schoolmate recalls that he and other members of the team would always scuffle over the right to sit next to Nixon at the meal served the football players before each game. The main course was always steak, and Nixon invariably was "too tensed up" to eat. "I always tried to grab the seat so I could eat my steak and his too," said the teammate.

Dr. Paul S. Smith, then professor of history and politics and now Whittier president, tells of the enthusiasm with which Nixon devoured a ten-volume history of America. Its emphasis was on Lincoln. The professor said he dared to give such an advanced assignment only to two students—Nixon and Leonidas Dodson, now professor of history and archivist at the University of Pennsylvania. At that stage of his college career Nixon also learned French and took to reading the classical French philosophers.

"As a young student Dick had the uncommon capacity to brush aside the façades of a subject and get to the heart of it," says Dr. Smith. "He always completed on half a page what would take a normal 'A' student two pages. He also perfected a skill he was developing, perhaps unconsciously, as an undergraduate. He has a fantastic capacity to communicate with people eye to eye, shoulder to shoulder."

Dr. Albert Upton said he twinged when he saw pictures of Nixon weeping on the shoulder of Senator Knowland at the Wheeling, West Virginia, airport after General Eisenhower had come to greet him in the wake of his telecast about the Nixon Fund during the 1952 campaign.

"I taught him how to cry," said Dr. Upton, "in a play by John Drinkwater called *Bird in Hand*. He tried conscientiously at rehearsals, and he'd get a pretty good lump in his throat and that was all. But on the evenings of performance tears just ran right out of his eyes. It was beautifully done, those tears."

In his senior year Nixon was elected president of the student body. Since graduating he has been awarded an honorary degree at Whittier and the college has established "The Richard M. Nixon Chair of Public Affairs." But the students remember him best for two accomplishments: one dealing with dancing and the other with the annual bonfire. It was Richard Nixon who junked the blue-nose regulation that forbade dances at Whittier by convincing the hierarchy—the trustees, preachers, faculty and rich alumni—that students would either dance under honorable auspices on the campus or go to "dens of iniquity in Los Angeles." He secured a place for himself in the annals of Whittier bonfires when he was a junior. He was chairman that year of the traditional undergraduate escapade—the annual bonfire on a mound of earth called Fire Hill. The custom was for everyone in the student body to pile things for burning on the allotted site, for days, with the chairman tossing on the last item. The chairman provided the crown for the heap, and his status as a leader of men was judged over the years by the style and size of the country privy he could purloin for that purpose.

Normally the bonfire was topped by a one-holer. Occasionally a really superior chairman would drag in a two-holer. In 1933 Richard Nixon established a record that still stands. He produced a four-holer.

William Brock, one of Nixon's Orthagonian fraternity brothers, says that bonfire was the hottest thing that ever happened at Whittier. Brock is an electrical engineer in Pasadena, and a Democrat. He is a Negro, and was a football star. "I remember Dick as being a lot better player than he's given credit for," says Brock. "He was little, but he had more fight and spunk than the big man."

Brock says he sticks by Democratic candidates in elections, except when Nixon runs. "And I really get mad when I hear Democrats or anybody accuse him of bigotry. That sort of thing is fantastic. Dick was my buddy in college many years before he or anybody else figured him to become a politician. He was one of the fellows who got me into the Orthagonians."

Nixon graduated from Whittier in 1934. The New Deal had already generated some cautious hope—but no jobs. Nixon was among the fortunate few who did not need one. All he wanted was a law school where you could get by without money, and by happy coincidence a school across the continent, in Durham, North Carolina, was looking for bright students on whom to spend its newly acquired abundance. James Buchanan Duke, the tobacco multimillionaire named for the pre-Civil War Democratic President, had left a huge endowment to Trinity College. The austere little Methodist institution took its benefactor's name, becoming Duke University, and then adopted his mode of living.

Nixon applied for one of the law scholarships available to high-honor college men throughout the country. In a letter of recommendation Dr. Walter F. Dexter, then the Whittier College president, wrote: "I believe Nixon will become one of America's important, if not great leaders."

Nixon got a full tuition scholarship and a National Youth Administration job which paid 35 cents an hour. There were 44 students in his class from 37 states, practically all scholarship students. To develop high standards for the school, Duke offered fewer scholarships to the second- and third-year students than to the first-year students. That also developed strenuous competition. "In those Depression years few families found it easy to raise tuition money," says Dean E. R. Latty. "Richard Nixon demonstrated his superior legal ability by maintaining his scholarship for his entire three years." He also became a member of the Order of Coif, the national scholastic fraternity for honor law students.

A month or so after matriculation he was studying late one night in the library. His mind wandered from the book—to his homesickness, the seven courses he was determined to master that semester, the troubles ahead if he did not achieve a high enough average to keep his scholarship. William Adelson, an upperclassman who happened by, asked him, "What's wrong?"

"I'm scared," said Nixon. "I counted 32 Phi Beta Kappa keys in my class. I don't believe I can stay up top in that group."

"Listen, Nixon, you needn't worry," said Adelson, a high honor man himself. "The fact that you are studying so late yourself shows you don't mind hard work. You've got an iron butt, and that's the secret of becoming a lawyer."

None of Nixon's friends in law school expected he would go into politics. Basil Whitener, a tall, backslapping North Carolinian, the number-one politico in the class and now a Democratic congressman from the North Carolina hill country, says: "Nixon was not outward, but seemed shy. He was friendly in a quiet way. He was no smiler then; quite the contrary. Like most others, I figured he would wind up doing a wonderful job in a big law firm, handling securities or other matters that need the attention of a scholar, not a politician."

Nixon's ambition was to join a "great" law firm. During the Christmas holidays of 1936 he and two fellow seniors—Harlan Leathers and William Perdue—went job-hunting in New York. They applied at practically all the well-known law offices: Donovan, Leisure, Newton and Lombard; Root, Clark, Buckner and Ballantine, now Dewey, Ballantine, Bushby, Palmer, and Wood, with former Governor Dewey of New York as senior partner; Coudert Brothers, of which the prominent Democrat Thomas K. Finletter is a senior partner; Davis, Polk, Wardwell, Gardiner and Reid, which was headed by the late John W. Davis, Democratic candidate for President in 1924; Millbank, Tweed, Hope and Webb; Lord, Day and Lord, of which Herbert Brownell, Jr., was then a member and is now a senior partner; and others.

Leathers landed a place with Millbank, Tweed. Perdue wound up with a large oil corporation of which he is now vice-president.

Nixon got only an "iffy" response from the Donovan firm. His highest hope was to find a place with Sullivan and Cromwell, of which John Foster Dulles was a senior partner. Nixon recalls that he was attracted more by the "thick, luxurious carpets and the fine oak paneling" of the Sullivan and Cromwell reception room than by the possibility of being a low-echelon associate of Dulles, however.

"If they had given me a job," he said in 1958, "I'm sure I would have been there today, a corporation lawyer instead of Vice-President."

Nixon classified himself as "liberal" in college, "but not a flaming liberal." Like many law students of that period, his public heroes were Justices Brandeis, Cardozo and Hughes, then the Supreme Court's progressive minority.

Through his three years at law school Nixon's morale rose and sank to peaks and valleys that are characteristic of him even today. Friends gave him the nickname "Gloomy Gus" because he would sometimes complain, "I'll never learn the law; there is too much of it," at the very time his grades were highest. Years later, during the 1952 presidential campaign, when he delivered the television speech about the "Nixon

Fund" that reversed national sentiment in his favor, Nixon at first adjudged his performance a flop.

The Depression had not eased up much by 1937. As graduation drew near, Nixon decided to apply for a job with the FBI. "The FBI looked very good to a young lawyer wanting work that year," he recalls. On May 3, 1937, Dean H. Claude Horack wrote J. Edgar Hoover: "Some time ago you suggested that I might refer to you any exceptional young man who has an interest in the work of the Federal Bureau of Investigation. I have such a man in mind who is to graduate in June. . . . Richard Nixon, one of the finest young men, both in character and ability, that I have ever had the opportunity of having in my classes. He is a superior student, alert, aggressive, a fine speaker and one who can do an exceptionally good piece of research when called upon to do so. His position with his fellows is shown by the fact that he is this year president of the Duke Bar Association. . . ."

In June, when the FBI job had not materialized, Nixon decided to try his luck in his home town. He had to cram five months of detailed California law into two months of study. He did it successfully.

Meanwhile, there was the Duke graduation. His mother and grandmother, then 89, drove across the continent to be there. Witnesses say the pride those ladies felt showed through their Quaker composure. Only 25 of the 44 students who started with the class graduated. Nixon stood third in the class scholastically.

Four months later he wrote Dean Horack that he had taken the FBI examination. "They have been investigating my character since that time," he added. "But unless my present prospects fall through, I shall not accept the job even if it is offered to me." Long afterward Nixon jokingly asked his friend J. Edgar Hoover why the FBI never came through with the job. The explanation was simply this: the FBI was preparing a form notifying him to report for duty when an unexpected appropriation cut forced the bureau to stop hiring.

3 ❋ *Whittier Lawyer, 1937–1942*

WHITTIER, known as "Ye Friendly Town," was becoming a Los Angeles suburb and had grown to a population of about 25,000 when Nixon returned in 1937 to practice law. The founding Quakers and their progeny were already far outnumbered, but the quiet tone of the community had not changed. The Chamber of Commerce still boasted, justifiably, that Whittier "tolerates no establishments that may be an invitation to hoodlumism."

Nixon wore a sharply pressed blue serge suit his first day as a member of Wingert and Bewley, Whittier's oldest law firm. Before settling down at his own desk, however, he went after the years of accumulated dust in the firm's library. Mrs. Evelyn Dorn, a secretary who became a devoted friend, said he rearranged all the books—several hundred of them. "He took every one of them out, cleaned up all the shelves, and I think he even used some varnish on them."

When cases started coming to him, Mrs. Dorn says, he would work without letup. During particularly busy periods he would live on pineapple malts and hamburgers. At first Nixon was given all the firm's divorce cases. The intimacies confided to him by some clients would often cause him to blush. He became hardened to hearing these facts of marital life, but he cost Wingert and Bewley more fees than he earned because he saw to it that most of the prospective divorces ended in reconciliation. Later Nixon took to handling much of the legal work that he liked best—he became the firm's chief trial lawyer and he also became its specialist on estates and federal income taxes.

After he had become established he set up a branch office in nearby La Habra, a lawyerless community of 4,000. Nixon's office in La Habra was a desk in a real-estate office, but he made a good enough impression to be chosen as the town attorney. Furthermore, his senior partner, Tom Bewley, the town attorney of Whittier, appointed Nixon as his assistant. "Dick's duties were to draft the ordinance and keep the council happy," Bewley recalls. He also had to act as town prosecutor in police court and a sort of overseer of law enforcement. Whittier was dry then, but permitted wine to be sold with food in restaurants. A certain café became a public nuisance, it was said, because customers often drank too much and staggered out into the street. This was a sight Whittier's citizenry would not tolerate. Nixon posted the small police force in the vicinity of the café with orders to arrest for intoxication tests anyone who seemed to stagger. Within a week practically every customer had been picked up at least once. The café closed, and the owner moved his sinful trade to Los Angeles.

Nixon was not only a thorough police prosecutor, but also as a corporation and tax lawyer he impressed juries because, Bewley says, "he was more legalistic than dramatic in his courtroom manner." His first big civil case concerned an oil-gas lease. It was a complicated affair involving intricate and finely drawn points of law. Associates in the case say Nixon won it simply because he was more zealous than the opposition in researching every conceivable angle of the subject.

When his law practice had been safely established, Nixon branched out into business. The Whittier area had a particularly troublesome oversupply of oranges that year, so he and a group of local plungers decided to try to market them as frozen orange juice. The Citra-Frost Company was formed with Richard Nixon as president and attorney and a total of $10,000 of invested money in the bank. The product showed great promise. Two large shipping lines became interested and agreed to buy tons of it—if more satisfactory means of preserving and packaging it could be found.

"Dick worked his heart out on the thing," says Bewley. The Nixon company was preserving whole orange juice, not the condensed variety now available everywhere. The major problem was finding a container that would hold it and preserve it at the same time. Everything imaginable was tried from cartons and cans to cellophane bags. In trying to save the business until the container and preservative experiments might succeed, Nixon and his associates cut costs by picking and squeezing oranges themselves. The venture folded in a year and a half. A few disappointed investors blamed Nixon for the failure—and still vote accordingly.

Meanwhile Nixon had been elected president of the Whittier Alumni Association. The following year he was made a trustee of the college. He was 26, the youngest member of the board and already a leader of several civic and church groups in the community. He also conducted a course in practical law at the college and when he was 29 a movement was started to make him president of the college. There had been dissension on the board. A president had quit and left town. One of the biggest donors withdrew his support until "things are done right." Nixon became his choice at the behest of a young faculty group headed by Dr. Upton. Dr. Upton says Nixon would have become president if the war had not intervened. (He could have had the post after the war, too, but by then he was already committed to run for Congress.)

Nixon never had the time or the money as a young fellow to be a ladies' man. A classmate in high school and college said she and the other girls admired him but thought "he was too intelligent to be much fun." He dated the daughter of the local police chief steadily before going east to law school, and at Duke he attended occasional dances as a stag. Shortly after his return to Whittier as a graduate lawyer, he met Pat Ryan.

It happened at tryouts for a Little Theater play. "I was a new teacher in Whittier, and they encouraged teachers to take part in the local events in town, including the Little Theater which was quite thriving at the time," Mrs. Nixon recalls. "I wasn't too anxious, but this friend of mine decided that she would go down to try out for a part, so I went with her. In the meantime she had told Dick that this 'glamorous' new schoolteacher was going to be in the play. Consequently, he just thought, 'Well, I'll go down and take a look.' So he went down too. I'm sure he didn't have time to be in any plays, because he was a struggling young lawyer, and he wouldn't necessarily want to come right back and start being in plays rather than getting down to business. So, I met him there at the Little Theater. He decided to take the part. I did too—not because of him, but because I was sort of pressured into it."

That very night Nixon proposed, and his wife said long afterward, "I thought he was nuts or something. I guess I just looked at him. I couldn't imagine anyone ever saying anything like that so suddenly. Now that I know Dick much better I can't imagine that he would ever say that, because he is very much the opposite, he's more reserved.

"I admired Dick from the very beginning," Mrs. Nixon added. "I was having a very good time and wasn't anxious to settle down. I had all these visions of doing all sorts of things, including travel. I always wanted to travel."

Thelma Ryan was born in Ely, Nevada, two months after Richard Nixon was born. Her father, who worked in a mine, nicknamed her Pat. "There were accidents in the mines, so we moved out to California, and my father bought this little farm which we called a ranch [at Artesia, 18 miles from Los Angeles]," Mrs. Nixon said. "I was just a baby, so I don't remember Nevada. Of course, I've been back since. We all helped out on the ranch, and it was a good kind of life when you look back on it. It was truck garden. All irrigation. There was a lot to do. And I loved to be out of doors, so I worked right along with my brothers in the field, really, which was lots of fun. We picked potatoes; we picked tomatoes; we picked peppers and cauliflower. When I was real tiny I just tagged along. But when I got older I was able to do more. I drove the team of horses and things like that. We didn't have a tractor then. You had to use the horses for a number of things. For instance, when you went down rows of cauliflower you had to have a special cart with high wheels so that you didn't injure the cauliflower heads. I remember we used to take our produce over to ship, like the tomatoes were shipped, and we would ride up on top of the wagon. Things like that were the fun we had.

"The farm was ten and a half acres, but we were able to make a living on it. And, of course, all my friends lived on little ranches, as they are called there, too. Consequently, they did about the same things that we did. We also had the work horses which we rode. We thought that was great sport—to get on them and ride them bareback. All the fun that we had was more or less connected with our little farm there. Then we would raise peanuts. My father would put in just enough for family use. We would have a roast of peanuts in the yard, and all the children would come. My mother baked a lot. She was very good. She baked bread and cinnamon rolls and all sorts of things like that. I helped her too. I was the only girl home at the time. I have another sister, who was older and away. We used to eat up the whole baking. All the children used to play in the yard, 'Run, Sheep, Run' and all the other fun games, and we would get hungry and come in and eat up the whole baking.

"The school was a mile away. We walked a mile each way, to and from school."

Pat Ryan's mother died when she was 12, and she took charge of the house. Her father died five years later, the year she graduated from high school. She worked in the local bank for a year. Then she drove East with relatives and had a job in a hospital near New York for a year or so before returning to Los Angeles to attend the University of Southern California.

"I took merchandising, and while I was in college I worked holidays and vacations at the Bullock-Wilshire store," she said. Her work schedule also included occasional bit parts in movies. "I was a good student, so I was able to miss classes and do this extra work in the movies," Mrs. Nixon recalled. "I was in quite a number of them, but mostly just in mob scenes. You would have to hunt real hard to find me, but I made quite a bit of money. I was in *Small Town Girl*. In *Becky Sharp* I had a little walk-on part and got $25. I just walked on, but at least I could be seen. I did have a line. I can't remember what it was though, because it was cut before it reached the screen. What I do remember about that movie is that I got $25 for it, rather than the usual $7. I made quite a bit of extra money that way. To earn the regular $7, you would have to stay out there [on the studio lot] for the whole day. I never thought of movies as a career because it seemed so very boring. It was those retakes and retakes, and you would see those stars going over and over and over about three words until you almost went mad. I did the extra bit playing only for the money. But I did all sorts of interesting things to earn a little extra money then, you know, secretarial work and other things because I was earning my way through school."

Pat Ryan graduated from the University of Southern California the year Nixon finished law school. Both were honor students. She wanted to become a buyer for a large store. "I had trained to be one and I loved that field of merchandising very much," she said, "but I was offered this job teaching. The pay was $190 a month, which was fabulous in 1937, and much more than was offered in the other field. So, you see, my coming to Whittier wasn't planned at all. I only went four years to college and the requirement was five years at that time to teach in high school. But I had a special credential because I had a great deal of business experience. Consequently, out of a clear sky I just decided to accept this teaching job because it would be a lot of fun and I received all this money, and I had great visions of those free summers when I could do what I wanted to. I really dreamed about those summer months. But now I've decided that the only reason that I accepted the teaching job was destiny. Through it I met Dick in his own home town."

At the high school she taught commercial subjects, was faculty adviser for the "Pep Committee," coached the cheerleaders, directed school plays, and became generally involved in most of the school and community activities. She also met most of the town's eligible bachelors and had a fine time. After the Little Theater tryouts, Nixon stopped dating anyone else. But not Pat. He hung around dutifully even when she had other dates and would drive her to Los Angeles if she was to meet someone there, and wait around to take her home.

"I don't think that Dick had done a great deal of dancing, but he swung into it all right," Mrs. Nixon says. "We had a young group, mostly my friends from college. He became part of that group when we dated. We liked to do active things like sports of different kinds. We were taking up ice skating. The artificial ice rinks had just opened up and it was the gay thing to do. But it was awful for Dick. He almost broke his head two or three times, but he still kept going.

"Our group used to get together often. Of course, none of us had much money at the time, so we would just meet at someone's house after skating and have food, a spaghetti dinner or something of that type, and then we would sit around and tell stories and laugh. Dick was always the highlight of the party because he has a wonderful sense of humor. He would keep everybody in stitches. Sometimes we would even act out parts. I will never forget one night when we did 'Beauty and the Beast.' Dick was the Beast, and one of the other men dressed up like Beauty. This sounds rather silly to be telling it now, but in those days we were all very young, and we had to do home entertainment rather than go out and spend money. We used to put on funny shows. It was all good, clean fun, and we had loads of laughs."

Mrs. Nixon said, "There was no talk of politics or anything of that type" in those days. "I didn't even think in terms of that. He was doing well as a lawyer. He was well liked by everybody. He was always president of some group like the 20–30 Club and this, that and the other thing, so I knew that he would be successful in whatever he undertook."

Pat Ryan finally said "Yes" in the spring of 1940. Nixon brought her engagement ring on May 1 in a lovely May Day basket, and they were married June 21, 1940, at the Mission Inn, in Riverside. It was a fine wedding, Mrs. Nixon says, and after the ceremony "we just took off in our car . . . heading, generally, for Mexico City, but without any particular destination. We didn't have a trip outlined. We just went. We felt really splurgy. That's what we still like to do— to get in the car and ride off just to be going, without any particular destination. It is always a lot of fun . . . but because of television we can't go anywhere now without being recognized. It seems everybody has seen our faces on television. I had the girls at the beach one day and I looked a sight. They wanted ice cream, so we went up to this little corner drugstore. The minute I stepped out of the car, two elderly ladies said: 'Why, there is Pat Nixon.' I thought no one would recognize me, dark glasses, beach skirt and everything, but they did. We are even recognized at night. People blow their horns and wave to us. It gives you a good feeling —it always does with us—to have people be so friendly, so kind, to give us a cheery wave . . . but then, too, it means no more private automobile trips."

The Nixons rented an apartment above a garage, and their circle of friends became the other young married folk of Whittier. Frequently they attended performances at the Los Angeles Opera. Often their group would get the same seats in the gallery, one of which was behind a post. They named it the "post seat" and proceeded to take turns using it. Jack and Helene Drown were their closest personal friends. Drown practiced law. (He now has a large magazine- and newspaper-distributing business in Los Angeles.) Mrs. Drown was on the Whittier High School faculty with Mrs. Nixon.

Mrs. Nixon continued to teach after her marriage, and Nixon confided to a few intimates that he aimed sooner or later to get into a big city law practice. He kept looking over the field, quietly, and even during a brief trip to Cuba he spent a bit of his vacation time exploring the possibilities of establishing law or business connections in Havana.

Then the Japanese attacked Pearl Harbor. Nixon was determined to serve in the war effort but, considering his Quaker upbringing and family, it had to be done slowly. In January, 1942, he went to Washington and applied for a job in the tire-rationing section of the Office of Price Administration, the many-tentacled OPA bureaucracy which later was to become the butt of many Nixon attacks on the Democratic administration. Thomas I. Emerson, a member of the Yale University law faculty, was in charge. Emerson told John Harris, then Washington correspondent for the Boston *Globe,* "Dick Nixon came into my office without warning. My secretary had been making appointments for applicants. I don't recall that Nixon had any letter of introduction from anybody. He just walked in and said he had come to Washington to get in the war effort. I found he had a very good record at Duke and a good law practice in Whittier. He gave that up to enter the war effort. He was a nice-looking boy, seemed intelligent and had an excellent record. He was obviously a person we could use. I gave him the job right then and there."

Nixon's immediate superior recalls he was "very quiet, self-effacing, conservative and competent. . . . He had a desk out in one of the open bays." His starting salary was $61 a week. By August, when he left to join the Navy, he had gotten two raises and was making $90. Nixon's six months as a minor government bureaucrat shattered some of his illusions and reshaped a bit of his political philosophy.

"I came out of college more liberal than I am today, more liberal in the sense that I thought it was possible for government to do more than I later found it was practical to do," Nixon said. "I became more conservative first, after my experience with OPA. . . . I also became greatly disillusioned about bureaucracy and about what the government could do because I saw the terrible paper work that people had to go through. I also saw the mediocrity of so many civil servants. And for the first time when I was in OPA I also saw that there were people in government who were not satisfied merely with interpreting the regulations, enforcing the law that Congress passed, but who actually had a passion to get business and used their government jobs to that end. These were of course some of the remnants of the old, violent New Deal crowd. They set me to thinking a lot at that point." In the OPA, Nixon said, he learned firsthand how "political appointees at the top feathered their nests with all kinds of overlapping and empire building."

As a lawyer Nixon was entitled to a direct commission in the military service, so he joined the Navy as a lieutenant, junior grade.[1] After routine training he was shipped to New Caledonia and detailed to the Naval Air Transport organization, known as SCAT. Lester Wroble, a Navy friend and now vice-president of a paper company in Chicago, says Nixon earned a three-pronged reputation at their first war theater outpost, a place called Green Island. With supplies and materials wheedled out of visiting naval craft he set up what

---

[1] He was promoted to full lieutenant a year later. In October, 1945, he became a lieutenant commander and in June, 1953— six months after he had taken office as Vice-President—he was raised to full commander in the Naval Reserve.

became known as Nixon's Hamburger Stand, where officers
and men supplemented their less appetizing service rations
without charge; from time to time he got hold of various
items not on the government issue list, like bourbon whiskey,
priceless to the men, and shared everything with all hands;
and Nixon also became known as the only sane and sensible
poker player in the South Pacific. Nixon's Quaker upbringing
excluded card playing as an unnecessary frivolity, and gam-
bling as a sin. (He never smoked, either, until the war, when
he took to puffing an occasional cigar. Now he lights a cigar
when it seems to be the thing to do at a banquet or a ceremonial occasion, and about once a month he actually smokes
one.) "I played bridge in law school for the first and last
time," he said. "I never knew what poker was until I joined
the Navy." When he was a member of the House and a
Senator, he played a few times with fellow congressmen. As
Vice-President he had time for only one game. However,
there was plenty of time for poker during his Navy days, particularly on Green Island.

The Green Island games ran to high stakes, as they did
at other lonely outposts around the world. Wroble remembers
one pot of $1,100. But Nixon steered clear of the wild hands.
"Dick never lost, but he was never a big winner," said Wroble.
"He always played it cautious and close to the belt. If you
stood behind him or were kibitzing, he had no prejudice and
was not superstitious about showing you his hole card. He
seemed always to end up a game somewhere between $30 and
$60 ahead. That didn't look like showy winnings, but when
you multiplied it day after day after day, I'd say he did all
right."

Wroble and other wartime friends say that what they
recollect most clearly about Lieutenant Nixon is that "he was
one guy who knew where he was going." "Most of us had
big, grandiose schemes," said Wroble. "Dick's plans were
concise, concrete and specific." He was a good lawyer before
the war and he intended to be a better and more successful
one after it.

4 ❀ *Congressional Campaign, 1946*

BEFORE the war, when the state assemblyman from his district was appointed a judge, Nixon considered running for the vacancy. Someone else was endorsed by the Republican party leaders, however, and his only campaign venture was in the 1940 presidential election when he made some speeches locally for Wendell Willkie. Nixon recalls harboring "no grandiose ambitions" in the political field. "I wanted to enter the law, but I wasn't a youngster who wanted to be President of the United States," he says. "Even in college political battles as such never appealed to me, but I always seemed to get dragged into them to run for some office or another."

Mrs. Nixon remembers distinctly that "there was no talk of political life at all in the beginning," either before or after their marriage. When opportunity was offered Nixon to run for Congress, she adds, "I didn't feel strongly about it either way. . . . I felt that a man had to make up his mind what he wants to do, then after he made it up, the only thing I could do was to help him. But it would not have been a life that I would have chosen."

Nixon registered as a voter in 1938. He was 25 and had missed four voting years. But his job as assistant city attorney of Whittier was a political plum, so to speak, and therefore he had become, in effect, a politician. But it was the late fall of 1945 before he went into politics in earnest.

Whittier and his environs, then the 12th Congressional District of California, was stanch Republican territory. Yet in 1936 it elected a Democrat for Congress, and kept re-electing him. Jerry Voorhis, the congressman, was mild-mannered,

34

conscientious, likable and extremely popular. He was respected by fellow congressmen and the press corps in Washington. He worked hard at his job, answered his mail promptly, dealt with personal problems of his constituents on an eagerly non-partisan basis, and when Congress was not in session he seldom passed by opportunities to be guest teacher of Sunday-school classes or to address church and civic groups. Furthermore, the congressman faithfully remembered births, anniversaries and other happy occasions in his district. And, of course, that kept his name in the minds of many voters. In short, Jerry Voorhis was a smart politician.

As was customary for candidates in the crazy quilt of California politics, Voorhis always sought both the Democratic and the Republican nomination. He never ran as an out-and-out partisan Democrat. In fact, the word "Democrat" rarely appeared in his advertisements and other paraphernalia (just as the word "Republican" almost never showed up on the material of his opponents). Several Republican organization leaders were among Congressman Voorhis' loyal supporters. This galled other rock-ribbed Republicans because, well known to the party faithful, Voorhis was no ordinary Democrat. He was raised in well-to-do circumstances, and that made him all the more sensitive to the woes of the poor. After graduating Phi Beta Kappa from Yale, he took a factory job at 39 cents an hour, worked as a freight handler in a railroad yard, where he saw two fellow workers killed for lack of adequate safety equipment, toured Europe, where he witnessed hunger everywhere, and then, after failing to get a job in a Southern textile mill, and working awhile on a Ford assembly line, he married and, with financial help from his father, opened a school and home for orphaned boys. In the mid-twenties Voorhis was a LaFollette Progressive. Then he became an active Socialist. And in the early Depression years he embraced the "End Poverty in California" program of Upton Sinclair and ran for assemblyman on the ticket which Sinclair headed for Governor. By 1936 Voorhis had become a bona-fide Democrat and ran for Congress as a follower of Franklin D. Roosevelt. Although he grew increasingly conservative in Congress and became an energetic foe of Communism, his record as a whole was bitter medicine for most stalwart Republicans. Worst of all to them was his espousal of cooperatives and a Voorhis plan for altering the monetary system. They called the latter a "funny money scheme."

When all else failed, the Republican hierarchy in California turned to the 1940 census for salvation. Since the legislature was Republican, the plan was to gerrymander Voorhis and several other Democratic congressmen out of office simply by redefining their districts. Two communities which Voorhis normally carried by a ratio of five to one were sliced from his district. Even so, Voorhis was re-elected in 1942 by a 13,000 vote majority and again in 1944, for a fifth term, by the same impressive margin. Other Democrats also survived the gerrymander. Therefore, in 1945, Republican professionals agreed to let complaining amateurs try their hand. These, most of them successful business, industrial and professional figures, traced the trouble to low-grade candidates, known in the trade as "turkeys." It was decided to form a fact-finding committee of leading citizens in each troublesome district. This committee would interview potential candidates, weed out the perennials and the misfits, and support with all available resources "sound-thinking, articulate and respected" individuals, preferably newcomers. Murray M. Chotiner, a resourceful Beverly Hills lawyer-politician whose enterprises included a public relations firm, was designated by the party organization to help the amateurs. Chotiner had masterminded several exceptionally successful campaigns for Republicans, including Governor Earl Warren, and later was to become Richard Nixon's political manager.

Meanwhile, the citizen fact-finders in the 12th District bestirred themselves well ahead of schedule. In the late spring of 1945—a full year and a half before the target election— a group met in Arcadia. Stanley Barnes, an attorney who has since been appointed to the United States Circuit Court of Appeals, as chairman and Frank E. Jorgensen, a vice-president of the Metropolitan Life Insurance Company, were the spark plugs. Later, to assure unity, leaders of various regular Republican party organizations were added to the committee in time to hear the first aspirants for nomination. As might be expected, none of the eight applicants was satisfactory. In fact, Jorgensen and his group already knew the man they wanted. He was Walter Dexter, a former president of Whittier College who had become California's superintendent of education. To run for Congress Dexter would have had to resign his state position and, as Jorgensen recalls, "he couldn't afford to risk the financial loss that would result if he was not elected." Dexter therefore suggested one of his former students, Richard M. Nixon, whom he described as one of the most promising young men he had ever known. Jorgensen and two associates, Boyd Gibbons and Rockwood Nelson, drove over to the Nixon grocery store to make inquiries. Frank and Hannah Nixon were more than willing to talk about their oldest living son. They noted that a good friend in town, Herman L. Perry, manager of the local Bank of America branch, also had mentioned that their son would be an ideal candidate.

Perry telephoned Nixon in Baltimore, where he was renegotiating Navy contracts while awaiting release from the service. Nixon flew to California, and on December 4, 1945, he formally accepted the fact-finding committee's endorsement in a letter to Roy O. Day, district Republican chairman. It was evident from his letter that the 32-year-old Nixon was eager to be out of uniform and running for office. "I am going to see [Congressmen] Joe Martin and John Phillips and try to get what dope I can on Mr. Voorhis' record," he wrote, in part. "His 'conservative' reputation must be blasted. But my main efforts are being directed toward building up a positive, progressive group of speeches which tell what *we* want to do, not what the Democrats have failed to do." The neophyte politician advised Day to "bring in the liberal fringe of Republicans. We need *every* Republican and a few Democrats to win. I'm really hopped up over this deal, and I believe we can win."

In January Nixon was released from active duty, and he came west with a satchelful of ideas and a set of electioneering pictures from which he learned a fundamental political truth. It was that the great majority of veterans had been enlisted men for whom a politician campaigning in the uniform of an officer held little attraction. The photographs were thrown out, and the simple words "Dick Nixon" or just "Nixon" replaced "Lieutenant Commander Richard M. Nixon" on proposed literature. Nixon began his active campaign immediately. Shortly thereafter the Nixons' first daughter, Patricia, was born, and within three weeks Mrs. Nixon left the child with her mother-in-law and joined her husband.

Murray Chotiner was the principal professional member of Nixon's campaign organization. Chotiner was Senator Knowland's southern California campaign manager, in itself a full-time job. Roy Day retained him as publicity director for Nixon, on the side, at a fee of $500.

Voorhis and Nixon took advantage of California's peculiar cross-filing system to become candidates for the nominations of both parties. But while Nixon worked at it energetically, Voorhis sent word that he was very busy looking after the people's welfare in Washington and therefore could not spare the time to campaign in the spring primaries. As usual, that was fine strategy. Voorhis won the Democratic nomination, got a substantial vote in the Republican primary and gained the psychological advantage of beating Nixon by 7,000 votes in the over-all count. Normally this would have meant sure victory in the November general election. But Nixon's morale went up when a Los Angeles political reporter pointed out that Voorhis' vote, 53.5 percent of the total, was quite a drop from 1944, when he polled 60 percent.

"Keen political observers . . . thought we ran a darn fine race, and this was the best Republican primary showing in years," Nixon wrote Chairman Day. "Frankly, Roy, I really believe that's true, and it is time some of the rest of the people began to realize it. All we need is a win complex and we'll take him in November."

The general election campaign flared up early in September, much like many others being fought throughout the country that year of meat and housing shortages, labor unrest and general postwar disenchantment. The Republicans were the "outs," and their battle cry was "Had enough?" The theme of the 12th District campaign followed the national pattern in most respects—that is, the incumbent Democrat was branded as a tool of Sidney Hillman's CIO-Political Action Committee, a promoter of controls and an enemy of free enterprise who would socialize America.

But the Voorhis-Nixon battle developed distinctive nuances of bitterness. The veteran congressman had never before been confronted by a buzz-saw opponent, and the tenderfoot candidate had never before debated so totally for keeps. Both candidates electioneered on three fronts. Most exciting to them and the voters were five debates. Meanest of the three fronts was a battle of newspaper advertisements and statements. Most strenuous for the candidates were handshaking and coffee-hour tours.

While Voorhis believes, in retrospect, that he would have lost anyway, Nixon believes the turning point for him, as the underdog, was the first debate. "It was tough," Nixon says. "I was the challenger, and he was the experienced incumbent. Once that debate was over, I was on my way to eventual victory." Nixon went into the debates against the wishes of all his advisers except Chotiner. The others feared Voorhis was too experienced and Nixon too green. Chotiner insisted the gamble had to be taken because, at worst, Nixon would lose and, at best, he might strike the spark his campaign needed so badly.

The first debate did just that—thanks to a Political Action Committee endorsement of Voorhis which is still the subject of controversy. There had been a small Nixon advertisement which declared, in part, "A vote for Nixon is a vote against the Communist-dominated PAC with its gigantic slush fund." Voorhis vigorously insisted he had not sought and did not have the endorsement of the regional Political Action Committee of the CIO. At this Nixon leaped to his feet, drew a paper from his pocket and read a report in which the Los Angeles chapter of the *national* Political Action Committee recommended that the national group endorse Voorhis. Nixon also read off the names of officers of the national organization's chapter who were also officers of the regional group. Then, dramatically, he thrust the paper at Voorhis.

Shortly afterward Voorhis issued a long, poignant statement declaring that, while he cherished the support of labor, he did not have and did not want the backing of the California

CIO because "under present top leadership of the CIO in California, there is at least grave question whether the Communist party does not exercise inordinate if not decisive influence over state and county organizations."

A few days later he telegraphed the national Political Action Committee demanding that it withdraw its "qualified endorsement" of him.

For the remainder of the campaign Voorhis expended much of his time and energy denying that he was the CIO's errand boy, while Nixon jabbed or punched, as the occasion demanded, with observations about "lip-service Americans" and high officials "who front for un-American elements, wittingly or otherwise, by advocating increasing federal controls over the lives of the people." In mid-October Nixon warned voters against being "fooled" by the "very conservative" tone Voorhis was adopting. "In the last four years, out of 46 measures sponsored by the CIO and the PAC, my opponent has voted against the CIO and PAC only three times," declared Nixon. "Whether he wants it now or not, my opponent has the PAC endorsement and he has certainly earned it. It's not how a man talks, but how he votes that counts."

The PAC controversy reached its shrill peak three days before the election, when Republican campaign headquarters issued a statement in behalf of a former lieutenant governor accusing Voorhis of "consistently voting the Moscow-PAC-Henry Wallace line in Congress." The statement also mentioned "the insolence of Moscow in telling the American voter to elect PAC candidates, such as Mr. Voorhis," and it pronounced Candidate Nixon to be "a man who will talk American and at the same time vote American in Congress . . . and fight in and out of Congress to perpetuate American ideals and American freedom."

There were, of course, other issues in the campaign, and in the context of those times it is not unlikely that some were more decisive with voters than exchanges about the PAC. There was, for example, the veteran issue. Nixon pointed to his own wartime service (and indirectly to Voorhis' civilian status) in an often-repeated promise "to preserve our sacred heritage, in the name of my buddies and your loved ones, who died that these might endure." For his part, Voorhis referred to his opponent at times as "the lieutenant commander" and the "subtlety" escaped no one.

As an "in," Voorhis was compelled to harp on only one positive theme. It was that he had achieved seniority and experience and to turn him out for a newcomer "wouldn't be good sense and would be damaging to popular government in these critical days."

On the other hand, as an "out," with no record to defend, Nixon was free to attack and promise at the same time. Thus he became "thoroughly committed to a program of federal tax reduction" and promised that a Republican Congress would solve the meat, housing and controls problem.

(It was during this first campaign that Nixon developed the knack of repeating verbatim questions asked of him from the floor. It requires the vocal apparatus to operate on one track while the thinking apparatus operates on another. Nixon does it to give himself time to think of the answer.)

Voorhis had 296 inches of campaign advertising and Nixon 162 inches, in the *Post-Advocate*, the daily newspaper of Alhambra, largest city in the district. It is noteworthy that not one line in a Nixon manifest mentioned the fact that he was a Republican, and none of Voorhis' alluded to his membership in the Democratic party.

Nixon won by a vote of 65,586 to 49,994 and carried Whittier, 5,727 to 2,678. He was one of seven Republicans to unseat incumbent Democrats in California. All told, the Republicans picked up 55 House seats and won control of the Eightieth Congress. In reflecting on the campaign 12 years later Nixon said the race was, in effect, a contest between a well-known New Dealer and a conservative Republican. "Voorhis lost because that district was not a New Deal district," he said. "Our campaign was a very honest debate on the issues." [1]

[1] Six years after the election, when Nixon was running for Vice-President, a story in the *New Republic* stated that there had been anonymous telephone calls accusing Voorhis of Communism. Nixon insists he had never before heard of such calls. Voorhis says several people told him they had received the calls, but he did not know their source. It is possible that some or all of the calls were designed to hurt Nixon as well as Voorhis by making him appear guilty of vicious tactics.

At the same time Voorhis offered this opinion: "I'm frank to say that I felt a little bit this way: I had been the congressman ten years. I'd done the best I could. And I really felt if the voters wanted to throw me out, by golly, okay. I'm afraid this was on my mind the whole time, to some extent. I hated a fight like that, especially because of its effect on my family."

On the whole, Nixon's record in Congress was a moderate one. During his first two-year term 91 percent of his votes conformed with Republican party policy, according to a survey by the nonpartisan *Congressional Quarterly*. In his second term it was 74 percent. After the campaign, becoming a freshman congressman was tame stuff, and Nixon admitted to "the same lost feeling that I had when I first went into the military service." Nixon requested assignment to the Labor Committee and, although he did not ask for it, he was also placed on the Un-American Activities Committee. One of his first specific jobs concerned civil rights. At the request of Adam Clayton Powell, Democratic congressman from Harlem, he was made a member of a five-man subcommittee which had one mission: it was to answer immediately anything said by Congressman John Rankin, the vehement racist from Mississippi. His work on the Herter Committee, whose reports led to the Marshall Plan, has been particularly significant for Nixon. As the only freshman representative on it, he visited Europe and learned something of America's international responsibilities. He was a leading proponent of the Herter program in Congress and, surprisingly, in his own isolationist district—which nominated him later in both Democratic and Republican primaries. Nixon considers his service to the Herter Committee the most important of his congressional career.

At the outset Nixon's favorite work was as a member of a small subcommittee that drafted the Taft-Hartley Labor Law. That was where he became friendly with a freshman Democrat from Masachusetts named John F. Kennedy. Nixon and Kennedy were on opposite sides of the Taft-Hartley question, and in the spring of 1947 they went to McKeesport, Pennsylvania, to debate the issue.

Meanwhile Nixon's interest in the Un-American Activities

Committee was not very great. But it warmed up on August 3, 1948, when Whittaker Chambers, a former Communist, listed among his one-time fellow conspirators a man named Alger Hiss.

5 ❋ *Hiss Case, 1948*

ALGER HISS was first mentioned to Nixon in February, 1947, a few weeks after his arrival in Washington as a congressman. A colleague had introduced him to the Rev. John F. Cronin, a newcomer to Washington from Baltimore, where he was professor of philosophy and economics at St. Mary's Seminary. Father Cronin had been helping to organize labor unions, and he became so alarmed at the extent of Communist infiltration in war plants that he took time off from his teaching to make an intensive study of Communist party activities. That led him to Washington, where he ran across all the names and episodes that subsequently became familiar to the public through congressional hearings—Alger Hiss, Elizabeth Bentley and the whole litany. The information was not at all difficult to come by, and Father Cronin was startled by the apparent indifference of responsible officials. It was on his mind when he met Congressman Nixon, and he talked about it.

Nixon was interested. But he had other interests—too many, in fact, for a fledgling legislator. It was a year and a half before the incidents Father Cronin had discussed were aired by the House Un-American Activities Committee. On July 31, 1948, Elizabeth Bentley, who said she had been a courier for a Communist spy ring, was the first to testify. Afterward a man she named as part of the apparatus contradicted much of what she said. That led to the calling of Whittaker Chambers, a confessed former Communist who had become a senior editor of *Time* magazine. Although Chambers had shown no inclination to cooperate with the committee, its members felt he might corroborate some of the Bentley testimony. Chambers had been interrogated by the FBI five years before. But the information he provided was in the files of the Justice Department. Since Justice was an agency of the Executive Department, its files ostensibly were not available to the congressional committee.

In 1939, after breaking with the Communist party, Chambers had gone to Assistant Secretary of State A. A. Berle, Jr., with his story of government employees with whom he had operated as a Communist party member from 1934 to 1937. This information was known indirectly to the House committee. But in January, 1948, two of its investigators got practically nowhere in an effort to convince Chambers that he should repeat it to them.

Nevertheless, Chambers was summoned before the committee on August 3. The story of his testimony and of the people he named as associates in his Communist party activities is well known. But additional material has become available from a memorandum Nixon prepared when a friend urged that he set down privately any otherwise unrecorded facts about the case, and also his impressions, while they were still fresh in mind. Nixon saw Chambers for the first time in the committee counsel's office before the session. "He impressed me as being extremely shy and reticent, and also as if what he was doing was being done because he thought he should, rather than because he wanted to." The committee heard Chambers in executive session. "He was not a crackpot and was, in fact, a very responsible person, at least as far as his background was concerned," Nixon wrote in his memorandum. The session then was made public—and, though Chambers spoke softly and had to be prodded repeatedly to raise his voice, he produced his list of names clearly enough for them to be speeded into headlines and over air waves.

For Nixon, who was to make of the Hiss investigation a phenomenal political success, the high spot of Chambers' testimony came toward the end of his prepared statement. When Chambers said he knew the consequences of what he was doing but felt that duty to his country compelled him to do it, Nixon recalled, "His voice broke and there was a pause of at least 15 to 20 seconds during which he attempted to gain control of his emotions before he could proceed.

"This one incident was to have a considerable bearing upon my own attitude toward him because I did not feel that it was an act. . . . On the contrary, I felt he indicated deep sincerity and honesty."

Alger Hiss, the most important name uttered by Chambers, asked the committee immediately for an opportunity to deny the charge, and it agreed to hear him August 5. Chambers had not impressed all the committee members as favorably as he had Nixon, and there was considerable anxiety.

The year 1948 brought a presidential election. Truman, Dewey and their forces were warming up for November. The Communist issue had not yet been tried nationally as a campaign weapon and, since the Soviet Union had so recently been America's ally, there was serious doubt as to whether Republicans would gain or lose by accusing Democrats of "softness" on Communism. In control of the Eightieth Congress, Republicans were running the committee now pointing a finger at Alger Hiss and others. And, although Hiss was not well known to subway straphangers, coal miners or cotton pickers, he was highly respected in the government, and also in legal and diplomatic circles. Only the year before he had been appointed president of the Carnegie Endowment for International Peace at a salary of $20,000, which was $5,000 more than what was then paid Cabinet members and congressmen. The Carnegie board which hired him was composed of eminent men. Its chairman was John Foster Dulles, the Republican party's foremost expert on foreign affairs. Hiss had been principal adviser to the American delegation at the first United Nations General Assembly Session. Before that he had distinguished himself as secretary-general of the conference in San Francisco which created the United Nations. Furthermore, he had accompanied the Roosevelt party to Yalta and had been executive secretary of the Dumbarton Oaks Conference in 1944. Hiss had graduated from Johns Hopkins University and the Harvard Law School. After a year as clerk to Supreme Court Justice Oliver Wendell Holmes he practiced law briefly in Boston and New York; then, in 1933, he began his government career in Washington.

From the moment he walked into the congressional hearing room on August 5, 1948, and raised his hand to be sworn, it

was obvious to everyone that Alger Hiss was quite different
from run-of-the-mill types that usually paraded before those
microphones. Before the day was done, Nixon realized that
this was his "first real testing." "Very few men get in the
merciless spotlight of national publicity in a case that may
make or break a party, or for that matter even a country,"
Nixon said 12 years later. "The Hiss case was a very rugged
experience in some ways. Considering the amount of time I
spent on it, it's as difficult an experience as I've ever had.
From the standpoint of responsibility . . . the resourceful
enemies I was up against . . . the battle day in and day out
. . . the terrible attacks from the press, nasty cartoons, editorials, mail . . . and there was always a great doubt whether
you are going to win and whether you are on the right side
or not. I was convinced that I was."

When Hiss concluded his testimony, the general feeling in
Washington was that the long-controversial Un-American Activities Committee had made its final blunder, and was finished.
Hiss had impressed practically everyone with the implication
that the committee had been duped into permitting Chambers
to use it as a forum from which to slander people. Congressman Rankin, the crusty old Mississippi Democrat, was so
moved that he left his seat to shake Hiss's hand. That morning
President Truman declared at a White House press conference
that Republicans had cooked up spy hearings "as a red herring
to keep from doing what they ought to do" about inflation
and the nation's other serious problems.

When the committee went into executive (secret) session
that evening, "virtual consternation reigned among the members," Nixon noted. All, except Nixon, felt Hiss was telling
the truth. F. Edward Hébert, a Democrat from Louisiana,
suggested the committee wash its hands of the case at once
and send the files to the Attorney General to determine
whether Hiss or Chambers should be charged with perjury.
Karl E. Mundt, a South Dakota Republican and acting chairman, suggested nervously that the committee develop a col-
lateral issue at once to take itself off the spot. Nixon recorded
that he and Robert Stripling, the committee counsel, insisted
that "although we could not determine who was lying on the
issue of whether or not Hiss was a Communist, we should at

least go into the matter of whether or not Chambers knew Hiss." Nixon was of the opinion that "Hiss was a particularly convincing witness that day . . . the committee had no real facts to use as a basis for cross-examining him and consequently he was able to dominate the situation throughout." Nixon suggested that a subcommittee examine Chambers again, in executive session. Stripling said that could be done very easily in New York because a witness in the Elizabeth Bentley case lived there and the committee could go there purportedly to see into that matter.

On August 7, according to the Nixon memorandum, Chambers "gave the information which eventually was to be responsible for breaking the Hiss case." In reply to questions Chambers had provided a mass of details about Hiss, the Hiss family, their hobbies and habits, and additional material that Nixon and other committee members were almost certain could be known only by someone who was as friendly with Hiss as Chambers said he had been. Representative Hébert still had doubts. And so did Representative John McDowell, a Pennsylvania Republican.

Nixon recorded several reasons for his skepticism about Hiss from the outset:

Hiss was much too smooth . . . much too careful a witness for one who purported to be telling the whole truth without qualifications. . . . I felt he had put on a show when he was shown a picture of Chambers . . . his statement "This might look like you, Mr. Chairman," seemed to me to be overacted . . . when I asked him who had recommended him for his government position, he attempted to keep the name of [Supreme Court Justice] Frankfurter out of the testimony and this indicated to me he might be following a general practice of testifying apparently forthrightly and openly on all matters, but actually giving the committee what information he wanted to and refusing to give information which he did not want the committee to have. He was rather insolent toward me from the time that I insisted on bringing Frankfurter's name in, and from that time my suspicion concerning him continued to grow.

Furthermore, Nixon wondered about rumors which spread immediately "to the effect that Chambers had spent some time in a mental institution, was insane, was an habitual drunkard and a homosexual . . . it seemed to me that this was a typical Commie tactic and though, of course, Hiss might not have been responsible for it, I was convinced that at least we should look into the matter further. . . ."

Between the secret interrogation of Chambers and August 16, when Hiss was recalled, also in secret, Nixon and the committee staff tried to double-check all the new material Chambers had provided. Nixon wanted "to convince myself and other members of the committee that Chambers had at least made a *prima facie* case which required that we bring Hiss back to rebut it." The fact that two members were still skeptical was "probably quite a good thing because it kept the rest of us from going off half-cocked."

On August 10 Nixon visited Chambers at his farm at Westminster, Maryland. He said it was "mainly for the purpose of attempting to convince myself on the issue of whether or not Chambers, in speaking of Hiss, was speaking of a man he knew, or was telling a story which he had concocted." Two hours of conversation just about convinced him. The clincher came when Chambers walked to the porch with Nixon as the congressman was leaving. "I was still trying to press him for any personal recollection which might help us in breaking the case," Nixon's memorandum reads. "The conversation came around to religion and he said that Mrs. Hiss was a Quaker and that he also was a Quaker at the present time. I told him that I was a Quaker, and then suddenly Chambers snapped his fingers and said, 'Here's something I should have recalled before. Mrs. Hiss used to use the plain language in talking with Alger.' As a Quaker I knew that Chambers couldn't know such intimate matters unless he had known Hiss, although, of course, there was a possibility that some friend of Hiss's might have told him of this. He pointed out that Alger was a genuinely kind, intelligent individual. That was the reason that Chambers was attracted to him—probably because they were both in the movement for the very highest motives."

It was then that Nixon went to several outsiders for confirmation of his own judgment. One of the first was William P. Rogers, counsel for the Senate Internal Security Committee, who had had considerable experience in assessing the veracity of witnesses. Nixon told Rogers that if he found Chambers was not telling the truth he would admit the mistake and apologize to Hiss. On the other hand, if Chambers was right, his story had to be proved. Rogers agreed and, after reviewing the transcripts, said he felt the Chambers testimony was provable.

Bert Andrews, chief of the New York *Herald Tribune* bureau in Washington, was another to whom Nixon turned. In 1947 Andrews won a Pulitzer Prize for a story that exposed damage done to a government employee because of unfair security procedure. Like most newspapermen and public officials in contact with Hiss, Andrews regarded him highly as a public servant. When Dulles sought his opinion of Hiss before appointing him to the Carnegie Endowment presidency, Andrews gave a fine recommendation, as other prominent Washington correspondents had done. Andrews was amazed by Chambers' testimony. When he checked the hearing transcripts at Nixon's request he became as convinced as Nixon was that Chambers told the truth. He had the impression, however, that Chambers still had not told all he knew. Thereafter, Andrews became an informal adviser to Nixon.

Christian Herter's advice was also sought and that of Foster Dulles, an adviser to candidate Dewey. Charles J. Kersten, a Republican congressman from Wisconsin and a friend of Nixon's, recalls how Nixon received word that the Carnegie Endowment and several important men associated with it were preparing to come vigorously to Hiss's defense. "We talked in the caucus room of the old House office building at the end of a day's hearings of the House Labor Committee," Kersten said. "Dick decided to see Dulles immediately, and he asked me to go with him."

They visited Dulles at the Roosevelt Hotel in New York where Dulles had a suite in the Dewey campaign headquarters. With Dulles as foreign policy aides to Dewey were his brother, Allen Dulles, later director of the Central Intelligence Agency, Herter and banker C. Douglas Dillon. Nixon brought along the transcript of testimony. The Dulles brothers read it very carefully, then discussed the matter with Nixon, well into the night.

"Hiss had a reputation at the time that was very high indeed," Secretary of State Dulles pointed out in an interview many years later. "Dick had gotten a lot of evidence, but it was clear he did not want to proceed with Hiss until people like myself had agreed that he really had got a case to justify his going ahead. Dick wanted to proceed cautiously, and he did not want to jeopardize a person's right."

As he reviewed the evidence Dulles walked back and forth in front of a fireplace in the large hotel room. He and Allen examined and re-examined sections of the transcript. "We went through the evidence to the end, and I told Dick that I thought it was a case that ought to be followed up," Secretary Dulles recalled. "I was greatly impressed. Many people in that position, who appeared to have something sensational, would go ahead. But Dick wanted to be careful about hurting reputations and sought the opinions of people who knew Hiss as to the weight of the evidence. It was the first time Dick and I had any intimate association. I formed a very high judgment of the sense of responsibility under which he operated."

When Hiss appeared before the committee again on August 16 and was questioned closely about the personal data Chambers had provided, Nixon saw practically every answer as a confirmation of Chambers—and his last doubts were cleared away. In a discussion that night with Bert Andrews, according to a note in his memorandum, he agreed "that it was best to have the confrontation [between Hiss and Chambers] at the earliest possible date before Hiss could build up his story."

The committee staged the confrontation hurriedly on August 17. Nixon and Hiss differ widely in their interpretations of the dramatic confrontation at the Commodore Hotel, New York. According to Nixon, the scene was this:

The committee members and staff went up to Suite 1400, which consisted of a living room and a bedroom—I would imagine they rented for about $15 a day. The living room was decorated with Audubon prints. We had one of the investigators take Chambers to another room and keep him in readiness for the hearing. We then proceeded to set up the room.

When Hiss arrived, he obviously was very upset. He said that he had a dinner engagement and asked permission to make a call so he could let them know how late he would be. We told him that the hearing would probably not take too long. On the previous day Hiss had been much less smooth than on August 5. Some of us seemed to sense that when Hiss brought up the name of George Crosley [a free-lance writer Hiss said he had known who looked like the photograph of Chambers] he was extremely glib. Now, when Hiss was seated, we told the investigator to go to get Chambers. Chambers entered at Hiss's rear and walked behind him over to the davenport, where he sat down. Hiss did not once turn around to get a good look at the man he claims he did not know. Instead he looked at all times stonily straight ahead at the members of the committee.

From the record it appears that I had no reason to criticize Hiss for suggesting that Chambers be sworn. The record fails to show just how the incident occurred. Hiss actually interrupted me as I made the suggestion and of course his manner and tone were insulting in the extreme. By this time he was visibly shaken and had lost the air of smoothness which had characterized most of his apperances before. In fact, this hearing, I think for the first and probably the last time, showed the committee the real Hiss because, except for a few minutes at the beginning and for possibly a few minutes right at the end as he was leaving, he acted the part of a liar who had been caught, rather than the part of the outraged innocent man, which he had so successfully portrayed before then.

When Hiss and Chambers stood up to confront each other, they were not more than four or five feet apart. Incidentally, we put the windows down so as to keep the street noises out, but at the last minute we raised the blind so that there would be ample light when the two men saw each other. When Hiss asked Chambers to open his mouth so he could see his teeth, he took two or three steps toward him and I would say was about a foot from his face as he peered into his throat. When he asked to have Chambers open his mouth wider, he actually reached up with his hand and made a gesture of opening the fingers to indicate what he wanted Chambers to do. I would say that his hand was not more than six inches from Chambers's teeth. In fact, I wondered why Chambers didn't reach out and bite his finger.

When Hiss finally admitted that he knew Chambers, he did so in a very loud, dramatic voice as if he were acting in a Shakespeare play. In fact, he rose from his chair and pointed his finger. When he walked over toward Chambers at the time that he dared Chambers to speak where he could be sued, he actually shook his fist and gave the appearance of one who was about to attack. But I was convinced it was purely a bluff. A staff member walked up behind him and actually touched only his clothes and asked him to sit down. Hiss wheeled on him as if he had stuck him with a hot needle in a sensitive spot, and shouted to take his hands off.

Chambers as contrasted to Hiss was very quiet throughout the hearing. He showed no fear when Hiss walked toward him. He was rather nervous, I would say, when he was reading [so Hiss might check his voice] but settled down as the hearing progressed, and after a time, I would say, he seemed secretly to be enjoying the situation. He was completely in command of himself throughout the proceedings.

At the conclusion of the hearing Hiss was completely unnerved, and my only regret is that we more or less agreed to let him go at an early hour so that he could make his appointment, because I feel that if we had continued to press him we might have gotten even more contradictions out of him, if not an actual break.

Nixon noted at this point that Hiss always insisted on having both the executive and the public session testimony before he would be interrogated at another hearing. On the other hand, Chambers did not want to see the transcripts and refused to have an attorney. Hiss, a lawyer himself, always insisted that an attorney sit by him.

In his book, *In the Court of Public Opinion,* Hiss stated that the committee on August 16 had given him "a clear commitment in time and place for me to see Chambers face to face." This, he added, gave him an unwarranted sense of having accomplished something. "The committee's delay in bringing Chambers and me together and their substituted procedure of separate secret hearings proved far more damaging to me than I then realized," he wrote. "I had been concerned because the impression was being created that I had categorically denied ever having met the man Chambers by any name or under any circumstances. . . . By taking Chambers' testimony of August 7 in secret, where it could not be promptly corrected by me, and by characterizing all of his testimony as accurate, the committee created an impression that Chambers and I had had a close association, and that what one supposedly intimate friend did the other might be expected to do also. This might be called a theory of 'guilt by close association.' "

Hiss then traced the hurriedly called session of August 17 to Harry Dexter White. He noted that White was frequently applauded by the audience in the hearing room when he appeared before the committee a week before and denied the charges both Chambers and Elizabeth Bentley had made against him. White had sent a note to the chair which said, "I am recovering from a severe heart attack. I would appreciate it if the chairman would give me five or ten minutes rest after each hour."

At this the chairman snapped, "For a person who had a severe heart attack you certainly can play a lot of sports."

"Flying back from Washington after my testimony of the afternoon before," wrote Hiss, "I had had time to read the fully reported accounts of White's appearance and had been impressed by his courage in voluntarily facing, despite his illness, the ordeal of a public grilling in the circus-arena atmosphere of klieg lights and flash bulbs. I had found unpalatable the committee's badgering of a sick man and its implication that he was malingering in privately asking for an occasional intermission." The next morning, Hiss continued, a staff member called to say Congressman McDowell was to be in New York that afternoon and hoped to see Hiss for ten or 15 minutes. During the day, Hiss recalls, he read in the newspapers that White had died "having over the weekend suffered a further heart attack, presumably brought on by his exertions before the committee."

At nearly 5:30, Hiss related, McDowell called.

Instead of saying that he would be along soon, he rather surprised me by inviting me to come to the Commodore Hotel and then added that Nixon "and one other" were with him. At this point I felt quite sure that something more than a casual conversation was planned and that the manner in which the arrangements had been made had been deliberately less than frank. A colleague, Charles Dollard of the Carnegie Corporation, was still in his office, and I took the precaution of asking him if he would walk over to the Commodore with me to see what lay behind this slightly mysterious maneuvering. I was by now highly suspicious of the good faith of various members of the committee. Biased accounts in the morning papers of my testimony of the day before were a plain and prompt repudiation of the protestations of secrecy by some members of the committee. I wanted at least one friend present who would be able to give his version of any further relations I might have with the committee.

We went to McDowell's hotel room and, as we entered, found that it was still in the process of being hastily converted into an improvised hearing room. McDowell and Nixon were there; [Rep. J. Parnell] Thomas arrived a good deal later. . . . Suddenly the connection between White's death and the hastily summoned hearings struck me. The impact of the press account of White's fatal heart attack was hardly favorable to the committee. . . . My experience with the committee up to this point led me to conclude that they had decided to meet the crisis of a bad press by a sudden and sensational move. . . .

When Chambers was ushered in, Hiss saw him as "short, plump, perspiring and very pale." Hiss added that "his appearance was certainly familiar, and I thought I saw Crosley in the added pounds and rumpled suit. But there was no expression, no spark of individuality as yet. I wanted to hear his voice and to see if he had Crosley's bad teeth before expressing my feeling that this was George Crosley . . . Chambers did not meet my eye, but stared fixedly before him or up to the ceiling. He had given his name in a tight, rather high pitched, constrained voice, barely opening his mouth. This seemed evidently not the man's normal voice, nor could I see whether his front teeth were decayed. In response to my request that in speaking he open his mouth wider, he was able only to repeat his name, again in a strangled voice, through almost closed lips."

Finally, the session ended with a sharp exchange between Hiss and the chairman.

"I had followed the traditional forms long enough out of respect for the Office of Congressman and out of habit," Hiss wrote subsequently, in his book. "I had tried to get the committee to follow the orderly procedure with which I was familiar. Now at the end of this hearing I wanted to make it quite plain that I resented the committee's callous and ruthless procedures. It helped, I felt, to clear the air in this fashion. As I told Mr. Dulles that evening in a telephone conversation, it was evident that the committee and I were now at war." [1]

The public hearing at which Hiss and Chambers were brought face to face was held on August 25. It produced the expected headlines and heightened the controversy over who was lying. But Nixon and the committee were aware that, for all their effort, there was still one big hole in the case. It was summed up in the word "Why?"

"The weak point in Chambers' story was that Chambers was unable to give a satisfactory explanation for what he talked about with Hiss and the other [Communist party] members of their group when he came down to see them each week [in the mid-thirties]," Nixon noted in his memorandum. "Chambers used to say that they discussed party policies, how to get new members for the ring and so forth. Of course, the explanation was that his group was engaged in espionage, and

[1] As a government witness at the Hiss perjury trial two years later, Dulles testified that on August 18, a day after the confrontation, he suggested that Hiss resign as president of the Carnegie Endowment Organization to save the foundation from further embarrassment. Dulles stated also that he had told Hiss he would not be fired, however. When Hiss was indicted in December, 1948, he offered to resign, but the board granted him a leave of absence with full pay instead of accepting the resignation.

although both Stripling and I discussed this possibility, we were not able to get any information from Chambers along that line."

Later Nixon added: "It now seems probable that the explanation for Chambers' letting out his story in bits was that he did not want to go into the espionage phase unless absolutely necessary, and he knew that the more of the story he told the more likely it was that a connection with the espionage activity would be established." The scene for that fatal phase was set on August 17 when Hiss dared Chambers to repeat his charge where he would not have congressional immunity from a libel suit. On August 27 Chambers did just that on a radio program, "Meet the Press."

A month later Hiss sued. And it was that civil suit which led to Chambers' production of handwritten, typewritten and microfilmed copies of classified government documents which, he said, Hiss passed to him to be relayed to the Soviet Union.

There were still anxieties for Nixon and his colleagues before the case was closed. Once early in December the so-called "Pumpkin Papers"—microfilm Chambers had produced from a hollowed-out pumpkin—were thought to be fraudulent, because the first test indicated the film was new, and not 11 years old as it would have been if Chambers' story was authentic. Another, more careful test verified the authenticity of the film.

Nixon concluded his memorandum with a notation about the reason Chambers gave for finally turning over the documents:

He said that he had become convinced that unless he did he would never be able to convince anyone of the seriousness of his charges and of their truth. He said that Hiss's lawyers [in the libel suit] had questioned Mrs. Chambers rather ruthlessly and that also he had resented the implications which Hiss's people had been making that he was a homosexual and had been crazy and the like, but he said that when he made the decision in a period of Quaker meditation he tried to put these personal animosities out of his mind, and he felt that he had reached the decision and made it primarily because of the public interest which was involved.

Although Chambers was always very relaxed and confident in giving his testimony, I seemed to sense that after he finally decided to go into the espionage phase of the case, he talked as if a great load had been lifted from his mind, and he seemed very free and almost elated by what he had done.

On December 15, 1948, a federal grand jury in New York indicted Hiss for perjury in denying that he ever turned over government documents to Chambers. The first trial took five weeks, and ended inconclusively on July 8, with the jury deadlocked eight to four for conviction. Nixon and three other members of the House Un-American Activities Committee accused Judge Samuel H. Kaufman of bias for Hiss and demanded that his fitness be investigated. The judge's "prejudice for the defense and against the prosecution was so obvious and apparent that the jury's eight to four vote for conviction frankly came as a surprise to me," Nixon declared. He accused the judge of refusing, for political reasons, to permit two witnesses to testify. "I think the entire Truman administration was extremely anxious that nothing bad happen to Mr. Hiss," he said. "Members of the administration feared that an adverse verdict would prove that there was a great deal of foundation to all the reports of Communist infiltration into the government during the New Deal days."

Congressman Emanuel Cellar, a New York Democrat and chairman of the House Judiciary Committee, vigorously defended Judge Kaufman's conduct, but admitted that if impeachment proceedings were brought in the House he would disqualify himself since Judge Kaufman had been his law partner. No positive action followed against the judge.

On November 17, 1949, the second Hiss trial began before Judge Henry W. Goddard, and on January 21, 1950, Hiss was found guilty by the jury. Among the hundreds of messages received by Nixon was one in which Herbert Hoover stated: "The conviction of Alger Hiss was due to your patience and persistence alone. At last the stream of treason that existed in our government has been exposed in a fashion that all may believe."

With the conviction, the Hiss case became a major political

asset to the Republican party, and to Nixon in particular. When he was nominated for Vice-President in 1952, General Eisenhower introduced him to the National Convention as "a man who has shown statesmanlike qualities in many ways, but has a special talent and an ability to ferret out any kind of subversive influence wherever it may be found, and the strength and persistence to get rid of it."

From some of the speeches during the Presidential campaign one might have thought that Alger Hiss was a candidate on the Democratic ticket. Nixon charged on several occasions and in several different ways that a Democratic victory would yield for America "more Alger Hisses, more atomic spies, more crises" instead of lasting peace. In a major campaign address, televised nationally from New York on October 13, 1952, Nixon reviewed the dramatic highlights of the Hiss investigation.

"We rented a room in the Commodore Hotel, Room 1400, incidentally, and in that room we called both Mr. Hiss and Mr. Chambers and asked them to give testimony as to whether or not one or the other could recognize each other," Nixon told his television audience. "Let me describe the room for you, because it is here that you can see the Communist conspiracy in action . . . twisting and turning and squirming . . . evading and avoiding. Imagine yourself in an ordinary hotel sitting room, with the windows to my back looking out on Forty-second Street, a couple of chairs here . . . a small hotel sitting room in front of us . . . a chair here facing us for Mr. Hiss, and a lounge over there where Mr. Chambers was to sit."

As a climax Nixon produced some of the documents obtained from Chambers and declared that the Russians had been given hundreds like them "from Hiss and other members of the ring," which meant "that the lives of American boys were endangered and probably lost because of the activities of a spy ring." That shows what "just one man can do to injure the security of his country when he owes his loyalty not to his own government but to a foreign power . . . and again this case is a lesson, because we see the action of the administration in covering it up rather than in bringing Hiss to book many years sooner as they should have."

Nixon got to the principal point of his story at the last minutes of his half hour:

Mr. Stevenson was a character witness, or should I say a witness for the reputation, and the good reputation, of Alger Hiss. He testified that the reputation of Alger Hiss for veracity, for integrity and for loyalty was good. . . . This testimony . . . was given after all these facts, this confrontation in which Hiss had to look into Chambers' mouth to identify him, after these papers came out of the pumpkin, after all of those facts were known . . . it was voluntary on Mr. Stevenson's part . . . it was given at a time when he was Governor of Illinois and the prestige of a great state and the Governor of the state were thrown in behalf of the defendant in this case. . . . It is significant that Mr. Stevenson has never expressed any indignation over what Mr. Hiss has done and the treachery that he engaged in against his country.

Then Nixon added:

Let me emphasize that there is no question in my mind as to the loyalty of Mr. Stevenson, but the question is one as to his judgment, and it is a very grave question. . . . In my opinion, his actions, his statements, his record disqualifies him from leading the United States and the free nations in the fight against Communism at home and abroad; because, you see, the election of Mr. Stevenson would mean four more years of the same policy which has been so disastrous at home and disastrous abroad for America.

Ten days later Stevenson replied with an assertion that General Eisenhower and John Foster Dulles had been far closer to Alger Hiss than he, Stevenson, ever was. In a national broadcast he asserted that he was doing his duty as a citizen and as a lawyer in giving a deposition about Hiss's reputation as he had known it. He pointed out that Senator Robert Taft, Senator John Bricker and Congressman Joseph W. Martin, Jr., had attested in far more complimentary terms to the reputation of a Republican congressman from Ohio who recently had been convicted of unlawfully receiving political contributions from his employees. "It is obvious that my testimony in the Hiss case no more shows softness toward Communism than the testimony of these Republican leaders shows softness toward corruption," Stevenson said. "At no time did I testify on the issue of the guilt or innocence of Alger Hiss. As I have repeatedly said, I have never doubted the verdict of the jury which convicted him."

Stevenson spoke of Nixon as "the brash young man who aspires to the vice-presidency" and declared that if Nixon "would not tell, and tell honestly, what he knew of a defendant's reputation, he would be a coward and unfit for any office. The responsibility of lawyers to cooperate with the courts is greatest of all because they are officers of the court. And Senator Nixon is a lawyer."

Stevenson added:

> I would suggest to the Republican "Crusaders" that if they were to apply the same methods to their own candidate, General Eisenhower, and to his foreign affairs adviser, John Foster Dulles, they would find that both these men were of the same opinion about Alger Hiss, and more so. . . . The facts are that the General and Mr. Dulles both demonstrated a continued personal faith in Alger Hiss in circumstances which imposed on them—as circumstances never did on me—the obligation to make a searching examination of his character and background.
>
> In December, 1946, Hiss was chosen to be president of the Carnegie Endowment by the board of trustees of which John Foster Dulles was chairman. After Hiss was elected, but before he took office, a Detroit lawyer [whom Stevenson never named] offered to provide Mr. Dulles with evidence that Hiss had a provable Communist record. No such report or warning ever came to me. Under date of December 26, Mr. Dulles responded. Listen to what Mr. Dulles said: "I have heard the report which you refer to, but I have confidence that there is reason to doubt Mr. Hiss's complete loyalty to our American institutions. I have been thrown into intimate contact with him at San Francisco, London and Washington . . . under these circumstances I feel a little skeptical about information which seems inconsistent with all that I personally know and what is the judgment of reliable friends and associates in Washington."

That, my friends, was John Foster Dulles, the General's adviser on foreign affairs. In May, 1948, General Eisenhower was elected to the board of trustees of the Carnegie Endowment at the same meeting at which Hiss was re-elected president and Dulles was re-elected chairman of the board. This was months after I had seen Hiss for the last time. I am sure the General would never have joined the board of trustees if he had any doubt concerning Hiss's loyalty.

After he had been indicted by the grand jury, Hiss tendered his resignation. . . . The board of trustees of which General Eisenhower was a member declined to accept his resignation and granted him three months leave of absence with full pay so that he might defend himself. . . . Alger Hiss, General Eisenhower and Dulles continued as fellow members of the board of trustees until after the conviction of Alger Hiss.

Before concluding his speech, Stevenson said, "I bring these facts to the American people," not to suggest that either Eisenhower or Dulles was soft toward Communists or even guilty of bad judgment, but "only to make the point that the mistrust, the innuendoes, the accusations which this 'Crusade' is employing, threatens not merely themselves, but the integrity of our institutions."

There were so many ramifications to the Hiss case that books already are being written about relatively small facets of it, and identical facts are being subjected to contradictory interpretations. On reflection, Nixon says that "looking back, I suppose the great lesson of the Hiss case is the personal tragedies involved for both Hiss and Chambers. They came from very different backgrounds, but both of them were sensitive, very capable men. Intellectually, Chambers was superior to Hiss, but Hiss was no slouch when it came to brains. Both were, I think, sincerely dedicated to the concepts of peace and the concept of bettering the lot of the common man, of people generally. They were both idealists. Yet, here are two men of this quality who became infected with Communism, infected with it to the degree that they were willing to run the risk, as they did, of disgrace in order to serve the Communist conspiracy. The fact that this could happen to them shows the potential threat that Communism presents among people of this type throughout the world."

Nixon all but dropped the word "Hiss" from his political lexicon after one of his earliest press conferences in the 1956 campaign when he praised Stevenson as being "forthright and direct," and acting "very creditably" in disassociating himself from an observation by Truman that Hiss had never been proved to be a spy or a Communist.

But both Nixon and the Republican party were to work a tremendous amount of political mileage from the sturdy treads of the Hiss case—and for Nixon, this road started in 1950, when he ran for the Senate against Democratic Congresswoman Helen Gahagan Douglas.

6 ❋ *Senatorial Campaign, 1950*

NOTHING in the litany of reprehensible conduct charged against Nixon the campaigner has been cited more often than the tactics by which he defeated Congresswoman Helen Gahagan Douglas for Senator. It is one of the most familiar stories of Nixon's political career, and the source of much dislike and mistrust of him. A searching study of that campaign, including a check of Mrs. Douglas' files in her New York apartment, reveals that the accepted account is only a fraction of what really transpired. It was indeed a ripsnorting campaign, overflowing with villains and political iniquity —or heroes and cagey maneuvers, depending on how one judges.

It began with a conflict of political ambitions—Nixon's, Mrs. Douglas', Senator Sheridan Downey's and others'. The Democrats had regained control of Congress in the 1948 election and, although the Hiss case focused enough national attention on Nixon for him to be recognized by Capitol tourists, he now was not only a junior member but a junior in the minority party of the lower house. Nixon raised his sights to the Senate.

Challenging Republican Senator William Knowland was out of the question. But California's other Senator was a Democrat whose seat would be at stake in 1950. Senator Downey wanted a third term, and most people felt he probably would win it. It is an axiom of California politics that an incumbent enjoys a great advantage regardless of party, record or office, because practically a third of the voters almost always go for the name identified with the office.

64

Three senior Republicans coveted Downey's post. But they decided against risking the race. That left only Nixon. He was a sad but earnest underdog until his lucky star came through in the form of Mrs. Douglas' candidacy, which meant a showdown fight among the Democrats.

Though California had many more registered Democrats than Republicans, the latter frequently won state elections because left- and right-wing Democrats had habitually clawed each other so viciously in their party primary that the survivor, or nominee, was too weak and demoralized to campaign effectively in the general election. The encounter between the conservative Downey and the liberal Mrs. Douglas was destined to be a prize show.

Earlier, before the Republican picture had brightened, Nixon toured the state quietly to muster backing for his candidacy. Former President Hoover encouraged him. Senator Knowland offered his own "unqualified support" and that of the Oakland *Tribune,* his family's newspaper. Principal figures in a Stassen political organization, "California Volunteers for Good Government," also were enthusiastic. They endorsed Nixon ahead of schedule, almost upsetting his timetable.

But the small band of original supporters in his congressional district were the principal holdouts. "We were against it," says Frank Jorgensen. "We thought Dick was firmly entrenched as a congressman, and there was too much risk in running for the Senate." Nixon called a meeting in his former law partner's office. Beforehand, he instructed Roy Day, local Republican chairman, to argue for his running for Senator.

Day obliged. This provoked Herman Perry, the old banker and family friend, to shake his finger excitedly and accuse Day of being "nothing but a politician!" Perry pleaded with Nixon not to "sacrifice" himself. It was an emotional and inconclusive get-together.

On November 3, 1949—a full year before the election—Nixon announced for Senator. The issue, as he declared it, was "simply the choice between freedom and state socialism."

Much of his speech was directed at conservative Democrats. Nixon paid tribute to the Democratic party's record of distinguished service in the past. Then he said: "But today, nationally and in our own state of California, it has been captured and is completely controlled by a group of ruthless, cynical seekers after power—committed to policies and principles completely foreign to those of its founders." If they could see "the phony doctrines and ideologies now being foisted upon the American people," Thomas Jefferson and Andrew Jackson would "turn over in their graves. . . . Call it planned economy, the Fair Deal or social welfare—but it is still the same old Socialist baloney, any way you slice it."

He also proclaimed his candidacy to be "a banner of freedom which all people, regardless of party, can follow."

Politicians treat California as two separate states. They electioneer through different campaign organizations in the south and in the north. Each of these normally has two sachems—a distinguished citizen, as a nonsalaried "chairman," and a professional operator, usually a public-relations man, as "campaign manager." The star Republican professional in 1950 was Murray Chotiner. Beginning with Warren's election as Governor, he had executed a dazzling run of Republican triumphs. Chotiner was engaged as Nixon's southern manager and also to oversee the whole campaign. A rapport developed between the two men and Chotiner became Nixon's closest political associate and campaign adviser. That relationship lasted until 1956 when Chotiner's name figured in a congressional investigation of influence-peddling. The Beverly Hills lawyer's emergence as a national political figure was followed, as it is for most lawyer-politicians, by an influx of clients from beyond his state's borders. One of Chotiner's new clients was a Philadelphia racketeer. Another was a clothing manufacturer accused of cheating the armed services. A third was a relatively small airline with an important case pending before a government agency. Nixon was in no way involved in Chotiner's private operations, but he was embarrassed. Chotiner became a political exile.

Although Chotiner respected Nixon as a master campaigner, he considered him the hardest candidate of all to manage. Nixon insisted on perfection, says Chotiner, which is impossible in the heat of a political battle, and he could not cure himself of a tendency to try to do everything. Chotiner recalls a showdown during the 1950 race for Senator. "I had to tell him: 'Dick, you can either be the candidate or the manager. You can't be both. A candidate's job is to think and to speak. You just go out and make speeches and get votes, and let us make the other mistakes.' "

The only way a Republican could win, Nixon had told friends, was with "a fighting, rocking, socking campaign." At the outset in 1950 all the rocking and socking was done by the Democrats—on each other. In the warm-up, Mrs. Douglas accused Senator Downey of a do-nothing record in Washington and of catering to big business and power interests. Downey charged she campaigned on "personal bias and prejudice," and he linked her with "extremists."

Two months before the primaries Downey withdrew from the race, stating that he was not physically up to "waging a personal and militant campaign against the vicious and un-ethical propaganda" which he accused Mrs. Douglas of using against him. In reply, Mrs. Douglas said she was sorry Downey was ill. At the same time she reminded the voters that the "illness gimmick" was not new to politicians facing defeat—and her fight switched to Downey's successor in the race, Manchester Boddy, editor and publisher of the Los Angeles *Daily News.*

"It is the same old plot with a new leading man," Mrs. Douglas declared, after Boddy filed for the Senate nomination.

As it turned out, the "new leading man" was accompanied by a new campaign assault that showed how easily and directly Democrats could use issues of Communism and subversion. In the weeks that followed, her fellow Democrats painted Mrs. Douglas every insulting hue of red. Few of them bothered to acknowledge, even obliquely, that she was actually a vigorous foe of the Communist party and had fought Henry Wallace's Progressive party in a congressional district where *that* took considerable courage.

In the keynote of his campaign Boddy stated: "There is indisputable evidence of a state-wide conspiracy on the part of this small subversive clique of red-hots to capture, through stealth and cunning, the nerve centers of our Democratic party—and by so doing to capture the vote of real Democratic citizens."

He warned that the "blueprint of subversive dictatorship" called for control of the Democratic party by the "red-hots" who would make the party "serve their own twisted purposes . . . good California Democrats who know the score . . . have taken up the banner to preserve the American way of life and protect the true liberalism and honest progressivism which has made the Democratic party great."

Thereafter, Senator Downey returned to the battlefront to declare in a state-wide radio broadcast that Mrs. Douglas "gave comfort to the Soviet tyranny by voting against aid to Greece and Turkey." The Senator also charged that she "opposed an appropriation to enable Congress to uncover treasonable Communistic activities" and that in this she "joined Representative Vito Marcantonio, an admitted friend of the Communist party." [1] Downey also commented that she wept when Henry Wallace failed to get renominated for Vice-President in 1944.

Linking Mrs. Douglas with Marcantonio became a part of every attack from the Boddy camp. A former American Legion commander "alerted" veterans to Mrs. Douglas' "consistent policy of voting along with the notorious radical, Vito Marcantonio." The vice-president of the California Democratic Women's League cautioned Democrats to "wake up and see where she is trying to lead us."

And so it went—in newspaper ads, speeches, billboards and even in a general letter to California's clubwomen. Ostensibly, the main purpose of the widely distributed letter was "to point out that Helen Gahagan Douglas is neither truly representative of her sex nor of her party," but a central paragraph told of how she was being "led by the notorious New York radical Vito Marcantonio" in opposing appropriations to fight Communism and voting "against the Truman administration."

[1] In the election campaign Senator Downey ignored White House requests that he endorse Mrs. Douglas as a sign of party loyalty. Like several other well-known California Democrats, he favored Nixon.

Meanwhile Nixon, with only token opposition for the Republican nomination, stumped the state. He shook hands, addressed street-corner audiences and set up his public-address system to invite questions in practically every town. His favorite speaking topic was the Hiss case, but in the major speech of his primary campaign, delivered in San Francisco, Nixon proposed that President Truman establish a foreign policy advisory board that would serve both the President and Congress, ensuring "a consistent, realistic foreign policy" and inspiring wholehearted bipartisanship.

Occasionally Democrats would come up for breath from their melee and take a swing at Nixon. He was often tempted to respond, especially when Mrs. Douglas stated, offhandedly: "I have utter scorn for such pipsqueaks as Nixon and [Joseph] McCarthy." Near the end Nixon almost abandoned his policy of ignoring the opposition. He thought of getting in a lick or two about Mrs. Douglas' votes against the Greek-Turkish Aid bill (the Truman Doctrine) in 1947 and appropriations to keep the House Un-American Activities Committee going. But he was persuaded to tuck away his ammunition for later use, says Chotiner, because "quite frankly, we wanted her to be the Democratic nominee on the basis that it would be easier to defeat her than a conservative Democrat. So nothing was ever said pertaining to Helen Gahagan Douglas in the primary."

The only controversy in the first half of Nixon's campaign was over his bid for the Democratic nomination. He had cross-filed in the Democratic primary, just as Mrs. Douglas and Boddy had in the Republican primary. But Boddy and Will Rogers, Jr., his campaign chairman, angrily denounced Nixon literature mailed to thousands of registered Democrats. They charged Nixon misrepresented himself as a Democrat in a leaflet entitled "As One Democrat to Another."

The campaign leaflet told of how he "broke the Hiss-Chambers espionage case" and quoted various endorsements of his record and activities in Congress. It also stated that Congressman Nixon had "voted and stands for—lower taxes and more take-home pay . . . strong national defense for real security . . . California ownership of tidelands [oil

rights] . . . protection of small business . . . Taft-Hartley
Act with Wood amendments . . . reciprocal trade treaties
with adequate protection for American labor, agriculture and
industry . . . jobs for unemployed . . . sound national pen-
sion system . . . strong United Nations . . . statehood for
Hawaii and Alaska . . . civil rights" and many other programs. There was no direct reference to Nixon's party
affiliation, but the names of the chairman and secretary of
"Democrats for Nixon for United States Senator" were
printed, in small type, under a photograph of the candidate's
name as it would appear in the Democratic column of voting
machines on primary day.

In his attack on this "viciously false circular," Boddy
printed a large photostat of Nixon's latest affidavit of registration, showing that he had declared himself to be a Republican.

Nixon won the Republican nomination handily, and also
got 22 percent of Democratic primary votes. Mrs. Douglas
won the Democratic nomination by a plurality, since her total
was slightly less than half of the votes cast by Democrats.
She also got 13 percent of the Republican primary votes.

The autumn of 1950 was ready-made for mean electioneering. Domestically, the postwar reaction had set in. The nation
was on the brink of recession. Spectacular congressional
investigations were depicting Washington as a haven of subversion and corruption. In the Democratic party, which
controlled both the White House and the Congress, the
traditional division between conservatives and liberals had
broken out into a rash of grim primary fights in which
accusations of subversion were bandied about with a looseness once used with the far less odious charges of nepotism
or welfare-statism. On top of all else, war erupted in Korea.

Under the circumstances the general election contest for
Senator from California, or "the final," as it is called there,
was a natural for the times. The issue—"Communism"—
embraced every nightmare of treachery a voter could conjure
up. Seekers after a variety of offices milked it as best they
could. Edmund G. (Pat) Brown, Democratic candidate for
attorney general, paraded his "anti-Communism" by praising
the state legislature's controversial appropriation of $25,000

for an antisabotage program. James Roosevelt, Democratic candidate for Governor, went further—he not only approved the appropriation but declared it should have been larger.

Nonetheless, it was clear from the start that the Communist issue was Nixon's, above all others. Mrs. Douglas, his Democratic opponent, tried first to wish it away. She declared that it was not an issue at all, but "a phony cover-up by Republicans for their failure to advance a positive program for true democracy." She strove to dislodge Nixon from his perch, insisting that she had been more effectively anti-Communist than he.

The Nixon-Douglas campaign had some strange roots and alliances. And invariably they worked to Nixon's advantage. There was, for example, the Democratic primary encounter in which Congressman George A. Smathers unseated Senator Claude Pepper, of Florida. Although Nixon and Smathers were "opponents" in the sense that they belonged to different parties, they were close personal friends and, on many issues, they had the same conservative outlook. At the same time Senator Pepper was a liberal Democrat in the fashion of Mrs. Douglas.

After Smathers' primary victory in May, Nixon carefully studied it and adapted what he could to his own campaign. (Thus "Red Pepper," a slogan in Florida, became "Pink Lady," in California.) Relatively, however, the Smathers plan was only a drop in the tidal wave of help Nixon got from Democrats.

"California Democrats for Nixon," headed by George Creel, publicity man for the Woodrow Wilson presidential campaign in 1916, became the vehicle for a series of assaults that compelled Mrs. Douglas to quote President Truman as proof that she *was,* indeed, a Democrat.

Nixon's greatest windfall, of course, was the mass of accusations her fellow Democrats had hurled at Mrs. Douglas in the spring. Chotiner and his associates gathered them all, added an embellishment here and a nuance there, and played it back in the fall campaign.

The campaign was the most hateful California had experienced in many years. Nixon kept on the offensive all the way—beginning with a statement in which his campaign chairman established the line that Mrs. Douglas' record in Congress "discloses the truth about her soft attitude toward Communism" and a speech in which he, personally, announced his decision to risk the penalty of criticizing a woman because "if she had had her way, the Communist conspiracy in the United States would never have been exposed . . . it just so happens that my opponent is a member of a small clique which joins the notorious Communist party-liner, Vito Marcantonio of New York, in voting time after time against measures that are for the security of this country."

The impact of that speech was such that next day Mrs. Douglas sent telegrams to about two dozen of her closest friends saying, "I have run into a frightening crisis. I need your help, your advice, your support. Will you come to dinner at my house Tuesday, September 26, 7 P.M., so that we can talk over this terrible situation and hopefully find a solution."

An analysis of the Nixon and Douglas campaigns shows that the most notable difference was in the adroitness and calmness with which Nixon and his people executed *their* hyperbole and innuendo. When the Nixon camp questioned her fitness to be even a Democrat, for instance, or bemoaned her inability to judge between what was good for America and what was good for Russia, it was like a team of experienced surgeons performing masterful operations for the benefit of humanity. On the other hand, when Mrs. Douglas characterized Nixon and his followers as "a backwash of young men in dark shirts," the inference of fascism did not impress anyone who was not already impressed. And while her charge that Nixon was one of the most reactionary men in Congress had a certain ring of accuracy, because, after all, he *was* a Republican, inferences that he was an isolationist and the charge that "on every key vote Nixon stood with party-liner Marcantonio against America in its fight to defeat Communism" simply sounded and read as false as they were.

For whatever reason—perhaps because Mrs. Douglas and her friends were less blasé and more conscience-stricken by improprieties—when compared with the surgeons of the Nixon camp, Mrs. Douglas' operators performed like apprentice butchers. In a strange election-eve boast, Mrs. Douglas' campaign manager said that the Democrats had wanted Nixon to attack Mrs. Douglas.

Lawrence E. Davies, of the *New York Times,* put it this way on October 31, 1950:

> As outlined by Harold Tipton, Mrs. Douglas' campaign manager, her strategy was planned at the outset to "needle" Mr. Nixon into showing his hand. Two sentences, one charging that her rival had "voted with Representative Marcantonio against aid to Korea," the other declaring Mr. Nixon had voted with Mr. Marcantonio to cut European aid in half, were thrown into Mrs. Douglas' opening speech in late July.
>
> "They fell for it," Mr. Tipton said. "Nixon was right back with a defense. By September 1 he flooded the state with phony voting records. But our theory was that he couldn't keep up the red smear indefinitely."
>
> Douglas strategists hope that the Nixon campaign will boomerang.

As is well known, it did not. The Douglas campaign's repeated linkage of Nixon and Marcantonio may have been forgotten, because it was overshadowed by the shrewder manner in which Nixon later tied the much-maligned New York congressman to Mrs. Douglas. Nixon did not rest his case with just two, three or five Marcantonio votes, as did Mrs. Douglas. Nixon's charges went before the voters as a carefully researched leaflet, filled with dates, reference data and lawyerlike analogies that were just confusing enough to convince laymen of their authenticity. At the top the document was labeled DOUGLAS-MARCANTONIO VOTING RECORD. An opening, explanatory statement implied that almost everyone in California was anxious to know the truth about "the voting records of Congresswoman Helen Douglas and the notorious party-liner, Congressman Vito Marcantonio of New York." Then came the revelation: they had voted the same way 354 times. This was followed by a statement that "while it should not be expected that a member of the House of Representatives should always vote in opposition to Marcantonio, it is significant to note, not only the greater number of times which Mrs. Douglas voted in agreement with him, but also the issues on which almost without exception they always saw eye-to-eye, to wit: Un-American Activities and Internal Security." [2]

The first order was for 50,000 copies of the leaflet. Chotiner says he was never able to figure whether its immediate popularity was due to the content or the suggestive hue of the paper he had selected, which was bright pink. Anyway, within a week he ordered another 500,000, and they are known to this day—in pride or in shame—as "the pink sheets."

One of the hitherto not revealed political milestones of that campaign is the strategy by which an endorsement, of sorts, was wormed out of Governor Warren. As all his Republican colleagues quickly learned, Warren was a lone-wolf campaigner whose rare public support of another candidate was always based on the help that individual could give Warren, and not on party affiliation. Warren appointed William Knowland to the Senate to fill a vacancy in 1945. The next year, when Knowland ran for a full term, Warren agreed to endorse him only at the last minute. His reluctance had been based on a desire not to alienate supporters of Will Rogers, Jr., Knowland's Democratic opponent. In the 1950 election Warren, seeking a third term, headed the Republican ticket on which Nixon was the candidate for Senator. Nixon and Warren had no particular use for each other since Warren indirectly had aided Nixon's Democratic opponent for Congress in 1946 while refusing to acknowledge Nixon. In the Senate campaign the Nixon forces felt a Warren endorsement important because of rumors that the immensely popular Governor actually wanted to see Nixon defeated. Any hope of convincing Warren to come through was com-

[2] Marcantonio represented a slum district in New York where the constituents judge him principally by what he did for them in a personal way, like cutting through red tape to get them on the relief rolls. He managed that well enough to feel secure in his office. In the California election, when Mrs. Douglas was first tied to Marcantonio by her Democratic primary opponent, Marcantonio went to a friend of Nixon's and said, chuckling, "Tell Nicky to get on this thing because it is a good idea." Marcantonio disliked Mrs. Douglas intensely and normally used an obscene five-letter word when referring to her in private conversations.

plicated by the fact that the Democratic candidates had not expressed any support for each other. Nixon strategists thereupon evolved a plan to anger Warren into saying something.

An earnest young Republican, subsequently elected to Congress, was assigned to follow Mrs. Douglas and ask her during question periods and at press conferences whether she thought James Roosevelt should be elected Governor. She ignored the questioner until the Friday before election, when she replied: "I hope and pray he will be the next Governor, and he will be, if the Democrats vote the Democratic ticket."

The word was swiftly conveyed to Chotiner. He, in turn, passed it to a friendly newspaperman traveling with Warren. When the Governor was asked for his reaction, he replied that he would have to think about it. Twenty-four hours later he issued the following statement: "I have no intention of being coy about this situation. As always, I have kept my campaign independent from other campaigns. The newspaper reports from San Diego that Mrs. Douglas has said she hopes and prays Mr. Roosevelt will be the next Governor does not change my position. In view of her statement, however, I might ask her how she expects I will vote when I mark my ballot for United States Senator next Tuesday."

Nixon's campaign manager thereupon declared: "Every voter in California who reads his statement will realize that Earl Warren intends to mark his ballot for Dick Nixon on election day."

Whether he actually did is a secret Warren has yet to divulge.

On election day, and also the day before, the Nixon organization offered "prizes galore" to individuals who answered with the words "Vote for Nixon" if the candidate's headquarters telephoned. As part of the game Nixon assistants placed telephone calls at random throughout the state, inspiring thousands of people to plug Nixon's candidacy whenever their telephones rang.

Nixon was elected by a 680,000 vote margin. This so delighted and surprised him that he went from one victory party to another most of the night and played "Happy Days Are Here Again" wherever there was a piano.

7 ✳ *Ike's Running Mate, 1952*

REPUBLICAN successes in the 1950 congressional elections had the impact of a cold shower on the groggy party. It had lapsed into shock two years before when Harry Truman unceremoniously crushed G.O.P. expectations just as the power-starved faithful in many cities were beginning their victory celebrations. Now, with the 1950 results, things were looking up. The party had gained five seats in the Senate and 28 in the House, and its center of gravity in Congress, Senator Robert A. Taft, had vanquished the political forces of organized labor which combined across the nation to defeat him for re-election in Ohio.

Furthermore, the articulate young congressman whom party professionals viewed as "a real comer" because of the skill in which he "got Alger Hiss" had accomplished something in California to hearten Republicans and concern Democrats nationally. Representative Nixon had demonstrated in winning his election for Senator that a "model Republican" could defeat a "model Democrat" in an industrial state where Democrats outregistered Republicans by a million votes.

Former President Herbert Hoover wrote Nixon: "Your victory was the greatest good that can come to our country." Herbert Brownell, Jr., manager of the two Dewey campaigns for President and later a chief strategist of the Eisenhower campaign, declared that Nixon's "brilliant campaign" in California laid the groundwork for Republican success nationally in 1952. Freshman Senator Nixon quickly became his party's most sought-after speaker and soon blossomed into a Republican meld of Paul Revere and Billy Sunday. Across the land he trumpeted Republican gospel and warned the countryside to stop the Democratic hordes or face disaster. The Republican party had to win the next election, or die, he declared.

On top of his Senate duties Nixon managed to squeeze up to a dozen speaking engagements a month in the year and a half from the convening of the Eighty-first Congress to the twenty-fifth Republican National Convention. The two most significant speeches were at a party fund-raising dinner in New York City, May 8, 1952, and before the National Young Republican Convention in Boston, June 28, 1951. His New York appearance stood out because of what happened rather than what he said, for Governor Dewey informed Nixon after the dinner that he should be the candidate for Vice-President on the Eisenhower ticket. The Boston speech a year earlier was important for its content. In it Nixon wrapped up a battle plan and a Republican program for the pending struggle with the Democrats. He entitled the address "The Challenge of 1952" and proposed that the party wage "the kind of a fighting, rocking, socking campaign that will bring home to the people the merits of our candidate and our program." The Truman administration had failed on many fronts, said Nixon. No diplomatic gaffe in history had been worse, for instance, "than the failure of our State Department to get the wholehearted support of our allies in Korea"; therefore, "the American people have had enough of the whining, whimpering, groveling attitude of our diplomatic representatives who talk of America's weaknesses and of America's fears rather than of America's strength and of America's courage." Nixon also chided the Democrats for "piously" talking economy while asking Congress for funds "so that administration officials can ride to work and to their social engagements in chauffeured government limousines." But "the most vulnerable point" against the Democrats was "the failure of this administration to develop an effective program to meet the activities of the fifth column in the United States." "Communists infiltrated the very highest councils of this administration," he charged, yet "our top administration officials have refused time and time again to recognize the existence of the fifth column in this country and to take effective action to clean subversives out of the administrative branch of our government."

In his discussion of "subversives in government" Nixon spoke in some detail about the Hiss case. "When the case went to the courts," he stated, "two judges of the Supreme Court; the Governor of Illinois, Mr. Stevenson; Philip Jessup, the architect of our Far Eastern policy and a host of other administration officials testified as character witnesses for Alger Hiss."

In the speech which was to become a model for Republican campaigners, Nixon not only attacked the Democratic opposition ("We have a duty to criticize and to point up the mistakes of the past"), but he also advised fellow partisans that they "should not stop with destructive criticism. We should go a step further and offer our own constructive program to meet the great problems of our times."

He admitted that "the Republican party has some faults" and suggested that they be recognized and corrected. "But one thing can be said to our credit which cannot be said for the party in power," he added, "that is, that we have never had the support of the Communists in the past. We have never asked for that support. We do not have it now, and we shall never ask for it or accept it in the future. And for that reason a Republican administration, we can be sure, will conduct a thoroughgoing housecleaning of Communists and fellow travelers in the administrative branch of the government because we have no fear of finding any Communist skeletons in our political closets."

Nixon said a Republican housecleaning program would have to be "fair, sane, intelligent and effective" because "indiscriminate name-calling and professional Red-baiting can hurt our cause more than it can help it."

In essence, Nixon's program was as follows: "A program which is designed to meet the threat which is presented to our security by the internationalist Communist conspiracy: keep the United States militarily strong. Keep the economy of this nation strong and sound and productive and free. And develop a fair and effective program of internal security. And, above all, mount a mighty ideological offensive which will prove to peoples everywhere that the hope of the world does not lie in turning toward dictatorship of any type, but that it lies in developing a strong, a free and an intelligent democracy."

Just a month before his Boston speech Nixon made a pilgrimage to General Eisenhower at Supreme Headquarters of the Allied Powers in Europe. In reality it was sort of a sideline pilgrimage, since the main purpose of Nixon's European trip was to attend a four-day conference of the World Health Organization in Geneva. He stopped briefly in Paris on the way home, and after a half hour with Eisenhower, the Senator offered two observations. One was that building an integrated defense force for the North Atlantic allies was a tough proposition and Eisenhower "is doing a fine job under very difficult circumstances." The other was that Eisenhower might be available for the presidential nomination in 1952, but the Senator was not altogether clear yet about the General's political identity.

Nixon's speechmaking invitations piled up faster and faster in the wake of his address to the Young Republicans in Boston. In the next five months audiences in 11 states heard Nixon tear into the Democrats.

As a member of the California delegation Nixon was pledged to vote for Governor Warren at the convention— and he did, although he favored Eisenhower. In preconvention maneuvers all presidential aspirants sought his backing, especially since at least a third of the 70 California delegates would vote as he did if Warren released them. Stassen, who produced polls and surveys to "prove" he would benefit from an Eisenhower-Taft deadlock, proposed a Stassen-Nixon ticket. Taft personally solicited Nixon, then assigned their mutual friend, Tom Shroyer, an architect of the Taft-Hartley Law, to bring Nixon into the Taft camp. "I thought he was quite sympathetic in our first conferences during the latter part of 1951 and early 1952," Shroyer said. "Nixon liked Taft, but he did seem to have a few doubts about Taft's chances to win." A principal figure in the organization promoting Eisenhower's candidacy recalled: "It was clear to us by April that Nixon was friendly to our group. His hands were tied [by the legal commitment to vote for Warren], but it came to a point where a relationship was established . . .

where one of us would see him on occasion on the Senate floor and sound him out, get his advice on various things, never going too deep, still going deeper than we could with someone who was completely on the outside."

As the Eisenhower-Taft battle lines tightened in the late spring of 1952, the usual array of "inside reports" by some "political experts" got wilder. None was more absurd than the yarn that Governor Dewey was not seriously supporting Eisenhower but really aimed to maneuver a third nomination for himself. Actually Dewey was not only working vigorously to get Eisenhower the nomination, but he and Brownell also had decided that Senator Nixon would be the best running mate.

"Nixon seemed an almost ideal candidate for Vice-President," Brownell recalled. "He was young, geographically right, had experience both in the House and the Senate with a good voting record, and was an excellent speaker.

"The original conception of the team had worked out very well," Brownell added. "It was to have the President, who was experienced on the world scene, running with a young, aggressive fellow, who knew the domestic issues and agreed with the President's policies. The President could be presented to the country as one who would stand up against the Communists in the international sphere, and Nixon would lead the fight in the discussion of the domestic issues."

When Brownell mentioned this to Nixon at a Gridiron Club dinner in Washington, the latter said he was flattered but did not expect to be nominated.

Dewey broached the subject to Nixon after a $100-a-plate New York State Republican dinner on May 8. "I had heard a lot of very fine things about him," Dewey said. "I checked with a lot of people who worked with him in both the House and the Senate. Everybody whose opinion I respected said he was an absolute star, a man of enormous capacity. They liked and admired him. So I pretty much made up my mind that this was the fellow." Before that decision, however, Dewey wanted to see Nixon in action before a large New York audience. So Nixon was invited to the party dinner. "He made a very fine speech, from notes, not a prepared text," Dewey recalls. "He demonstrated he does not speak

from what someone else writes and also has a very fine
understanding of the world situation."

Afterward the Governor asked Nixon to his suite on the
twenty-fourth floor of the Roosevelt Hotel for a private chat.
"The two of us sat around for about an hour or an hour and
a half before he took his train," Dewey said. "That was the
occasion on which I discussed with him briefly the possibility
of him becoming the Vice-President."

Nixon says he "couldn't believe Governor Dewey was serious."

The nominating convention was still two months off.
Eisenhower was to return from Paris in three weeks to take
an active role in his campaign for the nomination.

Governor Warren's slate of delegates, including Nixon,
won the California primary on June 3. In public statements
and in hundreds of letters to people who were urging him to
support either Eisenhower or Taft, Nixon emphasized that
he would switch from Warren only with the Governor's permission. When it appeared more and more certain that just
20 or 30 votes could make the difference between victory
and failure, some Eisenhower leaders tried to pressure Nixon
into splitting the California delegation, whether Warren approved or not. At one point Paul G. Hoffman, a leader of the
liberal, independent Republicans for Eisenhower, tried to
convert Knowland, who was so doggedly for Warren that he
ignored offers of the vice-presidency from the Taft camp and
decreed that no California delegate would so much as even
talk about an alternate to Warren for the presidency. Although he was not happy about it, Dewey recalls that he considered Nixon's refusal to "participate in any movement to
break the California delegation . . . a very fine attitude."
Dewey said, "Nixon maintained his aloofness with perfection." Some Warren devotees charged Nixon with a "double-
cross," however, for sending 23,000 questionnaires asking
California voters who they thought would be the strongest
possible Republican nominee. The answer confirmed Nixon's
own belief. Most said Eisenhower. Nixon regards the double-
cross allegation as "silly." He said he told Warren and Knowland, "I was an Eisenhower man from the beginning," yet
he stuck by his commitment to Warren even when he knew

beyond question that it would be best for California to start the inevitable bandwagon for Eisenhower by giving him the mere 19 votes he needed for nomination on the first ballot. (California did not switch.)

There already are two or three conflicting legends about the maneuvers that swirled around Nixon during the period immediately before he was nominated in 1952—and his reactions. People most intimately associated with it—including principal movers and shakers—reconstructed what actually happened as follows:

Nixon arrived in Chicago on July 1 as a member of the platform-writing resolutions committee. Like other committees of the convention with serious conflicts to resolve, the resolutions group began to meet a full week before the convention itself was to open. Nevertheless, Nixon's early presence on the scene added spice to rumors cropping up in political columns that he would be Eisenhower's running mate because he was regarded as an ideal "bridge" between the seriously divided Eisenhower and Taft wings of the party. (A couple of "experts" predicted Nixon would be Taft's running mate for the same reason.) The Californian scoffed at the speculation, publicly and privately.

On July 3 Nixon issued a statement condemning the Taft-dominated Republican National Committee for seeming to settle the pending fight over contested delegations from three Southern states by granting temporary recognition to the Georgia group committed to Taft with the right to vote on its own status as the permanent delegation. At the time Eisenhower was equating the Taft organization tactics with cattle rustling and horse stealing. Nixon charged that questions of honesty and lawbreaking were involved, and the National Committee's action could "ruin" the Republican party.

On July 5 Nixon flew to Denver to board a special train bringing the California delegation to Chicago. All the delegates were registered Republicans, of course. But personal loyalties had come to mean more in California politics over the years than devotion to party, and as a practical matter the Chicago-bound Californians were really either "Warren men," "Knowland men" or "Nixon men," bound together by an election law that seemed to require them to vote for Warren until he freed them to do otherwise. As the stream-lined train sped east, Nixon gave his own followers a run-down on the latest preconvention developments. In essence, he reported that the Eisenhower drive was picking up and said it looked as though the General could win on the first ballot. As expected, bits and pieces of the Nixon report filtered through the non-Nixon sections of the train. Warren men became furious. They complained that the junior Sena-tor had breached senior Senator Knowland's edict that Cal-ifornia delegates would refuse even to consider an alternate to Warren. Several Warrenites "confided" to some newspaper correspondents that Nixon tried to entice California votes away from Warren in return for second place on the Eisen-hower ticket.[1]

The convention opened on July 7 with a floor squabble between Eisenhower and Taft leaders over 68 Southern delegates that were temporarily seated by the National Com-mittee. The Eisenhower group offered a solution with a snappy title—"Fair Play Amendment"—which appealed to one of the least controversial of American emotions and neatly complemented the moral plane on which Eisenhower orators said they would pitch their arguments. The issue over a few Southern delegates thus was boosted into a struggle be-tween good and evil. The Eisenhower team had launched what the General was later to proclaim his "Great Crusade," and, as the nation's voters watched on television, the exasperated Taft team argued in vain that *theirs* was really the honest-to-goodness "Fair Play" position. By voting time Nixon, Knowland and Warren were united on the issue, and California cast its 70 votes for morality and fair play. As is well known, the vote was more a test of strength between Taft and Eisenhower than anything else, and the Eisenhower side won with the help of men like Warren and Stassen, who probably would have preferred to sit out that particular test. Nonetheless, it was an Eisenhower victory and, although the

---

[1] Before the convention was over a couple of angry Warren enthusiasts laid the groundwork for the "Nixon fund" sensation that was to dominate the headlines and air waves in mid-Septem-ber and threaten to ruin Nixon and defeat Eisenhower.

nominees were not selected until July 11, Taft was through by noon July 7—and so were the hopes of a Taft-Eisenhower deadlock nurtured by dark horses Warren and Stassen.

Eisenhower leaders were careful not to divert attention from their main goal until it was fully achieved. They avoided public discussion of side issues during the four convention days and nights before balloting was to begin for the presidential nomination. But published reports that the inner circle had agreed already on the General's running mate had to be denied to ensure the continued support of some contenders for the vice-presidency who controlled substantial blocs of convention votes. Thus Senator Henry Cabot Lodge, chairman of the Eisenhower organization, laughed off a column in which John S. Knight, editor and publisher of the Chicago Daily News, predicted two days before the balloting that Eisenhower and Nixon would win.

Murray Chotiner, who was with Nixon much of the time in Chicago, said he doubts that the Senator thought he would be picked. Chotiner was managing Senator Knowland's campaign for re-election in 1952, but it was over by convention time because Knowland won both Republican and Democratic nominations in the June primaries. "Herb Brownell had some conversations with me at the convention," Chotiner recalled. "He wanted my opinion as to Knowland and Nixon. He wanted to know who would be the better campaigner, who would add more strength to the ticket. I gave him my candid opinion, which was that Nixon had a shade as a campaigner and also appealed more to independents and young people. It was just a shade in favor of Nixon. Brownell asked how Nixon's nomination would react on Warren. I said I didn't know but that there had not been any warmth between the two. He asked me what Knowland's reaction would be. Nixon had said before the convention that, if it were a choice between him and Knowland, it should go to Knowland. When I told Helen Knowland [the Senator's wife] what Dick had said—that Bill would make a wonderful candidate, that he was entitled to it—Helen said, 'You tell Dick not to think of saying anything of it, to go right ahead, and if it is awfully close not to think for a moment how Bill would feel about it.' I reported that to Brownell, and he said, 'Well, if Bill Knowland's wife feels that way about it, why that must be it.' "

The night before the convention was to vote for nominees, Nixon reviewed his situation at great length with his wife. He had begun to feel that there was substance to all the talk and he might be offered second place. Mrs. Nixon stuck by her doubts.

At four A.M. Nixon telephoned Chotiner's hotel room. "What are you doing?" he asked. "Sleeping," replied Chotiner. "Do you want to come down?" Nixon asked.

Chotiner said: "I went down to his room, where he was sitting talking with Pat. He said, 'What do you think? If this thing is offered to me, do you think I should take it?' I said, 'Yes, I do.' He said, 'Why?'

"I could tell that Pat had been talking against it. I said, 'Dick, you're a junior Senator from California and you will always be a junior Senator from California. Bill Knowland is young and he's healthy, and unless something should happen to him, you will always be second man in California. The junior Senator from California doesn't amount to anything. There comes a time when you have to go up or out. Suppose you are a candidate [for Vice-President] and we lose? You're still the junior Senator and haven't lost anything. If you win, and are elected Vice-President, and at the end of four years you become all washed up, you could open a law office in Whittier and have all the business in town. Any man who quits political life as Vice-President as young as you are in years certainly hasn't lost a thing.'

"I urged him very strongly to take it," Chotiner added. "But he was still debating it at five A.M. when I left to go back to bed."

When the balloting for the presidential nomination began on July 11, the confident Eisenhower leaders labored mightily to hold their delegates while the desperate Taftites worked feverishly to pry some loose. By 1:50 P.M. all the palpitating was over and done with. The convention recessed until four P.M. to give the party's new standard-bearer time to pass the word about whom he wanted for a running mate.

As major-domo of the experienced political group running the Eisenhower operation, Brownell submitted Nixon's name to the General. Eisenhower agreed Nixon would be a good choice, Brownell said, but was "surprised" to learn "that the presidential candidate could choose the Vice-President as a matter of long-standing custom." After some other possible candidates were discussed, "it was clear that Nixon was the one to be chosen." Nevertheless, Eisenhower said he would leave it to Brownell "to get the collective judgment of the leaders of the party," and they were to understand that "Nixon would be very acceptable."

Brownell summoned about two dozen representative Eisenhower leaders to a meeting at the Conrad Hilton Hotel, across the street from the Blackstone, where Eisenhower was staying. At the same time proponents of various candidates for the nomination were invited to present their cases.

Paul G. Hoffman recalled, "The first person to be discussed was Taft." Several other names also were brought up "and knocked down," he said, "then Nixon's was offered." Everyone in the room had an opportunity to state his opinion. Hoffman's was: "Nixon fills all the requirements."

Dewey, the first powerful Republican figure to propose both Eisenhower and Nixon nominations, had this earnest recollection of the commitee session: "There were a lot of people with a lot of views. I waited until they had gotten down through the list. I didn't say much about it, until finally they had gotten from the East all the way across to the West. Then I named Nixon as the logical nominee."

The committee thereupon voted unanimously for Nixon, and Brownell picked up two different telephones to give the news simultaneously to Eisenhower and Nixon.

Nixon had lent his car to a newspaperman, Earl Behrens, of the San Francisco *Chronicle*. No taxis were in sight. On a plea from Chotiner, a parking lot guard produced both an automobile and a motorcycle escort.

"Dick was calm and pensive," Chotiner recalled. "As we were speeding to the General's headquarters, he said, 'Murray, when we get up there, will you call the folks at home? They're probably watching TV. Tell them it looks as if I'm going to be nominated for Vice-President.' I said, 'Sure.'

"We went up in the elevator at the Blackstone. I've never seen so many newspapermen in my life. The elevator doors opened, and the flash bulbs started popping. Nixon said, 'Boy! They already know it.' Dick went on into the General's suite, and I called Whittier and got his sister-in-law. She said, 'Oh, we know all about it already. It's been on television.' It seemed to me that Dick had been in the position of being the last to learn about it."

Eisenhower introduced Nixon to Mrs. Eisenhower, and the men sat down to talk. Then Nixon left to get ready for his appearance before the convention. There were many telephone calls to make. One of the first was to his senior colleague. Knowland said when he answered the telephone, "I was told by someone whose name I don't recollect . . . that Dick would like to talk with me. Dick came to the phone and he asked whether I would be prepared to place his name in nomination. I had already at that time been informed he was the choice as the nominee for Vice-President. I forget whether it was Brownell or someone else who informed me."

At the convention hall most of the morning's excitement and anger had subsided, and the delegates milled around, swapped rumors and ignored the speeches scheduled at the last minute to kill time. Finally, serious business was resumed at about 5:30. Mrs. Clare Boothe Luce announced she would not propose Senator Margaret Chase Smith for the nomination, as planned, because Mrs. Smith "does not wish to create on this floor any division of loyalties which have not already existed." Then Knowland presented the name of Nixon—the man whose "bulldog determination" enabled "the government to hunt out and unravel the Alger Hiss case" . . . a campaigner "who puts forth more of his heart into a campaign [than anyone else Knowland has known]" . . . and "a young man who gives to the Republican ticket an appeal to the young men and young women of this nation."

There were four seconding speeches, then Governor John S. Fine, of Pennsylvania, moved that Nixon be nominated by acclamation—and he was. Within an hour Nixon had delivered an acceptance speech which opened with the question: "Haven't we got a wonderful candidate for President of the United States?" and Eisenhower had proclaimed his "Great Crusade for freedom in America and freedom in the world" in an address of acceptance which began with words of congratulation to "this convention on your selection of the nominee for the vice-presidency."

The television audience that evening included Nixon's two daughters. According to friends, their reactions were mixed. Patricia, six, reportedly said: "I want everybody to vote for my daddy." Julie, four, is said to have wailed: "I want Mommy."

At the outset Eisenhower informed his running mate that he viewed the vice-presidency as an important, meaningful office and believed the Vice-President should be an active participant with full knowledge of all that went on in an administration and not a "figurehead." Nixon agreed entirely and started immediately to become the hardest-campaigning vice-presidential candidate in American politics. During his first day as the nominee he held a press conference (the platform was too ambiguous on civil rights and labor, he said, and the weaknesses would be remedied in campaign speeches); he met with congressional campaign leaders to devise a coordinated drive for the presidency and control of Congress; he told the Republican National Committee the main campaign issues were "the Truman record" and "Communism at home and abroad" and stated that "any Democratic candidate can be defeated on those issues"; and he joined General Eisenhower at the first of several precampaign strategy sessions in which the respective campaign roles of Eisenhower and Nixon were worked out, with Eisenhower to emphasize the positive and Nixon to lead the offensive against the opposition. Democrats called this a "high road-low road" strategy.

Two weeks after the Republican convention the Democratic National Convention nominated Adlai E. Stevenson for President and Senator John Sparkman of Alabama for Vice-President. Earlier Stevenson had compared Nixon unfavorably with the septuagenarian Democratic Vice-President, Alben Barkley, and remarked that "the Republican party makes even its young men seem old; the Democratic party makes even its old men seem young." Now, Nixon described Stevenson as "a 'me-too' candidate in reverse." Futhermore, he said the Democratic nominee was "Jack Kroll's candidate; Jake Arvey's candidate and—this is his greatest handicap—he's Harry Truman's candidate." (Kroll was director of the CIO-Political Action Committee; Arvey was Democratic boss of Illinois.)

On July 28 practically the whole of Whittier turned out for a Nixon homecoming celebration in the Whittier College stadium. Governor Warren, the chief welcomer, declared, "All the people of California are rejoicing at your success, Dick." A week later the Governor told a meeting of the California Republican Central Committee in Sacramento that Nixon's nomination "is like a breath of fresh air to this country, and I believe the people will respond to it."

Nothing remained for Chotiner to do as Knowland's campaign manager since the senior California Senator was reelected by virtue of winning both parties' primaries in June. So Chotiner became manager of Nixon's campaign. According to the master plan developed at Eisenhower-Nixon strategy sessions, Nixon was to begin on September 17 with a whistlestop tour of the West Coast. Nixon wanted first to test his "basic speech" and rub the rough edges from his relatively inexperienced campaign organization, so he introduced something new to politics—the trial run. He scheduled a four-day barnstorming tour of then-safely-Republican Maine, much as plays try out in New Haven before opening on Broadway. "It paid off," said a Nixon strategist. "It was good for the candidate, the campaign manager, the trip men, the advance men, the publicity men, radio and TV men, and everybody else in the campaign." Among things the candidate learned was to be more cautious in complying with requests of photographers. At a lobster plant in Rockport the Nixons were asked to pose picking up lobsters. Mrs. Nixon hesitated. Nixon said there was nothing to it, that the big ones are fat and lazy and move slowly. Then he picked up the biggest one he could find—and its claws flashed open and went for his throat. Mrs. Nixon screamed. The lobster clutched at the candidate's lapel. Flash bulbs exploded. And then everyone laughed as Nixon finally freed himself.

Shortly before the all-out campaign began, a Gallup Poll reported that only 45 percent of the voters could name the Republican candidate for Vice-President. Just 32 percent could name the Democratic candidate and only one in four knew the identity of both. This was not unusual for vice-presidential nominees—or even Vice-Presidents. But Nixon's name managed to move swiftly from the relatively unknown to the well-known.

Within a week of embarking on his first major whistle-stop tour Nixon became the most talked-about, most controversial and, as it developed, the most politically fortunate vice-presidential candidate in history—thanks to a nationwide uproar over an $18,000 "fund" maintained for Nixon by his political friends in California.

8 ※ *The Fund, 1952*

IN establishing the "Nixon fund" the Senator's boosters tried to envision any troubles it might cause. "We endeavored to set it up so that any possible criticism of it would be completely disarmed," recalled Dana C. Smith, the Pasadena lawyer who became trustee and manager of contributions and expenditures. The objective was to provide money to enable Nixon to campaign continuously for the Republican party and his own re-election instead of waiting until his newly won Senate seat was at stake in 1956. Nixon approved.

Neither he nor his California admirers divined in 1950 that he would be candidate for Vice-President within two years. Even then, the fund might have gone unnoticed if Eisenhower and Nixon had not sold their Crusade for Political Purity so well. America had to choose, they averred, between looseness and corruption under the Democrats and angelic honesty under the Republicans.

General Eisenhower was stressing the need to change the moral climate in Washington and the need for unsullied public officials the day the first stories about the Nixon fund appeared. It was Thursday, September 18. The General, campaigning in Iowa, promised to drive the "crooks and cronies" from power and bring a Republican "Honest Deal" to Washington to replace the Democratic "Fair Deal." "When we are through," he declared, "the experts in shady and shoddy government operations will be on their way back to the shadowy haunts in the subcellars of American politics from which they came."

The issue was further highlighted that day by Adlai Stevenson, who was electioneering in Connecticut, and by Governor James F. Byrnes, of South Carolina. Byrnes, once a power in the Democratic party and still a significant force in its Southern wing, put Dixie's stamp of approval on General Eisenhower. Stevenson would be "under too great an obligation to those responsible for the 'mess in Washington,'" he said. "It will take a man like Eisenhower" to clean it up.

Stevenson made a speech on campaign ethics. Ethics were more important than victory, he said. "Victory can be bought too dearly." Observers assumed this was a jibe at Nixon, who had launched the major assault phase of the Republican campaign the night before with a rally that resembled a religious revival.

"What corruption means to all of us is that every time we pick up our paper, every day, we read about a scandal," said Nixon. "You know, as a matter of fact, this administration is going to go down in history as a scandal-a-day administration because you read about another bribe, you read about another tax fix, you read about another gangster getting favors from the government . . . and are sick and tired of it."

Bernard Brennan and Murray Chotiner, then Nixon's principal political lieutenants, had proposed the year-round campaign in 1950. Creating a special fund was Dana Smith's idea. He was acquainted with arrangements to finance public figures of modest means whose expenses for off-season politicking could not be paid from formal campaign treasuries. He knew how to shake the money tree in their behalf. In 1950 Smith was treasurer of Nixon's campaign and during the uproar in 1952 he was chairman of Volunteers for Eisenhower in southern California. "I do not know of any instance in which . . . Senator Nixon . . . ever did anything for any contributor to his political expenses, whether or not strictly campaign funds, which he would not have done for any responsible constituent," Smith stated.

Senator Nixon's gross salary was $12,500. He was also provided $2,500, tax-free, for general expenses, a maximum of $2,000 for telephone, telegraph and stationery bills, $70,000 for a staff and one round-trip home per session. Furthermore, he earned a bit more for lectures and after-dinner speeches, but it all could hardly finance his operations. In his freshman year as a Senator he crossed the continent three times on speaking tours, went halfway across—and back—13 more times, made three visits to the South, and ten up and down the East Coast. His bill for Christmas cards alone was $4,237.54.

"After the very difficult 1950 campaign," said Nixon, "the people who had been active—my finance committee as well as others—sat down with me and said: 'We want you to start campaigning right now for 1956, and we think that the way to do it is to have available the funds to make speeches, make trips to California and so forth.' We discussed the practical possibilities. They asked me, 'What can you do?' Of course, as you are aware, most congressmen and Senators have a campaign fund unless they are independently wealthy. I didn't ask them for any money. The idea of the year-around campaign was theirs. They said: 'We want you to keep in touch with all your [campaign workers].' They knew that when I was in the House I had sent out Christmas cards [to all who helped in the House campaigns], for example. I said, 'Do you realize that we had over 25,000 people as workers in the Senate campaign?' So it was worked out. [What was created] was simply a campaign fund."

Smith agreed to become its manager. A special trust account was opened in Smith's name at a Pasadena bank. Audits were scheduled. And an estimated budget of $16,000 a year was agreed to. An orthodox public appeal for money was felt to be too complicated and unnecessary, so it was decided to solicit the more generous backers of Nixon's campaigns for Congress and the Senate.

Donations were solicited by telephone, personal contact and mail. "A group of us here, after the dust of battle had settled and we found that Dick was safely elected, began to realize that electing him was only part of what we really wanted to accomplish," Smith wrote potential contributors. "We not only wanted a good man in the Senate from this state, but we wanted him to continue to sell effectively to the people of California the economic and political systems which we all believe in. It was immediately apparent to us that this would take money and that Dick himself was not in a position financially to provide it. We have therefore set up a pool, to which a considerable number of us here are contributing on an annual basis, to meet expenditures which seemed necessary to accomplish this object. . . . We have limited contributions to a minimum of $100 a year and a maximum of $500 . . . so that it can never be charged that anyone is contributing so much as to think that he is entitled to special favors."

The type of activities the fund would support were listed as transportation and hotel expenses, airmail and long-distance telephone charges, preparation and dissemination of Nixon's speeches, questionnaires, newsletters and the like, the Senator's Christmas cards to campaign workers and contributors, radio, television, advertising and general publicity.

Smith assured those he solicited that "nobody is drawing any salary or other compensation out of this, so you can count on it that the money will be effectively used where it will do all of us, including Dick, the most good." Furthermore, he wrote, "we have only included in our group [of contributors] people who have supported Dick from the start, so that it does not provide any way for people who are 'second guessers' to make any claim on the Senator's particular interest."

Many responded more liberally with praise than with cash, so the base was broadened. The privilege of contributing was extended to latecomers on the Nixon bandwagon, and Smith asked the United Republican Finance Committee of Los Angeles County, the regular party organization's treasury unit, to take over the Nixon fund—contributor lists, bankbooks, bills and all. However, the committee said it could not because its powers were too limited.

On June 28, 29 and 30, 1951, Smith, Chotiner and Brennan went on a barnstorming operation to urge state-wide support. They addressed Republican groups from San Francisco to San Diego. Everywhere the party faithful acclaimed the program. But the response was disappointing. In September Smith again solicited individuals by mail. The fund was solvent mostly because Nixon was spending less than anticipated.

By primary day in June, 1952, Nixon's associates had explained the fund to about 500 possible donors, who, in turn, told another 500 or more throughout California. Yet checks had come from fewer than 100, and they added up to a total far below expectations. So Nixon decided that the regular party fund-raising organization had to assume the responsibility if it wanted any more cooperation from him. Nixon wrote Smith on June 9, 1952:

> I think the time has now come for us to have a showdown with Republican Finance on obtaining assistance for our programs. I believe that we should make our requests modest.

He suggested $10,000 a year from the southern California organization and $5,000 from the northern.

> I think that this request can be justified on several grounds. The most important one is that the purpose of all these off-year expenditures is, in the final analysis, to assure the election. Another good argument is that this type of expenditure is taken care of customarily by [the] Republican Finance [Committee] in other states like New York and Pennsylvania.
>
> I feel very strongly on this matter, and, frankly, I intend to condition my future cooperation with Republican Finance on whether they support our program. After all, I am the only man who appeared at the various Republican Finance dinners who has received no benefit whatever from them. This, of course, was due to the fact that I did not happen to be running this year. As you are aware, appearing at such a dinner is not politically advantageous and by reason of having to accept such engagements it became necessary for me to turn down some open meetings which would have been much better from a political standpoint for me to accept.

Nixon added that he felt "tremendously indebted to our special group for what they have done to make our programs possible in the past, but I don't feel that they should continue to bear this burden indefinitely."

In a confidential reply dated June 11, 1952, Smith complained to Nixon that the Republican leaders in San Francisco had been promising a $5,000 contribution for eight months, but "it is apparently more convenient for them to forget about it." Despite these and other collection troubles,

Smith suggested that the fund goal be raised to a "minimum of $20,000 rather than $15,000 because we know that it is very desirable to step up your activities after this year, as your own re-election year begins to come closer and you would not have to soft-pedal your activities on account of a Knowland campaign coming up." (Senator Knowland had, in fact, been re-elected by virtue of winning both the Democratic and Republican nominations in the primaries a week before Smith wrote this letter.)

"As things stand now, I still have not paid the last $1,000 of that printing bill at the Capital City Engraving Company and have on hand $879.24," Smith continued. "I do not like to cut this fund down any lower than that to make a further payment on the Capital bill. I do not see much additional money coming in, short of another general appeal to the previous contributors, which I had hoped to avoid. Bernie [Brennan] said he had a promise of an additional $500 a couple of weeks ago, but it has not shown up. If that comes in promptly, I could clean up the Capital bill and still have a little in the bank to take care of your convention expenses and so forth. After the convention I might have a little more time to scare up enough more money here and there to see us through the summer, even if northern California continues not to come through."

Stray whispers about the fund were started at the Republican National Convention in July by a couple of California delegates who made a project of confiding to strangers that Nixon was despised by fellow Californians, that he "double-crossed" Governor Warren and that he was being "kept" by a brand of favor-seeking millionaires. Variations of the story soon reached some news correspondents, of course. But the 1952 Republican Convention was a scandalmonger's paradise and the Nixon story was lost, like a nursery rhyme in a sea of garish murder mysteries. In the fierce battle between Eisenhower and Taft partisans no reputation of importance was spared, and gossipers among the Republican faithful became as suspect as the dirt they peddled.

One version of the Nixon story, as heard by Peter Edson, Washington political columnist for Newspaper Enterprise

Association, appeared to merit checking, however. It was that Nixon got a "supplementary salary" of $20,000 a year from 100 California businessmen, each of whom chipped in $200. Edson asked several California political correspondents and editors, including James Bassett, of the Los Angeles *Mirror,* who later became Nixon's campaign press secretary. None put any credence in the story. Two months later—on September 14—Edson appeared with Nixon on the television program "Meet the Press" and afterward he asked the Senator about the alleged supplementary salary.

"Without a moment's hesitation, he told me that the rumor as I had it was all wrong," Edson wrote subsequently. "But there was a story there and it would be all right for me to use it. He didn't attempt to duck the question in any way." The Senator suggested that Edson telephone Dana Smith in Pasadena for details, because Smith ran the fund and knew much more about it than Nixon himself did. Edson called the next day, and Smith discussed the general background and specific aspects of the fund. He also suggested that other states adopt the plan to keep Senators who had no independent incomes from having to bow to outside "pressure."

Later that day Smith reviewed the fund operation again, this time with Leo Katcher, of the New York *Post*; Richard Donovan, of *Reporter* magazine; and Ernest Breasher, of the Los Angeles *Daily News.* These reporters were digging into Nixon's background for biographical material that went beyond the mostly favorable sketches previously published. Smith told them substantially what he had told Edson.

Meanwhile, Nixon left Washington for California, with a stop in Denver to review with General Eisenhower final plans for the campaign offensive which was to begin at 8:30 P.M. on September 17. After the chat with Edson, Nixon turned his mind to other matters. Senator and Mrs. Nixon arrived in California at nightfall, September 16. A representative of the Los Angeles *Daily News* mentioned to Bassett, Nixon's press secretary, that his paper had a story for release on Thursday about a Nixon fund, Bassett told Nixon, who said it probably was Edson's story and therefore an accurate one because Edson was to get the complete picture from Dana Smith.

Richard Nixon is about as superstitious as the average successful politician. He is respectful of the mysterious power called "luck." Thus his first stumping tour of the presidential campaign began at Pomona, a community in Los Angeles County where he had started his surprisingly successful campaigns for Congress and Senate. The send-off rally on Wednesday night brought 15,000 well-wishers to the railroad heading. A flag-waving delegation from Whittier was led by Nixon's aging parents. Governor Warren officiated. The Senator's whistle-stop route was up central California through Oregon and Washington, the same route Governor Stevenson had followed the week before. Nixon promised to "nail down those lies" told by the Democratic candidate. He paraded the basic Republican assault weapons, labeled "Korea, Communism, Corruption and Costs." And he declared that "no administration with the greedy, gouging, grumbling history of the Truman regime" could accomplish the great things for America which General Eisenhower proposed.

As the rally wound up, the 11-car campaign train started slowly to pull out of Pomona, with Nixon, on the back platform, imploring one and all: "If you believe as I believe, come along on this great Crusade. . . ." The tracks stood out under angled floodlights, creating a vision of the path to glory. Hundreds of magnetized listeners found themselves following behind the crawling train with Nixon's outstretched arms seemingly their goal. If it were possible, thousands of television viewers would have joined the trek which ended when the train rounded a curve a hundred yards from the starting point, and the trackside lights were turned off.

It had been a good meeting and all aboard the Nixon Special were gay in anticipation of the campaign ahead. Most of the staff had been through it before. The only newcomers to the entourage were William P. Rogers, who later was appointed Attorney General by President Eisenhower, and Miss Rose Mary Woods, the Senator's executive secretary. Neither had experienced a political campaign before. Rogers came along as a sort of assistant-without-portfolio on the campaign train after Nixon "assured me that nothing ever happens to a candidate for Vice-President."

A messenger from Republican headquarters in Los Angeles met the train at a water stop before midnight. He brought word that a "fund" story to be printed in newspapers the next day could cause trouble. Nixon summoned a few advisers to his private car at one A.M. The fund was reviewed in considerable detail. Rogers, who had not heard of it before, gave as his judgment that no impropriety was involved; therefore, "the facts" would neutralize possible criticism. Chotiner, who was reputed to possess an extra, supernatural sense that spotted things of political importance before they even germinated, was not disturbed either. "Hell, there's nothing to this thing; it's ridiculous," he said.

Because of a four-hour time lag between the East and West coasts, the Nixon fund story was already stirring political tempers in New York and Washington on Thursday, September 18, before Nixon had begun the first full day of his journey. The New York *Post* was on the streets at ten o'clock, its front page dominated by the words: SECRET NIXON FUND! The story was on the second page under a two-line banner headline that said: SECRET RICH MEN'S TRUST FUND KEEPS NIXON IN STYLE BEYOND HIS SALARY. Peter Edson's column was printed later that morning and afternoon in other newspapers. It was written as a straight news story, and lacked the speculative flamboyance that made the New York *Post* article seem more sensational. The United Press and the Associated Press relayed the substance of both reports to other daily newspapers.

Word reached the Nixon train at Bakersfield. Nothing had appeared yet in California newspapers, however, and the large, early-morning trainside audience was friendly. When the Senator concluded his speech with the *big* question, "Who can clean up the mess in Washington?" the crowd responded, "Ike can!"

The press contingent started to grow at Tulare, the second stop. Nixon refused to comment about the fund, however, and at Fresno, the third stop, reporters were barred from Nixon's private car.

Tension on the train mounted with the rumors, which multiplied as the morning wore on. In the early afternoon at Merced—the fifth stop—Nixon issued a brief statement outlining the "facts" of the fund and declaring: "I might have put my wife on the federal payroll as did the Democratic nominee for Vice-President . . . nor have I been accepting law fees on the side while serving as member of Congress. I prefer to play completely square with the taxpayers." [1]

Meanwhile, in Washington, Democratic headquarters, surprised and delighted by a windfall of incalculable value, rushed to the offensive. National Chairman Stephen Mitchell demanded—via a mimeographed statement, press interviews and radio and television appearances— that Eisenhower throw Nixon off the ticket at once or eat his fulsome observations on "public morals."

The Republicans, fearing the consequences of a possible scandal and at the same time hoping to mousetrap the excited Democrats, launched an offensive and defensive simultaneously. Robert Humphreys, public-relations director and senior staff member then at headquarters, issued a statement in the name of Senator Karl Mundt labeling the whole thing a "left-wing smear" and a "filthy" maneuver by a pro-Stevenson newspaper. He also called the Eisenhower train in the Midwest for permission (which Chairman Arthur Summerfield readily gave) to commit the national party organization to a policy of "down the line support for Dick." Late in the afternoon Humphreys accepted a call from Republican headquarters in Chicago. "We've been trying for days to interest someone in a Stevenson fund we have uncovered," said a voice. "It is worse than the Nixon fund we just read about." Humphreys replied, in effect, fine, but let's worry about Nixon now and deal with Stevenson later.

General Eisenhower's 18-car campaign train—the *Look Ahead, Neighbor* Special—was passing among the voters of Iowa and Nebraska. In reply to questions in the morning, Press Secretary James Hagerty said, "We never comment on a New York *Post* story." In the late afternoon he said the General would have nothing to say. The General's staff was saying plenty, however, in the privacy of compartments and washrooms beyond earshot of the candidate, at one end of the

[1] Senator John Sparkman, the Democratic candidate for Vice-President, campaigning some 3,000 miles away in Florida, snapped that there was "nothing *sub rosa*" about the job his wife had in his office. "She has given excellent service," he declared.

train, and the reporters, at the other. All day they held conferences, analyzed reports and rumors, and weighed the problems of switching vice-presidential candidates in mid-campaign.

At strategy meetings the month before, Governor Sherman Adams, chief of the Eisenhower staff, and Chotiner, the Nixon manager, formulated a new, foolproof liaison plan to keep the two campaign teams in intimate and constant touch during the final period of electioneering when a mistake by one of the candidates might be compounded unwittingly into a disaster by the other. The Adams-Chotiner plan set up direct communications between the respective echelons of the two teams. Thus Eisenhower would deal with Nixon, and vice versa; Chotiner would talk with Adams or Senator Fred A. Seaton; Hagerty and Bassett would discuss press matters, man to man; and so forth. As sometimes happens with even the best-laid plans, however, this one failed in the emergency of September 18 because Eisenhower simply did not call Nixon and Nixon did not call Eisenhower.

Newspapers picked up in the evening along the route of the Nixon Special in California reported that Midwestern audiences were reacting favorably to Eisenhower's charges that the Truman administration's legacies to the nation were "a problem of morality in government," "crazy federal spending" and "deficits that cheapen our money." A hoped-for statement of the General's unqualified support and faith had not materialized. Nothing had been heard from that direction, in fact, except questions—and, of course, rumors. The Nixon party might have viewed the General's silence more charitably if it had been privy to a decision of the Eisenhower strategists. The decision was to break the news about the fund to the General *after* his principal speeches so as not to risk upsetting him.

A large and friendly crowd awaited Nixon at Sacramento, the ninth and last stop that Thursday. But he sensed a strangeness in the reception committee of politicians. Instead of elbowing and maneuvering to be first in line, some seemed to hesitate when the time came to pose for pictures with the Senator. As his campaign special continued up the valley that night a gloomy and angry vice-presidential candidate sought the solitude of his compartment; and Pat Nixon, blinking back the tears she seldom tolerated, wondered if any political office was worth the sacrifice of a good name.

A half continent away that night *one* important individual on the Eisenhower train had reached a firm conclusion. Republican Chairman Summerfield had before him a report on the procedure for changing a candidate. In the mass of unnoticed resolutions adopted routinely during the rush to adjourn the National Convention was one that left the responsibility entirely to the National Committee. If Nixon withdrew, the Republican organization probably would split irretrievably in a fight over a successor. Summerfield redoubled his conviction that Nixon should stay.

Two newspaper articles set the mood on the Nixon train for Friday, September 19. One was an official announcement that the California franchise tax board would investigate the Nixon fund. The other was a "notice" issued by the Democratic National Committee to editors and correspondents citing criminal law on "bribery and graft . . . by members of Congress." The expense fund stories had blossomed overnight into implications of tax cheating, bribery and graft.

At Democratic headquarters in Sacramento early that morning the northern California campaign manager for Stevenson suggested that Young Democrats could strike a blow for the cause and enjoy themselves at the same time by heckling Nixon about the fund. Glen Wilson, a party field man, snapped up the idea, loaded his car with loud-voiced youngsters and streaked off for Marysville, Nixon's first stop. The Republican candidate had concluded his talk and the train was pulling away slowly when the hecklers arrived. They bounded from the car, and one of them shouted, "Tell 'em about the $16,000!"

Nixon wheeled around and yelled, "Hold the train! Hold the train!" It stopped; the crowd pressed forward; the grim-faced Nixon paused to control his anger, pointed to the questioner, recognizable in a spotted tie, and answered:

"You folks know the work that I did investigating Communists in the United States. Ever since I have done that work, the Communists, the left-wingers, have been fighting me with every smear that they have been able to. Even when I received the nomination for the vice-presidency, I want you folks to know—and I'm going to reveal it today for the first time—I was warned that if I continued to attack the Communists and crooks in this government they would continue to smear me, and, believe me, you can expect that they will continue to do so. They started it yesterday—you saw it in the morning papers. They tried to say that I had taken the money, $16,000.

"What they didn't point out is this: that what I was doing was saving you money, rather than charging the expenses of my office, which were in excess of the amounts which were allowed by the taxpayers and allowed under the law, rather than taking that money.

"Rather than using the money, the taxpayers' monies for those purposes, what did I do? What I did was to have those expenses paid by the people back home who were interested in seeing that the information concerning what was going on in Washington was spread among the people of their state. [Long applause.]

"I'll tell you what some of them do. They put their wives on the payroll, taking your money and using it for that purpose. And Pat Nixon has worked in my office night after night after night, and I can say this, and I say it proudly, she has never been on the government payroll since I have been in Washington, D.C. [Applause.]

"Point two: What else would you do? Do you want me to go on and do what some of these people are doing? Take fat legal fees on the side? During the time I've been in Washington—and I'm proud of this—I've never taken a legal fee, although as a lawyer I could legally but not ethically have done so. And I'm never going to in the future, because I think that's a violation of a trust which my office has. . . ."

The crowd cheered, the heckler scowled. Nixon waved and smiled, sternly.

Eisenhower ended his silence on the fund in Kansas City that morning. He predicted "the facts will show that Nixon would not compromise with what is right." The General's comment was relayed immediately to the Nixon train—and spirits were lifted a little, at least until the train reached Chico, where a telephone call was waiting. It was Senator Seaton, with Eisenhower's first message for his running mate since the fund uproar had started. Seaton told Chotiner, then Nixon, that the General was anxious to get to the bottom of this thing. Chotiner said that was mighty fine, but what more does the General require than the Senator's word? Seaton implied that the General might answer that himself in a direct telephone conversation which might be arranged in the next day or so.

The talk with Seaton delayed Nixon's Chico speech 34 minutes. But the crowd waited, and listened attentively, as Nixon beat the hecklers to the fund question by asking it himself. The answer was much like the one he gave in Marysville, and he followed it up with the safest promise a politician ever made on an American election stump: that a Republican administration would fire Dean Acheson as Secretary of State. The crowd roared approval, and the Nixon Special proceeded north.

The fund issue was becoming a national sensation. Commentators analyzed and speculated; radio and television programs were interrupted for late bulletins; the Democrats, sensing an opportunity to nullify the corruption issue, which they considered phony anyway, jibed sarcastically at Eisenhower's "Crusade"; Adlai Stevenson announced he would reserve judgment until the Republicans explained how Nixon had used the money; Democratic Chairman Mitchell wondered when the General would "cast away" his erring running mate. Among Republicans, Senator Taft flatly approved the Nixon action and scoffed at talk of changing candidates, and Oregon's Governor McKay demonstrated his backing by boarding the Nixon train with flags flying, a band playing and practically all the state's Republican hierarchy in tow. But most other Republicans of consequence either crossed their fingers and hoped for the best, in silence, or sent Eisenhower and his staff assessments of the situation that showed Nixon had to be dumped or the ticket would lose. At an Eisenhower whistle stop in Missouri a telephone call from General Lucius D. Clay, in New York, created a stir because the candidate halted his campaign speech abruptly to take it. Clay was an intimate of Eisenhower's and a key figure in Citizens for Eisenhower, a movement which rather looked down on regular Re-

publican organization people as *politicians*. Although the
nature of that September 19 telephone call was never disclosed, it was commonly believed—and frequently reported in
print—that Clay advised Eisenhower to get a new vice-
presidential candidate. Long afterward, in 1958, Clay said
that was not so. "I personally did not take a position on that
particular thing," he said. "All I asked [Eisenhower] to do was
please not to commit himself or make any statements until
Herbert Brownell had been able to reach him at his stop that
night and they could talk it over. I have complete confidence
in the sagacity and the intelligence of Herb. He did get there
that night and they talked it all over—and out of that came
the decisions which led to the radio talk [Nixon's nationally
broadcast explanation the following Tuesday]."

The most important telephone call made *from* the Eisenhower train on September 19 was to Paul Hoffman. Sherman
Adams made it at Eisenhower's direction. Adams reached
Hoffman in the Pasadena Hospital, recovering from a head
injury caused by a stray golf ball. "He asked me to begin an
immediate investigation of the Nixon fund, to find out if it
was clean," Hoffman recollected. From his hospital bed Hoffman retained Gibson, Dunn and Crutcher, a Los Angeles law
firm, and the Price, Waterhouse accounting organization.
Fifty lawyers and accountants—the cream of both firms—
went to work at once and stayed at it over the weekend.

Adams also had telephoned Senator Knowland in Hawaii
—as did Brownell—to urge that he join the Eisenhower train
as quickly as possible. Knowland was scheduled to do so in
about a week, but Adams and Brownell told him he was
needed immediately in the mounting crisis. Knowland was not
aware until after he arrived that there had been guarded talk
among Eisenhower strategists about having him on tap as a
substitute should Nixon be dropped. The moment Knowland
boarded the *Look Ahead, Neighbor* Special, however, he became a vigorous backstop for Chairman Summerfield, until
then the only unqualified pro-Nixon voice around Eisenhower.

During the afternoon of September 19 Eisenhower issued a
statement. He had "long admired and applauded Senator
Nixon's American faith and his determination to drive Communist sympathizers from offices of public trust." Nixon was

"an honest man," the General added, and would prove this by placing "all the facts before the people, fairly and squarely."

In California Dana Smith made public the fund donor list of 76 names and a report on the income—it totaled $18,250 —and disbursements—about the same amount. This bore out what Nixon had been saying, but the impact of a properly timed release was lost because Smith gave it out before getting a prearranged signal from Chotiner. Smith's explanation was that two reporters told him they were in a hurry to meet deadlines—and in late, low circulation editions, no less.

Meanwhile editorials calling for Nixon's replacement began to appear in some newspapers that supported the Republican ticket. The New York *Herald Tribune*, Eisenhower's favorite paper, called the fund "ill-advised" and suggested that the California Senator make a formal offer of withdrawal from the ticket, which Eisenhower could accept or reject as he saw fit. This was flashed to Chotiner at Medford, Oregon. It was the hardest blow yet, and Nixon's lieutenants decided to keep the news from him, at least overnight. Nevertheless, he heard about it from a Washington correspondent whose newspaper wanted a story on Nixon's reaction. Nixon shook his head; he had nothing to say. Pickets were at his last stop with taunting signs. He pretended to ignore them. He made his campaign speech and forced a smile as the town's organization of cave men initiated him into their order with a long ritual.

Saturday, September 20, there was a near riot at Nixon's rally in Eugene, Oregon. The signs carried by pickets read: SHH! ANYONE WHO MENTIONS $16,000 IS A COMMUNIST and NO MINK COATS FOR NIXON, JUST COLD CASH. While Nixon spoke there was a scuffle and exchange of insults between the pickets and people behind them who complained that the signs hid their view of the candidate. Nixon ignored it until his speech was concluded. Then, pointing to the "Mink Coat" sign, he said angrily, "That's absolutely right—there are no mink coats for the Nixons. I'm proud to say my wife, Pat, wears a good Republican cloth coat." The campaign train pulled away, a fight started and the "Mink Coat" sign was torn to shreds. No one was injured, to speak of, but there was one arrest—a "citizen's arrest" by Charles O. Porter, a

Democrat elected to Congress from the district four years later. Porter charged his "prisoner" with disorderly conduct, but nothing came of it beyond newspaper notices. "I was head of the local ADA [Americans for Democratic Action] chapter at the time and on the Democratic party executive committee," Porter recalls. "We were sitting there talking at our breakfast strategy meeting and my law partner and I got the idea that since Nixon was coming to town we ought to picket him to point up what the newspapers were saying about the fund. So we thought up a couple of good things to put on signs and got young Democrats at the University of Oregon to carry them." An elephant—the symbol of the G.O.P.—and about 1,000 people were at the rally, and the elephant keeper hit one of the sign bearers "with the elephant pick or something," said Porter. "I was surprised at the vituperation that this boy was taking. They were calling him a homosexual and such stuff. Just people coming up there and insulting him. At one point I held up the signs for him for a moment, but I did not picket Nixon myself. Not that it was below my dignity, but that just isn't the way the work was assigned. When Nixon pulled out, the crowd surged over with fists flying. I was mad because we had a right to be there and express our opinion. I was mad and disappointed that people should treat this boy like that for expressing an opinion. People kept calling, 'Dirty Communist!' This is what Nixon had done. It had repercussions for me. I even got accused of being an atheist. It broke up my law partnership." Porter said the partnership was subsequently resumed, however.

In the rash of public statements that day former President Hoover said, "If everyone in the city of Washington possessed the high level of courage, probity and patriotism of Senator Nixon, this would be a far better nation"; the CIO charged that Nixon had been bought by the real-estate interests who "knew a good investment when they saw one"; and Senator George D. Aiken, the liberal Republican from Vermont, said, "I know that no Senator can maintain a family in Washington and stay in the Senate on his present salary unless he has some outside financial help." Democratic Chairman Mitchell called Nixon "a Holy Joe that's been talking pretty big—now let him put up some facts."

On his campaign train late that afternoon General Eisenhower sent word to the press car that he would like to join the reporters in a glass of beer. That meant he would like to talk informally, and off the record—to give the press his views, as background information, with the understanding that what he said would not be quoted or attributed directly to him. The first question asked was "Do you consider the Nixon thing a closed incident?" Eisenhower frowned, and said, "By no means." He learned of the Nixon fund on Friday, a day after the newspapers printed the original stories, he explained, and was greatly disturbed. He had not known Nixon very long and still did not know him well, but the Senator seemed to exemplify the kind of honesty, vigor and straightforward aggressiveness that he admired and wanted to see more of in young leaders. Furthermore, he could not believe Nixon would do anything crooked or unethical, but Nixon would have to prove it—and convince "fair-minded" people. Then Eisenhower said, "Of what avail is it for us to carry on this crusade against this business of what has been going on in Washington if we ourselves aren't as clean as a hound's tooth?"

The resulting news articles attributed the "hound's tooth" quotation to "highest authorities," informed sources and the like.

When Nixon was told about the Eisenhower session, he forced a disbelieving smile and muttered something to himself. Mrs. Nixon, who had held back for three days her resentment, wondered to a friend, "Why should we keep taking this?"

In reminiscences, some of the campaign assistants have speculated that Eisenhower would not have gotten a single vote from the Nixon staff if the ballot had been cast that night, in Portland, Oregon.

When the Nixons returned from church on Sunday, September 21, there was a telegram from Harold Stassen stating that "After a thoughtful review of the entire situation, Dick, I have regretfully reached a conclusion"—you should offer your resignation from the ticket to General Eisenhower.

The Nixon party spent the weekend at the Benson Hotel, in Portland. Stassen's was one of several hundred telegrams Nixon got on Sunday. Most were from friends in California and congressional colleagues urging him not to quit the ticket.

But generally the messages throughout the day contributed to Nixon's weary despondency. Rogers, who manned the telephones, said, "We had calls from everybody, all offering advice. There were only a few of us that day who were reasonably sure it would work out all right." Governor Dewey agreed Nixon should bare his soul on national television as quickly as possible, then reported that seven of the nine people at his dinner table believed Nixon should resign from the ticket. It was obvious that Eisenhower felt the Dana Smith reports and Nixon's statements on the fund were not enough. The various "inner circles"—Nixon's, Eisenhower's and the National Committee's—talked about a radio-television report.

At six o'clock Nixon spoke at a dinner of the Temple Beth Israel Men's Club. "For all we knew, it was going to be the last speech of the campaign for him," Chotiner said. It was a low point for the Senator. "Dick was ready to chuck the whole thing, and frankly it took the toughest arguments of some of us to hold him in check," said another Nixon intimate. Before leaving the hotel for the Beth Israel speech, Nixon saw a survey that showed the newspapers to be two to one against him. When a "Have Faith" message was handed him from his mother, Nixon stepped into a vacant room to hide his tears.

Following the evening speech, Nixon's campaign doctor massaged his neck to ease painfully tense muscles. Then his staff advisers came to the bedroom for a full-dress discussion of what to do. Rogers said Nixon had no alternative but to resign if Eisenhower requested it. Chotiner disagreed. He said the General and a lot of people around him knew very little about politics, and if Nixon was dumped the Republican party was sure to lose the election. Nixon listened in silence. He got up once, during a pause in the discussion, and said, as though to himself, "I will not crawl."

The strategy session was interrupted at 10:05 P.M. by the long-awaited telephone call from Eisenhower, in St. Louis. Nixon sat on a couch and propped his feet on a table. Pleasantries were exchanged. The running mates talked a little about their respective whistle-stop experiences. The Senator told the General that Dewey also thought it would be good to put the fund story before the people on television. "I'm at your disposal," said Nixon. Then he told the General the important thing was for the Republicans to win. "I want you to know if you reach a conclusion either now or any time later that I should get off the ticket, you can be sure that I will immediately respect your judgment and do so." Eisenhower replied, in effect, that he did not think *he* should be the one to make that decision. At this Nixon stiffened and said sternly, "There comes a time in a man's life when he has to fish or cut bait." (Actually his words were stronger.)

At midnight Adams, Summerfield and Humphreys notified Nixon from the Eisenhower train that radio and television time now could be arranged—because three Republican party organizations had pledged the necessary $75,000. So Nixon broke off his campaign tour and flew to Los Angeles to prepare.

A small group of his original supporters and Young Republicans was at the airport to welcome him. They had banners and made a lot of noise—but the homecoming was quite a contrast to the hero's send-off just five days before.

9 ※ *Checkers Speech, 1952*

NIXON had been in politics only six years. Just a week before his arrival in Los Angeles on September 22 he was at a peak of his phenomenal career—and still headed upward. And now, as William Rogers put it, "he faced as severe a test as anyone could cope with. It was not just that his integrity was challenged; it was the possible consequences generally. If he got off the ticket, it would have been the first time in the history of the country such a thing happened; by the same token, if the Republicans lost, he would be the scapegoat."

The Senator exiled himself in the Ambassador Hotel to await the climax of "the worst experience of my life." Mrs. Nixon went to the home of Mrs. Helene Drown, a friend who had been her companion on the campaign train.

A national hookup of 64 NBC television stations, 194 CBS radio stations and practically the entire 560-station Mutual Broadcasting System radio network was contracted for by Batten, Barton, Durstine and Osborn, the Republican party's advertising agency. But getting the "perfect" time for Nixon's speech was a problem. Ted Rogers, the Senator's television adviser (and no relative of William Rogers), wanted a ready-made audience. The spot after the "I Love Lucy" program on Monday night was available, but Nixon could not be ready in time to fill it. So they got the half hour immediately following the Milton Berle show on Tuesday night. No event in history involving a vice-presidential candidate got such attention—before and after. For four days Nixon was talked and written about much more than the candidates for President. In the 48 hours that preceded his speech, rumors about him were "bulletin" material for the nation's news media. Radio programs were interrupted for "reports" that he had collapsed. They were interrupted again for his doctor's statement that he was "in perfect health." Eisenhower's deferred judgment was announced—and printed a dozen different ways. There were flat predictions that Nixon would stay on the ticket. There were also predictions that he would get off. The Los Angeles *Daily News* said, "Anything short of an enthusiastic burst of public support . . . will be interpreted in favor of what [Eisenhower and his strategists] have already decided—that corruption cannot remain a campaign issue as long as one of their candidates is tainted with the slightest suspicion. Thus, Nixon will probably be asked to resign. . . ."

On Monday afternoon the lawyers and accountants hired by Paul Hoffman sent their 18-page, single-spaced reports to Sherman Adams. The study was based on Dana Smith's files and, in effect, found everything to be legal and in line with what Smith had made public a few days before, except for about $11,000 deposited in the fund account after Nixon's nomination, and Smith said it would be accounted for as campaign contributions.

Monday was also the day of the "Stevenson fund" disclosure. An official of a mimeograph machine company doing business with the state of Illinois charged that Governor Stevenson "personally promoted" contributions from private businessmen. Stevenson immediately confirmed it, said it "has never been any secret," explained that the money supplemented the state salaries of members of his administration who left better-paying jobs in private business to serve Illinois. Stevenson insisted that none of the money went to him or any other elected official, and there was "no question of improper influence, because there was no connection between the contributors and the beneficiaries."

Nevertheless, the word "fund" had been battered into something that looked and sounded sinister, and the fact that he had a "fund" made Stevenson a target for the pointed questions, implied charges and innuendo to which Nixon had been subjected because of his "fund." It also gave Nixon an opportunity to suggest in a manner that could hardly be misunderstood that both Stevenson and his running mate, Sparkman, had better bare their financial souls, as Nixon was doing.

Normally, Nixon would work a full week, at least, on a major speech. There was less than two days for him to prepare the most important one of his life. He started on the airplane flight from Portland to Los Angeles. "I was pretty tired by that time," he recalls. "I tried to sleep, but after dozing a little while I woke up. I began to think about the broadcast, what could I say—how could I put this thing in a way people would understand. I pulled out some United Airlines postcards from the souvenir packet at the seat and made notes. It was not an outline of the broadcast, but of general ideas—the way I do it whenever I write a speech. I have a general idea of the theme I am going to hit, then I just let the thoughts flow into my mind and I write them down. That was when the idea came to me to mention the girls' dog, Checkers, the cloth coat and Lincoln's reference to the common people."

Nixon worked at it intensively for almost 24 hours before the telecast. Late the first night he rushed from his room looking for someone to double-check the Lincoln quotation. In the hall he bumped into Pat Hillings, a member of the campaign inner circle, who did not remember it. Nixon called his Whittier College history professor, Dr. Smith, who, in turn, called the English professor, Dr. Upton. The quotation was "The Lord must have loved the common people because he made so many of them." Nixon's reference to Checkers was inspired by Franklin Roosevelt's masterful use of his dog Fala in a 1944 campaign speech that made the Republicans a national laughingstock. Nixon tried his ideas on Bill Rogers and Chotiner. He credits Dewey with the proposal that caused more than a million Americans to write, wire and telephone after the speech. "Dewey suggested that I ask listeners to wire me indicating whether I should stay on the ticket or get off."

Shortly before Nixon was to leave for the studio, Sherman Adams telephoned Chotiner to find out, for Eisenhower, what Nixon would say. When Chotiner replied he did not really know, Adams said, "Oh, come now, Murray, you must know . . . he has a script, doesn't he?"

"No," replied Chotiner.

"What about the press?" asked Adams.

"We've set up television sets in the hotel for them, and we have shorthand reporters to take it down, page by page."

"Look, we have to know what is going to be said."

"Sherm," Chotiner replied, "if you want to know what's going to be said, you do what I'm going to do. You sit in front of the television and listen."

Eisenhower was campaigning in Ohio on Tuesday, September 23. His telegrams and messages were running three to one against Nixon. All day the General repeated to callers that he would not make up his mind until after the broadcast. Chairman Summerfield was at his office in Washington. Just after lunch he called Robert Humphreys over and said, "We have got to get to Cleveland immediately." He had just gotten word that one of Eisenhower's personal friends had boarded the campaign train with what seemed to be an impressive argument for replacing Nixon. Summerfield and Humphreys took the first plane. The General was to address a rally in the city auditorium that night. He planned to watch the Nixon telecast first, however, and arrangements were made to pipe it into the auditorium for the rally audience.

About an hour before the Eisenhower party was to leave for the auditorium, General Wilton (Jerry) Persons, an Eisenhower assistant, summoned Humphreys to the General's room. Eisenhower was reclining on the bed, his head propped up by pillows and the headboard. Adams stood on one side, Persons on the other. "One of the rumors we've gotten is a very difficult one," said Persons. "It is that when Nixon bought his house in the Spring Valley section of Washington, Mrs. Nixon paid $10,000 in cash for the decorations, the interior decorating." Did Humphreys have any information on that? Humphreys said the report had to be untrue. He had been at the Nixon home just a week or two before and seen the only "decorations" being hung. They were living-room draperies which had just arrived with a circular couch from the Nixons' house in Whittier.

"The General listened intently, said practically nothing and seemed to be satisfied with the answer," Humphreys recalled.

Before leaving for the auditorium the Eisenhower staff gathered for another inconclusive discussion of Nixon's fate. At the auditorium, the General and his party climbed three flights of stairs to the manager's office over the stage. A television set was perched in a corner. Eisenhower and Mrs. Eisenhower sat on a small couch in front of it. Next to the couch, on a chair, was William Robinson, publisher of the New York *Herald Tribune*. Summerfield, Hagerty and about 30 other campaign assistants stood against the walls.

An intensive rehearsal for the Nixon program was going on, meanwhile, half a continent away at NBC's El Capitan Theater in Hollywood. Nixon himself refused to rehearse—or even talk with the program director. So Ted Rogers hired a stand-in, a salesman Nixon's size, who had Nixon's coloring and was dressed as Nixon would be. The cameramen, electricians, control-room operators, directors—everyone having to do with the program, except the star, rehearsed all day Tuesday. Rogers put the stand-in through the movements Nixon might make, and instructed the cameramen to keep the lens directly on Nixon regardless of what he did. Just before going on the air Rogers told them to focus on Mrs. Nixon when the Senator talked about her. Draperies were hung over the glass "clients' booth" to keep Nixon from being distracted by the "audience"—Chotiner, Bassett and Ted Rogers.

About one hour before broadcast time a telephone call came from "Mr. Chapman" in New York. That was the code name Governor Dewey used during the campaign to avoid attention. Congressman Hillings said Nixon was not available. Then, according to Hillings:

"He said, 'Don't give me that business. I've got to talk to him. It's absolutely essential.'

"I said, 'My orders are, Governor, he's not to talk to anybody.'

"He said, 'You get him right now. I'm not going to get off this phone until you do it.'

"So I went out and told Chotiner. And Chotiner said, 'I think I know what it is.'

"Chotiner, who was particularly anxious to keep disturbing news from Nixon until after the telecast, took the phone and said, 'I'm awfully sorry. He's out someplace and I can't reach him.'

"He said, 'Well, I'll hold the phone.'

"I said, 'I haven't the slightest idea when he'll be back.'

"He said, 'I don't care how long it is, I'll hold this phone'—and if you know Mr. Chapman," Chotiner winked, "you know he's the kind of guy who will hold that phone."

Finally Chotiner got Nixon, who was across the hall. Dewey's message was that he had polled the campaign leaders and found that most felt Nixon should resign.

"Dewey didn't say that was his own feeling," recalls Nixon. "He said, 'I am reporting that the group feels you should. I regret this very much.' " Although Dewey did not say so flatly, and Nixon did not ask, it was implied that Eisenhower agreed with the majority.

"Dick looked like someone had smashed him," said Hillings.

That is exactly how Nixon felt. "The call was really a block-buster," he recalled. "I asked all the staff to leave me completely alone until time to leave for the broadcast so that I could decide what to do. I didn't describe the details of the call, but they knew who it was from and I told them I might require a complete change in approach. That is why my closest advisers told the literal truth—hard as that is to believe—when they said they actually did not know when the broadcast began what I was going to say.

"I sat alone for at least 30 minutes, debating as to what I ought to do. I had a tremendous respect for Dewey as a man and for his superb political judgment. The question I had to decide was whether I was justified in putting my judgment above his as well as possibly the General himself by not announcing my resignation from the ticket, which was the course of action the Dewey message seemed to imply so clearly."

Nixon added that "it was Chotiner who really saved the day as far as I was concerned. He was truly a tower of strength. He came into the room as I was shaving about ten minutes before departure time, and said, 'Dick, a campaign manager must never be seen or heard. But if you're kicked off this ticket, I'm going to call the biggest damn press conference that has ever been held. I'm going to break a rule. I'm

going to have television present. I'm going to break every rule
in the book, and I'm going to tell everybody who called you,
what was said, names and everything.' "

Nixon looked at him surprised, Chotiner recalls, and asked,
"Would you really do that?"

"I said, 'Sure.' 'Why?' he asked. And I told him, 'Hell,
we'd be through with politics anyway. It wouldn't make any
difference.' "

"Some way Chotiner's cold, realistic logic broke the tension," said Nixon, "and, while I didn't make a final decision
at that point as to what to do, I was able to think clearly and
decisively on the ride to the studio. By the time I got there I
had made my decision not to follow the course of action which
had been suggested by the General's advisers, but to submit
the case to the country and let the people decide."

By broadcast time the speech was scrawled, in note form,
on a lawyer's yellow note pad. His own mind was clear on
what to tell the country except for the item of quitting or
staying. His inclination was to leave it to the National Committee and hope for the best. "Even riding over to the broadcast I still hadn't decided for sure how I would conclude it."

In reminiscing six years later, Nixon said, "You have to
expect in a campaign that your integrity, your loyalty, your
honesty, your intellectual honesty may all be questioned.
That's fair game. You have got to be able to take it. But
what was involved was even more important than that. In
questioning my integrity and trying to prove it was bad, they
questioned the integrity of the Republican party, the judgment
of General Eisenhower in selecting me and approving me as
a candidate, and the whole 'mess in Washington' issue. I
realized that if I failed I would be off the ticket, of course. I
also believed there would be a great risk that the ticket would
lose, and that I would carry that responsibility for the balance
of my life."

The program opened with a picture of Senator Nixon's
calling card. Then the camera switched to the Senator, seated
behind a desk.

> My fellow Americans, I come before you tonight as a
> candidate for the vice-presidency . . . and as a man whose
> honesty and integrity has been questioned. . . .

. . . I am sure that you have read the charge and you've heard it that I, Senator Nixon, took $18,000 from a group of my supporters.

Now, was that wrong? . . . I say that it was morally wrong if any of that $18,000 went to Senator Nixon for my personal use. I say that it was morally wrong if it was secretly given and secretly handled. And I say that it was morally wrong if any of the contributors got special favors for the contributions that they made.

And now to answer those questions let me say this:

Not one cent of the $18,000 or any other money of that type ever went to me for my personal use. Every penny of it was used to pay for political expenses that I did not think should be charged to the taxpayers of the United States. . . .

. . . Let me point out, and I want to make this particularly clear, that no contributor to this fund, no contributor to any of my campaigns, has ever received any consideration that he would not have received as an ordinary constituent.

. . . Now what I am going to do—and incidentally this is unprecedented in the history of American politics—I am going at this time to give to this television and radio audience a complete financial history; everything I've earned; everything I've spent; everything I owe. And I want you to know the facts. I'll have to start early.

I was born in 1913. . . .

. . . Well, that's about it. That's what we have and that's what we owe. It isn't very much, but Pat and I have the satisfaction that every dime that we've got is honestly ours. I should say this—that Pat doesn't have a mink coat. But she does have a respectable Republican cloth coat. And I always tell her that she'd look good in anything.

One other thing I probably should tell you, because if I don't they'll probably be saying this about me too, we did get something—a gift—after the election. A man down in Texas heard Pat on the radio mention the fact that our two youngsters would like to have a dog. And, believe it or not, the day before we left on this campaign trip we got a message from Union Station in Baltimore saying they had a package for us. We went down to get it. You know what it was?

It was a little cocker spaniel dog in a crate that he sent all the way from Texas. Black and white spotted. And our little girl—Tricia, the six-year-old—named it Checkers. And you know the kids love that dog and I just want to say this right now, that regardless of what they say about it, we're going to keep it. . . .

. . . You have read in the papers about other funds. Now, Mr. Stevenson, apparently, had a couple. One of them in which a group of business people paid and helped to supplement the salaries of state employees. Here is where the money went directly into their pockets.

And I think that what Mr. Stevenson should do should be to come before the American people as I have, give the names of the people that have contributed to that fund; give the names of the people who put this money into their pockets at the same time that they were receiving money from their state government, and see what favors, if any, they gave out for that.

I'm going to tell you this: I remember in the dark days of the Hiss case some of the same columnists, some of the same radio commentators who are attacking me now and misrepresenting my position were violently opposing me at the time I was after Alger Hiss. . . .

And now, finally, I know that you wonder whether or not I am going to stay on the Republican ticket or resign.

Let me say this: I don't believe that I ought to quit, because I am not a quitter. And, incidentally, Pat is not a quitter. After all, her name is Patricia Ryan, and she was born on St. Patrick's Day—and you know the Irish never quit.

But the decision, my friends, is not mine. I would do nothing that would harm the possibilities of Dwight Eisenhower to become President of the United States; and for that reason I am submitting to the Republican National Committee tonight, through this television broadcast, the decision which it is theirs to make.

Let them decide whether my position on the ticket will help or hurt; and I am going to ask you to help them decide. Wire and write the Republican National Committee whether you think I should stay or whether I should get off; and whatever their decision is, I will abide by it.

Just let me say this last word: Regardless of what happens, I am going to continue this fight. I am going to campaign up and down America until we drive the crooks and Communists and those that defend them out of Washington.

And remember, folks, Eisenhower is a great man, believe me. He is a great man. . . .

Mrs. Nixon sat at one side, her eyes glued to her husband. ". . . I am submitting the decision to the Republican National Committee. . . ." Ted Rogers slipped into the studio and signaled vigorously, "Your time is almost up!" Nixon looked at him, but did not see. He kept coming, and talking to the camera. ". . . Wire and write the National Committee on whether you think I should stay or whether I should get off, and whatever their decision is, I will abide. . . ." He was off the air, but still talking. "I'm terribly sorry I ran over," Nixon said to Rogers. "I loused it up, and I'm sorry." He thanked the technicians. Then he gathered the notes from the desk, stacked them neatly—and threw them to the floor. "Dick, you did a terrific job," beamed Chotiner, patting his back. "No, it was a flop . . . I couldn't get off in time," he replied. When he reached the dressing room, Nixon turned away from his friends—and let loose the tears he had been holding back.

A crowd outside cheered as he and Mrs. Nixon got into their car. There was great excitement at the hotel. Someone shouted, "The telephones are going crazy; everybody's in your corner!" Nixon accepted a call from Darryl Zanuck: "The most tremendous performance I've ever seen." Nixon began to come to life.

In Cleveland the Eisenhower group had watched, seemingly without drawing breath. Mrs. Eisenhower and several of the men clutched handkerchiefs and dabbed their eyes. The General had a small notebook in his hand. He jabbed at it with a pencil, his eyes never leaving the television screen. When the program ended, he said to Summerfield, "Well, Arthur, you surely got your $75,000 worth." Downstairs 13,000 people screamed and shouted, "We want Dick!" Eisenhower wired Nixon, "Your presentation was magnificent." Then the General explained that before he would "complete the formulation of a decision I feel the need of talking to you and would be most appreciative if you could fly to see me at once. Tomorrow night I shall be at Wheeling, West Virginia."

Shortly thereafter, when he appeared before the Armory crowd, the General's praise grew more lavish. As a "warrior," he had never seen "courage" to surpass that shown by Nixon, he said, and in a showdown fight he preferred "one courageous, honest man" at his side to "a whole boxcar full of pussy-footers."

The General did not get around to telling the crowd what it wanted most to hear, however. "I am not ducking any responsibility," he declared, "I am not going to be swayed by my idea of what will get the most votes. . . . I am going to say: Do I myself believe this man is the kind of man America would like to have for its Vice-President?"

The crowd shouted, "We like Dick!"

Telephone and telegraph lines were clogged across the land. Despite Nixon's plea that messages go to the National Committee, they were sent to everything that sounded Republican —from the Eisenhower train to local political clubs—and the sentiment seemed almost unanimous: "Keep Nixon." [1]

Reports of the reaction raised Nixon's spirits. He felt the ordeal was over and everything had turned out fine. "After this, nothing could seem tough," he confided to Bassett. The song "Happy Days Are Here Again" rang out in the hotel. Then a reporter brought to the Nixon suite an incomplete news bulletin about Eisenhower's telegram.

The telegram itself had not come, and the bulletin stressed Eisenhower's desire for a further face-to-face explanation from his running mate. Nixon read and reread it. His smile disappeared. He dictated to Miss Woods a telegram to National Chairman Summerfield resigning as candidate for Vice-President pending the selection of a successor. Chotiner followed Miss Woods out of the room and tore the telegram to

---

[1] All the messages were never totaled. Party headquarters in Washington, alone, got 300,000 letters, cards, telegrams and petitions, signed altogether by a million people. They have been given to Whittier College, where Dr. Robert W. O'Brien has studied them for clues to sociological motivations. Underclassmen have dubbed the huge collection "The Dead Sea Scrolls."

shreds. The secretary said she was not going to send it anyway.

An hour later Nixon got the full text of Eisenhower's telegram proposing a conference in Wheeling, West Virginia, the next night. In reply, the Senator wired that he intended to resume at once his campaign tour which would end Saturday, September 27. "Will be in Washington Sunday and will be delighted to confer with you at your convenience any time thereafter," Nixon added. This unusual show of independence delighted the Nixon staff and shocked more people than it pleased in the Eisenhower entourage.

At about 10:30 P.M., as the Nixon group was preparing to leave the hotel, Summerfield telephoned to urge that Nixon come to Wheeling, as requested. He was told that Nixon was going to Missoula, Montana, to campaign the next morning. Nixon would meet Eisenhower only after the General's mind was made up, one way or the other. "Dick is not going to be placed in the position of a little boy coming somewhere to beg for forgiveness," Chotiner said.

More calls followed from the Eisenhower train, and finally the General himself sought to reach Nixon. By then the Senator's party was en route to Missoula.

Dozens of messages forwarded from Los Angeles were at the hotel when Nixon arrived at four in the morning. A news report quoted Dewey as calling the Nixon telecast "a superb statement by a man of shining integrity and great purpose in the service of his country." A telegram from the Republican National Committee reported that 107 of its 138 members had been reached in a quick poll and all voted "enthusiastically" to keep Nixon on the ticket. There was also a telegram from Harold Stassen: CONGRATULATIONS ON A SUPERB PRESENTATION, DICK, AND BEST WISHES ALWAYS TO YOU AND TO PAT. SINCERELY.

Awaiting Chotiner was a telephone call from Summerfield, relaying Eisenhower's assurance that everything would be all right. So Nixon slept a couple of hours, campaigned briefly in Montana, then headed for the emotional reunion with his chief. The plane landed at Wheeling in the late dusk. Chotiner rushed off to find out where Nixon was to go. At the same time a lone figure in the waiting crowd darted up the ladder into the plane and asked, "Where's the boss of this outfit?"

Frank Kuest, a correspondent, pointed forward and said, "Up there, General." Eisenhower went up to his running mate as he stood helping Mrs. Nixon with her coat.

Nixon remembers he was "flabbergasted" to see him there. "What are you doing here, General? You didn't have to come here to meet us." Eisenhower put his arm around Nixon. "I certainly did, Dick. You're my boy." Nixon turned his head to the window and tried to keep back the tears. Mrs. Nixon patted her husband and said, "Shall we go?" Eisenhower and Nixon posed for pictures, shaking hands. Then Nixon spotted his senior colleague, Senator Knowland. "It was quite a tense and emotional situation," Knowland recalls. "I said, 'Everything's going to be all right, Dick,' and he came over and said, 'Good old Bill.'" The picture of Nixon weeping on Knowland's shoulder was one of the most poignant of the campaign.

The running mates rode together at the head of a large caravan to the Wheeling Stadium, where Eisenhower declared that Nixon had "completely vindicated himself." Nixon said, "This is probably the greatest moment of my life."

The next day—exactly one week after the uproar—all was peaceful, happy and harmonious in Republican ranks. "The Order of the Hound's Tooth" was founded, with Nixon as president and all in his entourage during the "fund" week as charter members. The membership card, designed by the candidate, featured a portrait of Checkers.

That summed up the new, high-riding attitude of the Nixon group. His staff was even more optimistic than the candidate. Nixon had transformed himself into a campaign asset. Within 24 hours the entire Republican hierarchy was singing hosannas, including the leaders who felt the program's emotional pitch to be revolting. His success sent the Republican campaign soaring, establishing him as a national figure and the best-known, largest-crowd-drawing vice-presidential candidate in history. Letters to the Republican National Committee included enough small donations to pay for the television and radio time. Dana Smith got $3,200 in sums of one to five dollars and sent it to the campaign treasury. Checkers became a national hero—or to others symbol of Madison Avenue sentimentality.

Newspaper support swung back heavily in Nixon's favor. "The air is cleared," said the *Herald Tribune*. The New York *Journal-American* called the speech "an eloquent and manly explanation." The Denver *Post* said, "Senator Nixon talked his way into the hearts of millions . . . by speaking plainly and honestly about the dilemma of a poor man and the rich sweepstakes of politics."

The favorable reaction was hardly unanimous. *Variety,* the newspaper of show business, considered the telecast "a slick production . . . parlaying all the schmaltz and human interest of the 'Just Plain Bill'–'Our Gal Sunday' genre of weepers." Walter Lippmann was disturbed, "for this thing in which I found myself participating was, with all the magnification of modern electronics, simply mob law . . . the appeal to the people should have come after, not before, the case had been judged by Eisenhower." And a year later the term "the New Nixon" appeared in print for the first time in an editorial saying Nixon was not as bad as his fund speech would indicate. "This mawkish ooze ill became a man who might become the President of the United States," said the Montgomery, Alabama, *Advertiser*. "We have found ourselves dissolving our previous conception . . . the New Nixon rejoices us."

In retrospect, the affair was bad for Nixon. The people who remember it most vividly thought it was horrible. The Democrats and Nixon's Republican enemies have kept the embers aglow. Much of the "I don't like Nixon, but don't know why" talk stems from the incident. But if it were not for the immediate impact of that speech Nixon probably would have been done for and Eisenhower might have lost.

No participant in the fund episode—Democratic or Republican—came out of it clean as a hound's tooth. One of the hoariest of American hypocrisies is our attitude toward political financing. Few candidates in closely contested areas—whether running for mayor, Governor, congressman or President—let themselves be hindered by codes regulating political contributions and expenditures. It becomes shameful only if you are caught in circumstances that could cost votes. The Eisenhower forces, with Nixon as combat commander, compounded the hypocrisy by going to ridiculous extremes in the "purity" barrages they fired at the Democratic administration's scandals. There was so much sanctimony and rationalization in the 1952 campaign that even the most notorious political rogues, of both parties, took to reaching for halos. Yet when the seemingly questionable "funds" became an issue—Nixon's and Stevenson's—the strong judgments, Republican and Democratic, were based on their immediate effect on the election. "Morals," "ethics" and even simple fairness to Nixon and Stevenson, as individuals, did not figure.

Mrs. Nixon never fully regained her taste for politics after that. She dislikes to think back on the experience. Nixon treats the day of his television speech as an anniversary. "After it, very few, if any, difficult situations could seem insurmountable if anything personal is involved," he said. "Nothing could match it. Nothing could top it because not so much could again depend on one incident."

10 ❈ *Communism and McCarthy, 1950–1954*

WHEN he took office as Vice-President a week after his fortieth birthday in January, 1953, Nixon symbolized a new generation of Republican politicians. Only John C. Breckinridge, a pre-Civil War Democrat, had been younger than he. None had been more eager to make something of the vice-presidency—and of himself. Despite his enterprise, however, the first year was a disappointment. But the second—1954—was far worse; the worst of Nixon's first 12 years in politics.

The 1954 congressional election had its dismaying aspects. People "liked Ike" and his one-year-old administration better than ever, and politicians had not yet forgotten the power implicit in the Eisenhower vote. It was plain, therefore, that 1954 was *the* year to build a strong, national Republican party—just as the Democrats had capitalized so effectively on the Roosevelt victory of two decades before. Eisenhower and his high command talked about it at Cabinet meetings. Proposals were made and accepted. Slogans were adopted, money raised, the Citizens for Eisenhower organization revived. But to Nixon's disappointment, few got around to *doing* much. Furthermore, when the campaign reached the bloodletting stage, Nixon found himself again at the point of assault, without defenders on his flanks and almost no supporting force behind. This time there was not even a Senator McCarthy off in the bushes slashing away independently at the Democrats and drawing some of their fire.

McCarthy had gone nonpartisan. The nonaggression pact Nixon had worked out between him and the Eisenhower administration collapsed early in the winter, and for 36 days the country watched on television as the Republican administration and McCarthy grappled for each other's throat. Though neither McCarthy nor the Eisenhower "team" ever quite measured up to the virility of their public reputations. Eisenhower remained aloof, of course; but his party could not. Nixon, who regarded party unity as imperative, would have preferred to give the voters a less disgusting view of "the Republican family."

Party politics and McCarthy did not cause all Nixon's doldrums that year. A new street in his home town was to be named Nixon Boulevard. A local organization objected. To avert a quarrel the city fathers called it Mar Vista Lane instead. During the winter Nixon's father became gravely ill. When his brother objected to a local union's organizing the butcher in the grocery store, enemies of the Vice-President charged this showed *he* was antilabor. In the spring Nixon delivered the commencement address at Whittier College and the school president had to form a second reception line after the ceremony for those not wanting to shake the Vice-President's hand. Only two students took it. At Duke University, Nixon's other alma mater, a faculty meeting for the first time exercised its prerogative in such matters to veto an honorary degree the trustees had voted for Nixon. (The vote was 61–42 against Nixon. Only 103 of the 606 faculty members attended, none from the Law School.)

All in all, Nixon had ample reason to re-examine the merits of politics as a career. In mid-February he and his wife discussed their future from all angles, and the Vice-President agreed to retire from politics after his term ended in 1957. At Mrs. Nixon's request he noted the date and the decision on a piece of paper that he tucked into his wallet.

Adlai Stevenson declared at a Democratic fund-raising dinner in Miami on March 6, 1954, that "a group of political plungers has persuaded the President that McCarthyism is the best Republican formula for political success." Therefore, he added, Eisenhower is personally responsible for the "demagoguery and deceit of McCarthyism." This was broadcast on radio and television networks, and the wall of Republican hopes for unity came tumbling down. Eisenhower quickly directed Republican National Chairman Leonard W. Hall to demand equal time on the networks, before McCarthy got it, which Hall did. Then the President chose Nixon to reply for the administration and the party. This ended what remained of the Vice-President's influence with the Wisconsin Senator and caused Nixon and Stevenson to square off again as the principal national campaigners of the respective parties, taking up where they had left off in 1952—with Stevenson soon calling Nixon "McCarthy with a white collar" and Nixon branding Stevenson a snob.

Nixon first met McCarthy in 1947 at a "cheese party" for newly elected Republican congressmen. Wisconsin backers of Harold Stassen for President were the hosts. For the next three years there was no particular contact between the two men. Nixon says he "began to know [McCarthy] well in the campaign of 1950." McCarthy had entered the anti-Communist arena with a speech at Wheeling, West Virginia, on February 9 in which he reportedly said: "While I cannot take the time to name all the men in the State Department who have been named as active members of the Communist party and members of a spy ring, I have here in my hand a list of 205, a list of names that were made known to the Secretary of State as being members of the Communist party and who, nevertheless, are still working and shaping policy in the State Department."

When the uproar began over that charge, McCarthy asked Nixon to help him prove it. "At the time," Nixon recalled, "I told him, 'Now, the important thing—when it comes to this field—is one rule I would urge you to follow: always understate, never overstate your case.' I told him this in the very first conversation. He said he was going to Los Angeles. That is the reason he called me. He said he was going to have a press conference there and was sort of on a spot. I said, 'As far as your statement in Wheeling is concerned, I haven't read it, but you will be in an untenable position if you claim that there were umpteen, or however many, card-carrying Communists in the State Department, because you cannot prove that. On the other hand, if you were to say that there were so many people whose records disclosed Communist-front affiliations and associations, this you can prove. You've got to state it in the context of what is provable and not the other way.' But he did not listen and from then on that case was out the window."

Nixon was running for Senator that fall. When McCarthy came to California he called Chotiner, Nixon's campaign manager, and asked "What can I do for Dick?" Chotiner explained that Nixon did not want outside help. "Some arch-conservative group had invited Joe to speak," Chotiner said. "We were sore because it could destroy our campaign strategy, which was to run our own campaign without anybody from the outside. I told this to Joe, and he said, 'You don't have to tell me again. I won't do a thing to harm Dick.' "

Meanwhile, after a Senate committee was instructed to investigate McCarthy's charges, Nixon lent his files to the Senator for whatever clues they might offer. Late in the summer Nixon charged the inquiry was "rapidly degenerating into a political squabble" and urged, as he had done a month after the McCarthy speech in Wheeling, that McCarthy's allegations were grave enough to merit "vigorous" investigation by an "impartial, nonpolitical commission" of eminent jurists.

Nixon's other contact with McCarthy that year was on December 12 at a party at the Sulgrave Club. Many congressmen and Washington personalities were there, including McCarthy and Drew Pearson, whose fifty-third birthday was the next day. The Senator and the columnist, who had been saying and writing uncomplimentary things about each other, soon were arguing. Subsequently, the angry discussion adjourned to the washroom. A few minutes later Nixon, on going for his hat and coat, found McCarthy and Pearson grappling. Nixon says that as he went over to part them, McCarthy slapped Pearson on the face and said, "That one is for you, Dick." Nixon, who was no friend of Pearson's, pushed between the combatants saying, "Let a Quaker stop this fight." Then he grabbed McCarthy's arm and said, "Come on, Joe, it's time for you to go home." McCarthy snapped, "No, not until he goes first. I am not going to turn my back on the s.o.b." Pearson left and, since McCarthy had forgotten where he had parked his car, Nixon searched the area with him for a half hour, and found it.

There was a flurry of criticism in January, 1951, when McCarthy, as senior Republican on the Senate Government Operations Committee, made room for Nixon on its investigating subcommittee by ousting Senator Margaret Chase Smith. Mrs. Smith had incurred McCarthy's displeasure some months before by issuing a "Declaration of Conscience" urging the Republican party not to "ride to political victory on the Four Horsemen of Calumny—Fear, Ignorance, Bigotry and Smear."

On becoming a Senator Nixon had requested assignment to the Labor Committee. "Senator Butler, of Nebraska, the chairman of the Committee on Committees, asked if I would like the Committee on Government Operations also," he recalled. "I told him that I would be delighted. So I went on it. After that I had nothing to do with the appointment of subcommittees. That was McCarthy's appointment [as a matter of seniority]. He named me to the Subcommittee on Investigations presumably because I had had experience in investigations. But the first I knew of any conflict with Margaret Smith was when I read in the paper that she had been shunted aside by McCarthy. Under the circumstances, of course, I wasn't going to argue with McCarthy about what he should do about his committee. As you know, a new member takes whatever assignment he can get."

The full flavor is lost if one judges incidents of the McCarthy era in the context of modern times. In the dawn of Senator McCarthy's impact—the late 1940's—case histories on Communists-in-government were lying around Washington easily available to politicians who could juggle hot potatoes without fumbling. In this period the Wisconsin Senator was toying with other matters such as housing and agriculture. In 1950 anti-Communism already had become a political asset. As McCarthy was rolling up his sleeves, the Red attack in Korea made it the principal C in the formula of that magic potion Republicans used so effectively: K_1C_3, representing one part each of Korea, Communism, Corruption and Costs.

For various reasons McCarthy quickly became the foremost name in headlines about the anti-Communist fight, and he managed to symbolize either a holy, unswerving crusade against Communist subversives or hate, character assassination and selfish political opportunism. Those who viewed him as the hero of the "crusade" outnumbered the others, however, and the McCarthy era became a historic fact with the Senate election in Maryland. In that usually strong Democratic state, the Wisconsin Senator fought out his assertions about Communists in the State Department with the chairman of the Senate committee that investigated those charges. The chairman, Senator Millard Tydings, a senior Democrat who had been powerful enough to withstand President Roosevelt's 1938 purge, was beaten. Almost overnight frightened Democrats elsewhere began to vie with gleeful Republicans for Senator McCarthy's smile—or, at least, his nonopposition. In Congress Democratic leaders rationalized their apparent insensitivity even to McCarthy's "20 years of treason" accusation by assuring each other again and again that "Joe is a Republican problem." By and large, the strictly "Eisenhower Republicans" disapproved of McCarthy—but not enough to turn down his two-fisted support of the General in the 1952 campaign. Many encouraged it (discreetly, of course). After all, McCarthy was said to carry great weight with some traditionally Democratic nationality and religious blocs. Furthermore, they told each other, a Republican administration would solve the McCarthy problem simply because the Senator would not dare accuse members of his own family of softness on Communism. Nixon made that point in a different way. Without agreeing or disagreeing publicly on the McCarthy issue, he said, "The way to get rid of so-called 'McCarthyism' is to elect a new administration which will deal with this problem [Communism in government] honestly, as has not been done up to this point."

The Californian spoke no ill of his Wisconsin colleague. He endorsed McCarthy for re-election, as he did all Republican candidates, and sometimes spoke well of him. McCarthy, in turn, asserted, "The Communists know Nixon's election will be a body blow to the Communist conspiracy." During the acrimonious exchanges over the Nixon fund McCarthy charged: "The left-wing crowd hates Nixon because of his conviction of Alger Hiss, the man for whom Adlai Stevenson testified."

As the one most responsible for the first effective anti-

Communist investigation, Nixon was not particularly awed, from a personal standpoint, by McCarthy's power. But he was anxious that the party benefit however it could from the Senator's influence with bloc-voting Democrats and extreme Republicans. Nixon also felt that an affront to McCarthy could split the Republican party. From the start Nixon was sympathetic to McCarthy's zeal in fighting Communists. He saw such vigor and enthusiasm as a decided long-term asset, if sensibly channeled. He never shared the belief of some in the Eisenhower administration that "Communism to Mc-Carthy was a racket." Nixon felt that the Senator "believed what he was doing very deeply."

With Eisenhower's election, preserving party harmony became a near obsession with Nixon. A split over McCarthy would damage the administration and the President's prestige; he felt it would also stunt the party's growth when its prospects of development were better than they had been in decades, and give the Democrats the 1954 congressional election. Nixon insisted that most of the columnists and commentators urging an Eisenhower-McCarthy showdown were not friendly to either, and an open fight with Eisenhower would serve only to increase McCarthy's stature and lower the President's. At Cabinet meetings and in private conversations the Vice-President suggested that each matter McCarthy might bring up should be treated on its individual merits, and the administration should cooperate when McCarthy proved to be right. In addition, he cautioned fellow members of the Eisenhower team to remember their campaign promises regarding a cleanout of security risks in government.

A few nights after Eisenhower's election McCarthy was invited to Bill Rogers' home. Nixon and Jerry Persons, of Eisenhower's staff, also were there, and it was a fine, friendly evening. McCarthy agreed that perhaps he had been a little extreme in some things he had said and maybe even a bit irresponsible at times. He explained also that he believed seriously in what he was doing. Nixon and the others applauded and said they did not want him to take his eye off a single Communist. In the interest of promoting the anti-Communist cause, they urged that he cooperate with fellow Republicans in the White House.

This aura of peace and good will lasted for almost a month after the Republican administration was inaugurated. Then McCarthy made it known he did not like Eisenhower's appointment of Charles E. Bohlen as Ambassador to Russia and James Conant as High Commissioner of Germany. He tried to block their confirmation despite Nixon's assurances that they were patriotic Americans. In May the Senator branched out into the international sphere. Angered by the administration's failure to stop our allies from trading with Communist countries, McCarthy issued critical statements, then summoned a group of Greek ship operators and had them sign a "treaty" by which they promised to stop sending their ships to Communist China.

After a public hearing on this subject at which Harold Stassen, then chief of the administration's Mutual Security Agency, denounced McCarthy for "undermining" the Eisenhower foreign policy, Nixon stepped in to mediate. He believed the public approved McCarthy's private boycott against Red China and that it was not really a bad thing anyway. He was certain, too, that it was not the issue on which the administration should have a showdown with the Senator. So he arranged a sort of summit conference between Secretary of State Dulles and McCarthy, at which Dulles issued a statement praising the Senator for acting in "the national interest" and McCarthy issued one pledging to touch base with the State Department before negotiating international agreements in the future. It looked like quite a victory for the Senator. But after he got to thinking about it and discussing it with advisers, McCarthy decided he had not *really* done as well in the Dulles negotiations as it appeared. His uneasy feeling was fortified by testimony that Europe's trade with Red China was increasing and two British-owned ships had carried Communist troops. Thereupon, the headlines proclaimed a new crisis—this one involving Eisenhower himself.

At the suggestion of Democratic Senators Stuart Symington and John L. McClellan, McCarthy sent a letter to the President formally requesting a clear-cut statement of the administration's policy on Western trade with Communist countries. This produced a dilemma for Eisenhower. The

President's reply had either to be a strong statement that would cause trouble between the United States and its allies or a noncommittal, evasive one that would seem to nullify campaign pledges of anti-Communist action. For two days the letter was unclaimed. Technically, it did not exist as far as the White House was concerned. Then Nixon telephoned McCarthy. He asked if the Senator really wanted to go through with this tremendous bonanza for the Democratic opposition. McCarthy agreed to pull back, and he asked Nixon to intercept the letter before it reached Eisenhower's desk.

A month later Nixon, Rogers and Persons were hosts at a private dinner for McCarthy. It was an amiable affair. The talk centered around the fine accomplishments that could follow if McCarthy joined the team as a constructive associate of the President. McCarthy agreed. And although Nixon soon was energetically heading off additional crises—including an assault on the supersensitive Central Intelligence Agency and a much-discussed investigation of Communist influences in the Protestant clergy—the Vice-President continued to have hopes, long-range hopes, that is. They were based more on wishful thinking than substance, for the odds against the harmony Nixon sought were tremendous. Aside from McCarthy's own quirks, some of his advisers were calling the Nixon peace project a sellout and, on the other side, important Republican forces were declaring that there was no alternative but for Eisenhower to slap down the Wisconsin Senator. The Denver *Post*, an enthusiastic Eisenhower supporter, typified that view editorially on June 29, 1954: "Mr. Nixon is an ambitious young man. He is supposed to be a smart politician. He seems to believe that for the sake of harmony Republicans should swallow their conscientious scruples against McCarthy-type smears and McCarthy-type attacks on civil rights. Mr. Eisenhower is not a politician. But he has been forthright in his opposition to all that McCarthyism means. We believe that he has made more votes for the G.O.P. by his attitude toward the Wisconsin Senator than Mr. Nixon can ever make with his amoral talk about the necessity for appeasing Joe."

McCarthy's quarrel with the Army, which finally led to the

showdown, had already begun when he visited Nixon and Rogers, then deputy attorney general, who were spending a few days at Key Biscayne, an island near Miami. McCarthy arrived December 30, 1953, for what became the most amicable of all his moderation sessions with the Vice-President. Nixon's advice was: "Don't pull your punches at all on Communists in government. It doesn't make any difference if they are in this administration or in previous ones; if they are there, they should be out. On the other hand, remember that this is your administration. That the people in this administration, including Bob Stevens [the Army Secretary], are just as dedicated as you are to cleaning out people who are subversive. Give them a chance to do the job. Go to these people, discuss the matters with them and give them a chance to do the job."

While still in Florida McCarthy announced at a press conference that his investigating committees would broaden their inquiries to include tax cases compromised "at ridiculously low figures" during the Truman administration. The following week, when newspapers indirectly quoted Nixon as saying McCarthy had agreed to place more emphasis on fields of inquiry other than Communism, the Senator blew up. "It's a lie," he said.

Meanwhile, the Senator's feud with the Army was gaining momentum. He charged the Army promoted a dentist, Dr. Irving Peress, from captain to major and honorably discharged him although it had information that he was a Communist. McCarthy demanded to know why the dentist was treated so well and implied that subversion in the military establishment was responsible. A major blowup came in mid-February when Secretary Stevens refused to permit Brigadier General Ralph W. Zwicker, commandant of Camp Kilmer, New Jersey, where Peress was stationed, to testify again before the McCarthy committee. The General had done so once, but McCarthy considered his testimony unsatisfactory and told him such conduct made him "unfit to wear the uniform." A week later, on February 24, Stevens, McCarthy and three other Republican members of the investigating committee had a two-hour luncheon in the Capitol. The food was chicken and the talk was compromise. From it came a written "memorandum of understanding" which, in effect, was the Army's capitulation.

In reflecting on the period Nixon said: "Frankly, we tried to mediate with McCarthy until we were blue in the face. At the famous so-called Chicken Luncheon which was held in my room [the Army problem] was supposed to be worked out that way. McCarthy and Stevens agreed to work this thing out without carrying it to the ultimate extreme of open warfare. Our efforts failed with the result which anybody could have anticipated—a suicidal bloodletting for both the administration and McCarthy."

Frantic peace efforts followed. The principals—Eisenhower and McCarthy—were not brought together. But Nixon, Rogers, Chairman Hall, Senator Knowland, who was party leader in the Senate, and practically every other prominent non-anti-McCarthy Republican participated at one time or another. Washington was the general locale. Much of the action took place in the Woodner Hotel, where both McCarthy and Hall had apartments. The peacemakers went about their project assiduously. So did the "warmongers"—that is, Democrats, anti-McCarthy Republicans who whispered in Eisenhower's ear and the anti-Eisenhower intimates of McCarthy who whispered in his.

It was in this atmosphere that Adlai Stevenson hit exposed nerves in Washington with a broadcast charging that the Republican party was "divided against itself, half McCarthy, half Eisenhower." Under the circumstances Nixon would have been delighted to answer Stevenson, as spokesman for the administration. But he made it clear to Hall and others that he wanted no part of this answer for fear of compromising his position as mediator. Furthermore, his goodwill tour of Asia had received favorable reaction and lifted his prestige generally. He believed that from a personal standpoint, no matter how well he did in replying to Stevenson, he was bound to lose more than he could gain. Nonetheless, when Hall, Sherman Adams, Hagerty and James Bassett, the Republican press director, met with Eisenhower to discuss the reply, all agreed Nixon was the ideal man to handle it. The President then and there telephoned his Vice-President to convey the assignment. Nixon exiled himself to a hotel suite to prepare.

He confided to a friend later that it was one of the toughest writing jobs he ever undertook. On the day of the speech Nixon discussed it for 45 minutes with Eisenhower, who then took off for a weekend at his retreat in the Maryland hill country which Roosevelt called "Shangri-la" and Eisenhower renamed "Camp David."

Nixon spoke from Washington's CBS studio and told the audience he chose that sedate setting because the issue was too important for handling the way Stevenson did, "with a riproaring political tirade." The speech covered several subjects, as had Stevenson's, but the highlight was McCarthy and Communism—and Nixon both praised and chastised the Senator by indirection.

"Men who have in the past done effective work exposing Communism in this country have, by reckless talk and questionable methods, made themselves the issue, rather than the cause they believe in so deeply," he said. "When they have done this they not only have diverted attention from the danger of Communism but have diverted that attention to themselves. Also, they have allowed those whose primary objective is to defeat the Eisenhower administration to divert attention from its great program to these individuals who followed those methods."

Without mentioning his name, the Vice-President also asked the question often posed by McCarthy—why worry about being fair when you are shooting rats?—and answered it this way: "I agree they [Communists] are a bunch of rats. But just remember this, when you go out to shoot rats, you have to shoot straight because when you shoot wildly it not only means that the rats may get away more easily—but you make it easier on the rats. Also, you might hit someone else who is trying to shoot rats, too."

(There was a delayed-action sentence in the Vice-President's talk that has been quoted in practically every criticism of his methods since then. It was: "Incidentally, in mentioning Secretary Dulles, isn't it wonderful, finally, to have a Secretary of State who isn't taken in by the Communists, who stands up to them?")

The televised Army-McCarthy hearings began the following month, to Nixon's chagrin and disgust. "I prefer professionals to amateur actors," he said when asked what he thought of the show. He always had opposed televising committee hearings because "there is inevitably too much of a tendency for both the witnesses and the committee members to play to the cameras rather than the facts."

From then on there was occasional contact between Nixon and McCarthy, but no serious effort at conciliation or friendship, and McCarthy proceeded to lump the Eisenhower period with that of Roosevelt and Truman in his "years of treason" attacks.[1] When censure charges were brought against McCarthy later, Nixon appointed to the bipartisan investigating committee Senators recommended by their respective party leaders and he subsequently praised the committee's report.

One of McCarthy's closest personal friends has said the Senator "had a conviction that Nixon could have helped him and not only didn't but was active in the opposition to him." In October, 1955, when a news service asked Republican Senators their choices for the presidential nomination, McCarthy placed Nixon last on a list of six names. After Stassen started his movement to prevent Nixon's renomination the following year, McCarthy issued a long statement which appeared to support Nixon but was devoted mostly to attacking "the left wing of the Republican party," notably Eisenhower, its "leader," and such other figures as Stassen, Sherman Adams, Dr. Milton Eisenhower, Dewey and Paul Hoffman.

In reflecting on his experiences with McCarthy, Nixon said: "My feeling is that the McCarthy thing was a tragedy. I think he was really a casualty in the great struggle of our times, as Hiss was a casualty on the other side. Both deeply believed in the cause they represented. The reason McCarthy became a casualty was because in dealing with this conspiracy it takes not only almost infinite skill, but also patience, judgment, coolness . . . it takes all this plus dedication and courage and hard work. He had the last three qualities in abun-

---

[1] There never had been a full measure of trust. From the beginning Nixon was careful to have someone with him whenever he saw McCarthy. Frequently it was Rogers, whom McCarthy regarded highly and invited to be his lawyer before the Tydings Committee.

dance. But in the other respects he was erratic. To an extent he destroyed himself, but he was also destroyed because of the very character of the force he was fighting. This does not imply that all those who were against McCarthy were Communists. On the contrary, many people just as honest as he was opposed him because they felt his methods hurt the cause to which they were dedicated. It is important to remember that when fighting Communists in the United States, domestic Communism, it isn't enough to be right on the merits. You have got to bend over backward to be fair in tactics because those who oppose you are smart enough never to attack you frontally. They always direct their fire at how you do it, rather than what you do. The reason I succeeded in the Hiss case when McCarthy failed in some others is because I was right on the facts and I did not give the opposition any target to shoot at on the tactics."

When the time neared, in 1954, for getting out to stir up the voters, Nixon confided to a few intimates the only consolation was that it would be his last campaign. To at least one friend, he added, "I'm tired, bone tired. My heart's not in it." Although some Democrats complained that their people knuckled under too much to Eisenhower, the Republican viewpoint was that the Democrats had been hammering at the administration without letup on Dixon-Yates, the 1954 recession, farm problems, seeming differences on points of foreign policy between Eisenhower, Dulles and Nixon, and other issues. "They have a 'murderers' row' to come out at the drop of a hat and issue statements and fight for their party," Nixon said at the time. "We have practically nobody to stand up and fight back." He was weary of being the lightning rod for Republican leadership. It was evident he would have to take on again the job of Republican hatchet man ("Every campaign has one out front slugging," he admitted) and the prospect was not a pleasant one.

Nixon wanted to campaign personally for all who requested his help. That meant practically every Republican candidate in the country. The schedule he mapped out for himself called for 48 days of electioneering in 31 states, beginning September 15.

A major effort was required simply to convince voters that an "Eisenhower Congress" meant a "Republican Congress." While the national Democratic strategy was to blast at the administration, many of the party's candidates were implying or flatly saying they would support the popular Eisenhower in Congress more effectively than their "right-wing Republican" opponents. Republicans, meanwhile, adopted a heated-up version of their 1952 strategy. The emphasis, as enunciated by Nixon, was that a Democratic Congress would impair the Eisenhower administration's policy of hardness on Communists and return the country to the days of Truman administration softness. Nixon dealt with the issue almost everywhere, even in New Jersey, where Clifford P. Case, the Republican candidate for Senator, was himself a victim of softness-on-Communism accusations.[2]

Eisenhower was a more interested participant in the campaign than his relatively limited speaking schedule and the news stories of that period would indicate. On September 29 he wrote from his vacation headquarters in Denver:

Dear Dick: Good reports have been reaching me from all parts of the country as the result of your intensive—and I am sure exhaustive—speaking tour. Now that I have just read the excerpts of the talk that Rose Woods [Nixon's executive secretary] has sent us, I understand more than ever why the comments I have had have been so enthusiastic. Please don't think that I am not unaware that I have done little to lighten your load. On the contrary, I am, in point of fact, constantly suggesting other places for you to visit. You will have to consider these burdens that I impose upon you as penalty for being such an excellent and persuasive speaker.

One thing that has come of this is that you are constantly becoming better and more favorably known to the American public. This is all to the good.

[2] No candidate got more vigorous support from Nixon than the liberal, frankly anti-McCarthy Senator Case. The Vice-President insisted to Republican doubters that Case proved himself to be a bona fide, anti-Communist Republican by helping to draft the Mundt-Nixon Communist Registration Bill in the late 1940's. Case was elected by only 3,200 votes. Without Nixon's help he would have lost.

I am looking forward to your visit to Denver (but not, in all honesty, to our television stint). I hope we will be able to have a golf game while you are here. Don't bother to bring your clubs unless they are already on your plane, but I would suggest that you pack your shoes.

Others also had been exhorting the Vice-President. Congressman Charles Halleck, Republican leader of the House of Representatives, said, "You've got to give 'em hell, Dick! Sam Rayburn's just been to town [Indianapolis]. He was murdering us!" In New York, Governor Dewey advised Nixon to "hit harder . . . people like a fighter." Harold Stassen sent a note October 11: "I wish to commend you on the splendid and hard-hitting contribution you are making to this campaign."

Meanwhile the campaign was developing a lead of invective uncommon to off-year elections. Nixon's barnstorming put Democrats on the defensive. In speech after speech he declared that "thousands of Communists, fellow travelers and security risks have been thrown out" of government jobs by the Republican administration. He warned that the Democratic "left wing" would take over if that party won the Congress. He listed five Democratic candidates for Senator in the West as "left-wingers" (two of them won, three lost). And he asserted the Communist party was fighting Republicans "desperately and openly" because "the candidates running on the Democratic ticket in the key states are almost without exception members of the Democratic party's left-wing clique which has been so blind to the Communist conspiracy and has tolerated it in the United States." In the climactic last week of the campaign the Vice-President invited Democrats and independents to "put their party in their pocket and vote for an Eisenhower Congress [because] we recognize the Communist menace and this administration is determined to crush that menace."

The Democrats spent much energy swinging back. Their charges centered on the words "smear" and "gutter campaign," but some added a local touch. A Colorado Democrat insisted, for instance, that Nixon opposed him for the "deceitful purpose" of weakening Colorado's fight against Nixon's native California over certain water rights. Democratic responses to Nixon's claim of mass Communist and security risk discharges ranged from countercharges of "fascist type attack" to a "numbers game." Their demand that the Republicans name the Communists and actual subversives they fired was denied. After much prodding from Nixon the Civil Service Commission reported three weeks before the election that 6,926 federal workers had been dismissed or had resigned under the security risk program, and 1,743 of them had data in their files indicating "in varying degrees" either "subversive activities, subversive associations or memberships in subversive organizations." The others were considered either sex perverts, alcoholics or undesirable for other reasons.[3]

Nixon worked as tirelessly for fellow Republicans as he had ever done for himself. He drove harder, in fact, than many of the candidates, and as the campaign ended it was clear to Nixon's friends that he was dissatisfied with much that had happened—or, more accurately, had *not* happened. He felt that too many in the administration had done nothing or next to nothing. Chotiner, who managed the Vice-President's activities, recalls that with a few exceptions "Dick was about the only man [in the top echelon] willing to stick his neck out and campaign for Republicans though he knew that if the party won, they would say it was because of the administration, and if it lost, they would say it was his fault. He felt the people didn't stand by him who should have." He was disappointed also in the caliber of many Republican candidates and the party's organization generally. "We're in tough shape," he confided to a friend while en route to Denver for the final, election-eve address. "This administration is giving the country the best government it has ever had—but the problem is to sell it."

The Democrats regained control of Congress by picking up 20 seats in the House and two in the Senate. This net gain was smaller than had been normal for the "out" party in an off-year election. Nixon interpreted that outcome as a Demo-

---

[3] Fifteen months later the Civil Service chairman told a Senate committee that a subsequent survey showed that 41.2 percent of the dismissed or resigned security risks actually had been hired *after* Eisenhower had taken over the executive department from the Democrats.

cratic victory technically but a dead heat in reality. McCarthy said it was "a bad defeat" for the Republicans and blamed the administration's "jungle warfare against those of us who were trying to expose and dig out Communists." Stevenson called it a demonstration of the people's disenchantment with the Republicans and their "resort to abuse, slander and distortion."

Nixon's campaign solidified his position as hero of organization Republicans and villain of organization Democrats. In ensuing months the Democrats promoted *their* picture of him with considerably more enterprise than the Republicans did theirs.

11 ❈ *"Dump Nixon" Movement, 1956*

IN the seemingly serene Republican year of 1956 Eisenhower decided to seek re-election, and he offered Nixon a Cabinet post instead of a second term. Nixon planned to quit public life in disgust, then resolved to run again, whereupon Harold Stassen tried to shove him out.

Eisenhower announced on February 29 that he would be a candidate again, but he refused to discuss what would happen to Nixon. Nixon immediately issued a statement praising the President and his decision to run. In a note of thanks Eisenhower said, "I do want you to know that this expression —characteristic as it is of everything you do—touches me deeply." At his next weekly press conference Eisenhower revealed he had asked Nixon to "chart out his own course."

That, broadly, is what he had told the Vice-President, in private. And it caused Nixon and those close to him many anxious (and some embittered) days during the six months until the Eisenhower-Nixon ticket was renominated on August 22. Weeks before the President had charted his own course he was getting advice on what Nixon's should be. It came inadvertently via the pollsters, columnists and political writers he read in newspapers and directly from Eisenhower friends and associates, some of whom bespoke Nixon's interests. Eisenhower's affection for his understudy had increased greatly because he felt Nixon had shown mature judgment and limitless tact in the delicate period after the Eisenhower heart attack. Thus no one dared attack Nixon frontally in Eisenhower's presence. Even Stassen, who ultimately brought his anti-Nixon position into the open, prefaced his observations with "Dick is a fine fellow, and is doing a grand job, but . . ." The "buts" varied. Some contended it would be "healthier" for the party and would keep the convention from looking like a dictated affair if the vice-presidential nomination was kept open; others said Nixon's future would be brighter if he headed a major department as a Cabinet member in the second term; still others believed Nixon was considered too partisan and would hurt the ticket, particularly in a year when the vice-presidency would be emphasized because of Eisenhower's health.

The Cabinet and "open convention" ideas appealed to Eisenhower. In a long, intimate conversation at the White House he reminded Nixon that no Vice-President had been elected President, directly, in more than a hundred years. He pointed out that, on the other hand, men like Herbert Hoover had done well enough as Cabinet members for the presidency to become their natural next step. He asked Nixon to consider whether a Cabinet position would broaden his experience as an administrator and suggested an immensely challenging spot —Secretary of Defense. He further indicated that Nixon might have almost any other except the State Department, which was reserved for Dulles.

The President was "being friendly" and was anxious that "I consider all the facts before I made up my mind," Nixon says, in retrospect. Dulles, who had the confidence of both Eisenhower and Nixon, thought that Eisenhower "did not want to seem arbitrary. He wanted to leave [the vice-presidential selection] to the convention. He wanted the convention to be free. This did not mean that he did not want Nixon. He did. But he did not want to appear to be dictating. This is the President's nature. This was a delicate situation." Dulles recalled also that it was "a very difficult time for Nixon." Other friends of the Vice-President agree wholeheartedly. One of them who suffered through the whole emotional ordeal with Nixon said Eisenhower's reluctance to come out flatly and ask Nixon to be his running mate was "one of the greatest hurts of his [Nixon's] career."

"I think it might have been naïve on Eisenhower's part, but I don't think it was innocent on the part of whoever advised him," added the friend. "It was definitely an effort to ditch

Nixon. I think the President was naïve and sincerely felt that Nixon had a better political future from a Cabinet post. But Nixon had a much shrewder judgment and reached the conclusion very early in the whole episode that either he had to go all the way and win through or get out and be finished."

After Eisenhower's "chart your own course" statement at his March 7 press conference, Nixon figured it probably would be best for him to leave public life and accept the presidency of a large California business enterprise or a partnership in a New York law firm that guaranteed him an annual income in excess of $100,000. Both positions had been offered him on an "any time you want to come" basis. He did not seriously consider entering the Eisenhower Cabinet. ("I would have been like Henry Wallace if I had taken a Cabinet job.") On a Wednesday he told two or three friends he would call a press conference the next day to make an announcement of retirement from public life. Victor Johnston, executive director of the Republican Senate Campaign Committee, chanced to hear it from Nixon when they almost bumped into each other in the Capitol. Johnston rushed downtown to tell National Chairman Hall and then to the White House to alert Major General Wilton B. Persons, the President's deputy for legislative affairs, who was to succeed Adams as chief of staff. Hall and Persons dashed to the Capitol. They cornered Nixon and persuaded him to put off his decision for a while. Their arguments, and those of several other major supporters who rushed to the Capitol like firemen answering a general alarm, were that his friends would regard him as a "quitter" if he let them down. They also insisted his departure would split the Republican party and would be interpreted generally as a suggestion of doubt about Eisenhower's chances of surviving a second term. Nixon agreed to defer his decision. Meanwhile, Senator Styles Bridges passed the word that Nixon should be shown how highly he is regarded by Republicans; that week he was given 22,202 write-in votes for Vice-President in the New Hampshire primary. (In May, this demonstration of popularity was repeated in the Oregon primary, where 30,000 voters "wrote in" Nixon's name on their ballots.) Previously, only an occasional vote was ever cast for Vice-President in primaries, usually by accident.

Nixon has said the New Hampshire primary and the Republican leadership's violent reaction later that year to the Stassen ouster efforts convinced him that he should seek re-election.

"If Stassen hadn't intervened himself in this, there would have been a much better chance that I would have gotten off, even after the New Hampshire primary," he added. "That primary was convincing mostly in that it changed the attitude of the opinionated, those who were saying and writing that I would be a drag on the ticket. They couldn't write that any more after New Hampshire. But the major factor was the mail, the telephone calls and the scores of political leaders around the country who came to me and said, 'Stay on or we are through. We've had it.' The New Hampshire primary convinced me from the positive standpoint; the letter writers and political leaders convinced me from the negative standpoint. You see, if Stassen hadn't been in it, the negative factor would not have been there. If I had decided on my own to get out, without appearing to be pressured by Stassen, then the so-called Taft people and the other Republican organization leaders wouldn't have been mad. They would have said, 'This is what Nixon wants to do; it is up to him,' but they were not going to have Stassen push me off. That's why Stassen made it inevitable that I stay on. The reaction in party circles to Stassen's activities convinced me that my getting off would be a liability to the ticket. So I decided to stay on if the President wished me to, and I knew that I had to make a necessary fight."

After lunch on April 26 Nixon went to the White House to tell the President he had charted his course—that he would be pleased to run again. "I guess I was the first to know after the President," said James C. Hagerty, the White House press secretary. "The President rang for me. I went into his office. The Vice-President was sitting there. The President and Dick had big grins on their faces. The President said, 'Jim, Dick just told me he would be happy to be on the ticket, and he has made up his mind that he would like to run again with me.' Adams came in, and we later saw Persons. We told them. The President said to me, 'What do you think we ought to do on the announcement?' I didn't have to think long about that.

'Why not let Dick go out and say it?' I replied. The President said, 'Jim, you go with him, and after he finishes his announcement, you say [to the press] I was delighted to hear this news from the Vice-President.' " Thereupon Nixon went into Hagerty's office to conduct his first press conference in the White House.

On June 9 President Eisenhower suffered an ileitis attack which required an immediate abdominal operation. This sharpened the health issue and further revived intense interest in the Republican vice-presidential nomination. Hagerty stated a month later, while the President was convalescing at Gettysburg, that neither Eisenhower nor Nixon had altered his plan to run again. But that did not impress Harold Stassen, Eisenhower's "secretary of peace."

Stassen himself is not certain when he actually decided to undertake his 1956 preconvention operation which the public came to know as a "Dump Nixon Movement"—although Christian Herter, ostensibly its intended beneficiary, preferred to call it "a comic opera."

"I had, of course, thought about it for some months," Stassen recalled. But he actually did nothing more than discuss the matter with an intimate or two until May 6, when he returned to Washington from a long and fruitless disarmament conference in London.

The anti-Nixon operation that appeared to be making headway when he left was petering out for lack of leadership, an alternate candidate and effective encouragement from the White House. Interest revived quickly when President Eisenhower became ill early in June. But no Republican of national standing would indicate it publicly, at least not until Eisenhower's own status had been clarified. Even Stassen hesitated for a while to challenge openly the Vice-President, who might succeed to the presidency any day. During the month after Eisenhower's ileitis operation, Nixon went about his business with tact and an outward show of confidence, while Stassen consulted frequently with his ever-diminishing knot of followers and had the popularity of various potential candidates tested, secretly, by a poll taker who had conducted such surveys for him in the past.

"I knew that Len Hall and Dick Nixon were pressing Chris

Herter about renominating Nixon," Stassen insisted. "Consequently, it was very late then, and you either took the stand
or that moment was forever gone when anybody could take a
stand. . . . It became a matter of either moving or never
moving, and I decided, all things considered, that I'd better
move."

On July 12 Chairman Hall was summoned to Gettysburg.
The President, the chairman and Hagerty decided Representative Charles E. Halleck, of Indiana, should make the presidential nominating speech at the convention in August. Hall
proposed that they also select someone to place Nixon's name
before the convention and announce both nominators at once.
The three men agreed Herter would be ideal. Eisenhower suggested it be cleared with Nixon and Herter. Hall telephoned
the Vice-President in Washington, as Eisenhower and Hagerty
sat by, attentive. Nixon hesitated. He was not sure a "package
announcement" was best, he said, and furthermore he understood Herter might be interested in the nomination himself.
Hall put Hagerty on the phone, but Nixon insisted on waiting
at least a day. Eisenhower said nothing.

July 13—Nixon and Hall met, and Hall called Herter.
Herter said he "probably will be glad to" nominate Nixon, but
he wanted time to think it over. Stassen learned about the call
that night through a friend of Herter's.

"He told me that he was calling merely to inform me that
he had been making some independent researches of his own,"
Herter noted in a diarylike memorandum in which he tried
to keep up with "this extraordinary performance" as it developed. "Stassen said he had come to the conclusion that
Nixon would be a substantial drag on the President if he
were the vice-presidential candidate; and that as a result of
the polls he felt that I would be the least drag on the President. He then added that he felt this situation was of such
importance that he was asking for an appointment to see the
President and had been promised one the following week. I
told him that I had been asked to put Dick Nixon's name in
nomination, and he requested that I defer decision on this
until he had talked with the President, which I agreed to do."

July 20—Stassen was admitted to Eisenhower's office at
9:31 A.M. The President was preparing to leave that day for

a meeting of Inter-American Chiefs of State in Panama. It was to be his first strenuous activity since the ileitis operation six weeks before. He was not particularly anxious to talk politics. Stassen declared that world peace hinged on Eisenhower's re-election. Eisenhower nodded. Stassen then reported that he had made an intensive study of the election prospects and his private poll showed that Nixon, being a controversial figure, would detract enough from the ticket to create problems, whereas others—Herter, for instance—would have little or no effect on the outcome. Eisenhower frowned. He mentioned his liking for Nixon, then pointed out he had closed no doors on the vice-presidential nomination because he would not dictate to a convention which had not yet even renominated him for President. Stassen thanked Eisenhower, wished him well on the Panama trip and left at 9:55 A.M. He had been with the President 24 minutes. By 10:30 A.M. he had notified friends that Eisenhower had given him a tacit go-head. "The President said he is for an open convention," Stassen told them. Eisenhower had said as much publicly, whenever asked, in the weeks before his illness. But the words appeared to assume meaning to associates when repeated by Stassen.

Stassen's report was justified, perhaps, on the basis of his intensive study of the President's characteristic responses to the proposals of various kinds. Stassen saw these reactions as "situations." He listed them later as follows: "You have a situation where [Eisenhower] asks you to do something, and if you can at all honorably do it, you try to carry it out. Or there are situations where he asks you not to do it, and if you are a member of the team, you don't do it. Or there are third situations where, in effect, he doesn't express a view either one way or another, and then you have to make your own decision and move under those circumstances."

In this case it was "situation" number three. Stassen made his "own decision," moved "under those circumstances," and Herter noted in his diary that night: "Stassen called me in Manchester . . . saying that he had talked to the President and that the President appeared very much interested in what he had to say. He said that he advised the President that he was planning to talk to both the Vice-President and Len Hall to give them the benefit of his own conclusions; and that the President had interposed no objections to his doing so."

Herter later appended to his July 20 entry: "This was the last time I had any direct communication with Mr. Stassen until ten minutes before the President's press conference in San Francisco on Wednesday, August 22." (That was the press conference at which Eisenhower announced that Stassen would second the Nixon nomination.)

On July 23, after failing to get an immediate appointment with Nixon, Stassen sent him a two-and-a-half-page letter. It read: "I regret that it was not possible for you to see me. . . . I would have preferred to advise you personally of a conclusion I have reluctantly reached after a thorough and thoughtful review of the political situation in these recent weeks, and of which I advised the President on Friday morning. I have concluded that I should do what I can to nominate Governor Chris Herter for Vice-President at the coming convention. I sincerely hope that after careful reflection during the coming weeks you will conclude to join in supporting Chris Herter. I have reached this conclusion notwithstanding my long and continuing personal friendly feeling toward you because of these reasons. . . ."

Party Chairman Hall thought this could be serious. "I didn't think Stassen would get anywhere," Hall recalled, "but he could create doubt in people's minds, and you'd have a lot of candidates. Dan Thornton [former Governor of Colorado] and Ted McKeldin [Governor of Maryland] were after the vice-presidential nomination anyway. Margaret Chase Smith wanted her name to be presented to the convention. Stassen even convinced Goodie Knight [Governor of California] that Eisenhower had a list of six names, any one of whom was acceptable."

Hall wasted no time in passing the word, publicly and privately. With confidence (and still with little more than intuition to go on) he stated: "Nothing has changed. The ticket will be Ike and Dick."

At three o'clock Stassen invited the press to his office and announced his undertaking "in loyalty to Eisenhower." His private polls showed Nixon would cut the Eisenhower vote by 6 percent, he said, while Herter would do practically no harm. He also stated that everyone would be happier, including "important portions of the population abroad," if Nixon was replaced. Stassen said he was "confident President Eisenhower will be pleased to have Chris Herter on the ticket." He also explained, quite carefully, that "the Republican party will realize I did them a favor" because he was giving those hoping to replace Nixon an active movement to join.

Among the things Stassen did not reveal at the press conference is the fact that he had told Eisenhower he would talk with Nixon, Hall and other principal party figures before going ahead with his movement. He planned to call a conference of the Vice-President, the National Chairman, Attorney General Herbert Brownell, Deputy Attorney General William Rogers, Ambassador Henry Cabot Lodge and a few others. Stassen believed he might convince them, with his poll, that Nixon's candidacy would be a handicap to Eisenhower. That, in turn, could lead to Nixon's voluntary withdrawal from the race, he figured. When neither Nixon nor Hall would see him, however, Stassen felt he had no alternative but to forget the conference and go ahead with the enterprise.

After his press conference Stassen again sought an immediate appointment with Hall. The chairman was "busy," but suggested lunch the next day. Then Stassen tried to telephone Herter. "For the first time in my life I was watching a professional golf tournament being played in Massachusetts," Herter recalled. "I was riding around in a little cart following the players when all of a sudden some of the newspaper boys came up with a walkie-talkie and told me what Stassen had done. He hadn't said a word to me about announcing it. He just went ahead and announced it. It was all a little confused, so I said until I knew what the score was I couldn't say anything. I went to the front office and tried to call Washington to find out what was going on. It was then I learned Stassen had tried to reach me by phone, but went ahead and shot anyway." In his diary-memorandum Herter noted: "Stassen did not call me that evening or any time thereafter."

Eisenhower learned of the Stassen announcement in Panama by way of a news-service correspondent whose office had cabled for the President's comment. Press Secretary Hagerty, clearly surprised, rushed the message to Eisenhower.

Frowning, Eisenhower dictated this statement: "Mr. Stassen did inform the President on Friday of his decision to make such a statement and also to inform the Vice-President of it before issuing it. The President pointed out to Mr. Stassen that, while he had every right as an individual to make any statement he so desired, it was also equally obvious that he would not make such a statement as a member of the President's official family."

July 24—This was a day of frantic stocktaking by top-echelon Republicans. By nightfall practically all who counted had taken sides—with Nixon. Nonetheless, Stassen smiled broadly and confidently, in public, as though his undertaking was a robust child with great promise, instead of a stillborn corpse.

At noon Herter advised Hall by telephone that he would be "glad to place Nixon in nomination." He also asked Hall for suggestions as to what should be in a formal statement. A few minutes later Nixon telephoned Herter. "He very candidly and sincerely explained to me that he had not himself asked me to put his name in nomination because he knew I had many friends who might want to consider me a candidate and that he felt it would be much less embarrassing to me to refuse to Len Hall than to him directly," Herter said. "Nixon was most cordial and straightforward and I think his explanation as to why he had not called me personally was entirely genuine." At this point Herter appended in his memorandum: "From that day until I had completed my nomination speech for Nixon I discouraged every individual who asked my opinion as to whether he or she should assist Stassen in his efforts just as strongly as I could."

Herter was the only principal participant to consider the matter closed, however. Leonard Hall, who had played a cat-and-mouse game of mutual distrust with Stassen, wanted Herter to announce at once his intention to nominate Nixon. Herter preferred to wait a day until his son would be available to help with a formal statement. Hall then announced it on his own.

Meanwhile, Stassen held two press conferences. In the first, prior to the news of Herter's action, he solemnly declared he hoped "Vice-President Nixon will think this over in the next weeks and decide to join and support Governor Herter." In the second, after the news from Herter, he said the fact that Hall had asked Herter to make the nomination "is a confirmation of Herter's very strong standing in the party" and did not mean any lack of interest by Governor Herter in obtaining the vice-presidency. When asked if he had consulted Herter on this, he replied, "I didn't say that I did not consult him."

July 25—Although well aware of its death, all the principals continued to act as though the Stassen movement was still quite alive. Both Stassen and Nixon could hardly have been busier that day. Stassen started at a seven A.M. coast-to-coast television program. His day was filled with declarations of devotion to Eisenhower and Herter. He also made statements promising to drop his enterprise if Eisenhower asked him publicly to do so, and he charged that Chairman Hall was antagonistic toward him. The highlight was a public memorandum in which Stassen urged "all voters" to support his movement by writing letters to newspapers, calling and writing to Republican party officials at all levels and sending contributions to an Eisenhower-Herter headquarters.

Nixon's office was like a political headquarters on election eve. Party leaders from everywhere came or called to affirm their loyalty and offer prescriptions for banishing the Stassen threat. Governor Dewey recommended that Nixon barnstorm the country. Senator Knowland proposed that Stassen quit his post at the White House. Several suggested a showdown with Eisenhower. Nixon listened attentively to all, and decided to operate quietly and prepare for the worst. A meticulous state-by-state check of convention delegates showed he could count, under any circumstances, on 800 of the 1,323 votes that would be cast for the vice-presidential nomination.

July 30—Stassen visited Eisenhower for a few minutes at the Gettysburg farm, then announced the President had granted him a four weeks' leave of absence.

July 31—Stassen predicted that Nixon's name on the ticket would cost Eisenhower "millions of votes." Nixon received a petition of endorsement signed by practically every Republican in Congress. (Representative Patrick Hillings, a close associate of the Vice-President's, confided that the petition's principal aim was to bolster Nixon's morale. "He is a pessimist, and was running scared," Hillings said.)

August 1—Eisenhower told a press conference that Nixon "is perfectly acceptable to me as he was in 1952." The President refused to name any other "acceptable" candidate but said, "I do uphold the right of the delegates to the convention to nominate whom they choose." Stassen greeted that with a statement declaring "the convention is now definitely open. The problem of the vice-presidential nomination can now be considered deliberately and thoughtfully for the next three weeks."

August 4—Governor Knight, of California, joined the Dump Nixon movement publicly—the only prominent Republican other than Stassen to do so. Knight said Nixon's home state would go Democratic if Nixon was on the Republican ticket.

August 13—Stassen announced $6,535 had been contributed to his crusade, and it was doing fine.

Meanwhile the Democratic National Convention opened in Chicago, with a keynote speech in which Governor Frank G. Clement, of Tennessee, described Nixon as the Republican party's "Vice-Hatchet Man," who went about his "double-faced campaign . . . slinging slander and spreading half-truths while the top man [Eisenhower] peers down the green fairways of indifference."

August 14—The latest Gallup poll said Nixon had slipped in popularity since May, but was still ahead of Herter. The polls said 74 percent of the nation's Republicans favored Nixon, a drop of 9 percent from May, and 14 percent favored Herter, an increase for him of 4 percent. Among independent voters the spread was 54 percent for Nixon and 22 percent for Herter, with 24 percent having no opinion.

August 16—With the Republican Convention only four days off, Herter announced categorically that he would forbid his name to be submitted for the vice-presidential nomination.

August 18—Nixon and Stassen arrived in San Francisco for the convention, but not together. Each established a headquarters and began a round of meetings with delegates. Both talked with reporters. Nixon claimed the Eisenhower administration had given Americans "the best three and a half years of our lives." Stassen claimed his latest poll showed Nixon continued to be a serious handicap to the Republican ticket.

August 21—Eisenhower arrived in San Francisco. After settling down in the St. Francis Hotel, he summoned Chairman Hall for a report on the Stassen situation. Hall said Stassen had gotten nowhere. Eisenhower anticipated as much, and asked what Hall would suggest to stop the foolishness and unify the party. Hall replied that Stassen should second Nixon's renomination. Eisenhower thought that was not a bad idea. He noted that Stassen was coming to see him the next morning, and he told Hall to talk with Stassen first and tell him about the decision.

August 22—This was the day of the grand finale—but its most dramatic climaxes were witnessed only by the participants.

At nine o'clock Stassen left his room on the ninth floor of the St. Francis Hotel to see Eisenhower, on the sixth. He checked in first, as was required, with Sherman Adams, who occupied an office suite close to Eisenhower's. Hall darted into the Adams rooms behind Stassen. When the two met, Stassen handed the chairman a written ultimatum demanding that nominations for Vice-President be postponed until the next day instead of following Eisenhower's renomination that afternoon, as scheduled. Hall took a deep breath to fortify his sense of humor and self-control.

"Are you a delegate?" he asked, as quietly as he could.

"No," replied Stassen.

"Are you an alternate?"

"No."

"Well, who the hell is running this convention, you or the delegates?" Hall thundered.

"All Republicans have responsibilities," Stassen said calmly. His purpose, he added, was to help bring about "an open convention" as proclaimed by Eisenhower.

Finally Hall and Adams told Stassen firmly he would be permitted to see the President only if he agreed, first, to restrict his conversation in the Eisenhower suite to a suggestion that he be permitted to second Nixon's nomination in the interest of party harmony.

At 10:53 A.M. Stassen agreed and at 10:54 he and Adams

walked across the hall to the Eisenhower rooms, Adams leading the way.

Within five minutes Stassen had slipped back to his own
room, and Press Secretary Hagerty had announced the President would hold a press conference.

At the press conference a half hour later Eisenhower stated:
"Mr. Stassen called to see me a few minutes ago . . . after
several days here he had become absolutely convinced the
majority of the delegates want Mr. Nixon. And in these circumstances he no longer—and particularly since his own candidate had withdrawn so decisively—he saw no reason for
going further with his effort, and he thought, in order to get
his own position clear before the convention and the American
public, he was going to ask the convention chairman for permission this afternoon to second . . . the nomination of the
Vice-President incumbent, Mr. Nixon, for renomination."

The unprecedented presidential press conference was televised nationally. Stassen watched it in his hotel room, then
sent Nixon a telegram:

"I have concluded that I would like to second your nomination for Vice-President at the convention and join wholeheartedly and cheerfully in support of the nominees of the convention—President Eisenhower and yourself—for November,
urging the voters who had felt as I had to join with me in
this result. I have so advised the President. Best wishes to you.
HAROLD E. STASSEN."

12 ❋ *Ike's Illnesses, 1955–1957*

NIXON's conduct during the weeks after President Eisenhower's heart attack had raised his prestige in the administration. Previously, Eisenhower had always spoken well of his deputy, referring to him usually as "a comer" and "a splendid type of the younger men we want in government." Afterward Eisenhower declared flatly, "There is no man in the history of America who has had such careful preparation . . . for carrying out the duties of the presidency." Several of Eisenhower's personal intimates who had serious misgivings about Nixon, including Dr. Milton Eisenhower, became supporters of the Vice-President. After the first month of Eisenhower's illness the judgment of a number of colleagues was summed up by Nelson Rockefeller, then a special assistant to the President. "All of us in the administration," he wrote Nixon, "are proud indeed of the job you have done during these truly difficult days, and are proud to be associated with you as the leader who is carrying on in the President's absence." Only a few friends were aware of how acutely uneasy Nixon was about his capacity to meet the challenge. He aged the equivalent of quite a few years during those three months—in his own estimation, as well as that of those with whom he worked.

It started after the Big Four chiefs of state had exchanged smiles and declarations at Geneva in July, 1955. Then Eisenhower had gone to Denver for a long vacation. The soothing aura of peace and plenty that late summer and autumn inspired the Republican National Committee to unfurl the slogan: "Everything is booming but the guns." Nixon was to make a goodwill tour of the Near East in the late fall—welcome duty, especially since there was no election campaign in 1955. On September 26 Nixon was to join Eisenhower in Denver at a conference to launch a nationwide physical-fitness crusade.

On Saturday, September 24, the Vice-President and Mrs. Nixon attended the wedding in Washington of a stenographer in his office. They were back home at about five, and Nixon read in the *Evening Star* that Eisenhower had an upset stomach. That did not disturb him for he remembered that only a year earlier the President also had a slight digestive upset in Denver. Nixon was musing about this and turning to the editorial page when the telephone rang. It was Jim Hagerty.

"Dick, are you sitting down?" asked the President's press secretary.

"No, what is it?"

Slowly, Hagerty said he had bad news. The President had suffered a heart attack. The press would be told about it in a half hour or so.

"My God!" Nixon whispered hoarsely. He caught his breath, then proceeded to tell Hagerty that heart attacks are not necessarily serious any more, that victims frequently recover completely.

"I don't see how I could describe those first few minutes except as a complete shock," he recalls. "I remember going into my living room and sitting down in a chair and not saying anything or really thinking of anything for at least five or ten minutes. For quite a while I didn't even think to tell Pat, who was upstairs."

The numbness receded gradually. Nixon went back to the telephone and called Deputy Attorney General William P. Rogers.

"I wonder if you could come over, Bill?" he asked. Rogers arrived in 15 minutes by taxi.

Meanwhile the news was released in Denver. Nixon's telephone began to ring and people showed up—reporters, photographers, sightseers. The white-brick house in the residential Spring Valley section of Washington had never before attracted such attention.

Nixon decided to say nothing to the press. Questions kept coming, however, and practically every move from one room to another in the house could be noted from the street. The commotion became such that after dinner Nixon suggested that he and Rogers go to the latter's house in nearby Bethesda. Mrs. Rogers was asked to come pick them up a block away. The two men slipped out a side door, moved quickly down an alley and reached the car undetected. Their escape was aided by one of Nixon's children who had gone outdoors at the other side of the house to look at the crowd. The crowd looked at her—instead of the door from which her father and his friend left.

Rogers and Nixon soon were joined in the Rogers' large living room by General Wilton B. Persons, who was in command at the White House because Sherman Adams was vacationing in Scotland. The three men reviewed pending business and tried to figure what, if anything, could not be put off. Informally, they decided there was nothing. Nixon suggested, and the others agreed, that all the principal administration officials should be informed at once that the "team" was to operate as Eisenhower had planned it should and that there should be no precipitate comments about politics or administration affairs. It was decided that the administration should continue to function on a business-as-usual basis if possible.

Throughout the night—and for the next two months—Nixon was kept posted on every development in Denver, and every medical bulletin was read to him before being issued publicly. Persons left Rogers' house at 12:30 A.M. Sunday. Rogers went to bed at 1:30. About an hour later Nixon drifted up to the spare room where a pair of his friend's pajamas were laid out for him on the bed. He washed, slowly, then stretched out on the bed and scanned several magazines, reading without seeing or knowing what he read. At four o'clock he went downstairs to take a telephone call from Denver. It was Hagerty. The situation was grave, but hopeful, because Eisenhower appeared to be reasonably comfortable under his oxygen tent.

Richard Nixon got no sleep.

After church Sunday morning Nixon stated, "The business of government will go on without delay. . . . The President's team will carry out his well-defined plans." That night he met again with Persons and Rogers at Rogers' house. They decided that a meeting of the National Security Council would be held, as scheduled, on Thursday, and Nixon said it would be a good idea to call a Cabinet meeting on Friday to demonstrate further that the government was continuing to function in an orderly way. The Vice-President spent that night in his own home, and he invited the press corps keeping watch in the chill outside to use his basement.

Within a week a political caldron was boiling. Nominating conventions were less than a year off. Republican plans had focused on Eisenhower. Now, as he fought for survival under an oxygen tent, everyone was certain there would have to be another candidate, including National Chairman Hall, who amazed political experts by insisting otherwise in public. Governor Goodwin J. Knight, one of California's three shadow contenders, was the first to move. He proceeded to aim verbal kicks at Nixon, his most formidable competitor. The Vice-President's adherents prepared a counteroffensive, but he sent word through Robert H. Finch, the Los Angeles Republican chairman, that there was to be absolutely no political activity for him, not even by indirection. Nixon meant to negotiate the trying days and weeks ahead with a maximum of naturalness and a minimum of fuss. He intended to encourage understatement of his role during Eisenhower's inactivity and to avoid any action that might substantiate a charge that he was trying to benefit politically from the situation. Therefore, he continued to come early for administration conferences and meetings and presided from his customary chair, instead of the President's. He worked mostly in his own office. At the White House he used a conference room, and avoided the President's office. When Cabinet members wanted to talk with him, or he with them, he insisted on going to their offices, turning aside their suggestions that they come to his.

Adams flew in from Scotland on Monday morning and had lunch at the White House with Nixon, Persons, Rogers and Gerald D. Morgan, special counsel to the President. There was another evening meeting in the Rogers' living room. Nixon, Rogers, Persons, Leonard Hall and his public-relations aide, Lou Guylay, sat in a circle, and Adams sat slightly off to one side. The news from Denver late that afternoon had been bad. Someone in the circle mentioned nervously that the mistakes made when Presidents Wilson and Cleveland were incapacitated should be avoided. Calls kept coming from Denver and were received in the kitchen. Each report was analyzed, and Hall emphasized several times that administration officials should be careful not to do or say anything that would set off a premature battle for the presidential nomination. Nixon stated that things should not be permitted to fall apart for lack of decision. Adams seemed to be in a daze, possibly as a reaction to the shocking news or weariness from his rush across the Atlantic. For four hours, whenever he spoke —even in reply to questions—it was about his fishing in Scotland, and nothing else.

On Wednesday Nixon signed several papers "in behalf of the President." None was of legal significance. At the National Security Council meeting on Thursday it was agreed that Adams should operate from Denver as boss of the White House staff.

The highlight of that first week was a two-and-a-half-hour Cabinet meeting on Friday. Nixon opened it with a silent prayer and read the latest medical bulletin from Denver. The report that Eisenhower had spent his first night out of the oxygen tent and had slept without interruption for nine and a half hours brought smiles of relief in the large White House conference room. The meeting then proceeded at almost a normal clip. As the session ended, Dulles, the senior member, turned to Nixon and said:

"Mr. Vice-President, I realize that you have been under a very heavy burden during these past few days, and I know I express the opinion of everybody here that you have conducted yourself superbly, and I want you to know we are proud to be on this team and proud to be serving in this Cabinet under your leadership."

Next day a letter came. "Dear Dick," the President wrote, "I hope you will continue to have meetings of the National Security Council and of the Cabinet over which you will preside in accordance with the procedure which you have followed at my request in the past during my absence from Washington. As ever, Dwight D. Eisenhower."

On Saturday, October 8, exactly two weeks after the President's seizure, Nixon visited him in his eighth-floor suite at

Fitzsimmons Hospital, the first time a Vice-President had been at the bedside of a seriously sick President. Meanwhile, the Cabinet and National Security Council, after marking time, proceeded to undertake serious business. With members having strong opinions on legislative programs and budget items, some sessions were spirited. Arthur Flemming, who was then the defense mobilizer, recalls a heated argument over the budget at one Cabinet meeting. He was impressed with Nixon's tact. When he complimented the Vice-President afterward, Nixon said he realized that some Cabinet members talked longer than they would have if the President had been present, but he intended to be especially careful because "it isn't my Cabinet; it is the President's Cabinet. I am just the presiding officer."

Nine months after the heart attack Hagerty had to break the news of another serious presidential illness to the Vice-President. It was early in the morning of June 8, 1956. The press secretary reached Nixon in his limousine as the Vice-President was heading for his office.

Eisenhower was operated upon late that night for ileitis, an abdominal ailment. When he recovered sufficiently to see members of his administration, the President asked that Nixon be the first official visitor.

Eisenhower's third illness—the stroke of November 25, 1957 —resulted in an unprecedented agreement by which the President commissioned the Vice-President to assume the powers of acting chief executive should the President ever become incapacitated again. The stroke was not severe, and the President was back at his desk within a couple of weeks. It had a singular side effect, however, in that Nixon now showed the self-assurance he had acquired since the period of the heart attack two years and two months before.

Eisenhower created the stand-by office of acting President because Congress dallied on his suggestion that it repair the flaw in the Constitution that left in doubt a Vice-President's constitutional status during a President's disabling illness. Eisenhower worked out his plan with advice from Dulles and Attorney General Rogers. He thought the matter through in great detail on his trip to Paris for the NATO Conference just a week or so after recovering from the stroke. Originally he believed the Cabinet should monitor the agreement and decide the question of a President's inability to do his job if, for some reason such as unconsciousness, the President himself could not. After weighing alternatives, however, he decided in January, 1958, that the Cabinet would be too cumbersome. He felt it would be simpler and more practical to make the agreement directly with the Vice-President. In essence, the plan worked this way:

If Eisenhower was to find himself unable to perform his duties he would tell Nixon and Nixon would become acting President with the full powers and duties of the office until Eisenhower himself determined he was able to resume his responsibilities. If for some reason Eisenhower was not physically able to tell Nixon to take over, Nixon would do so on his own authority and serve as acting President until Eisenhower decided he could go back to work.

Eisenhower committed the agreement to writing in the form of a letter to Nixon. A copy was given to Secretary of State Dulles, and another to Attorney General Rogers.

13 ❈ *Latin American Mission, 1958*

RICHARD NIXON'S most unusual role in the administration—his overseas missions—stemmed from an offhand suggestion by President Eisenhower. "What are you going to do this summer?" Eisenhower asked him early in 1953 during one of the new administration's first National Security Council meetings.

"Anything you say, Mr. President," Nixon replied.

"Well, I think you should take a trip to the Far East. Take Pat. . . ."

So Nixon added diplomacy to the extra chores he was accumulating for his once-tranquil office and launched his newest career with an around-the-world tour of 19 countries on three continents.

He and Mrs. Nixon headed for distant horizons much as they had often taken to the hustings back home. The first tour, covering 45,431 miles in 70 days, included one 24-hour rest stop at Melbourne, Australia. Free time on the next, a 30-day trip through Central America, was an afternoon in San Juan, Puerto Rico. A three-week African tour included a detour to Rome for a day of relaxation. But before Nixon reached the Eternal City he had scheduled visits with the Pope, the President of Italy, the Prime Minister and a few other people, and Rome became the busiest stop of the trip. There were no rest periods at all on the itinerary of the Latin American tour and visit to England in 1958.

During his world wanderings Nixon has been trapped in a Mexico City elevator, picketed in Burma, called "son of a dog" in Casablanca and plagued by dysentery and other maladies in Ethiopia, Afghanistan, Indonesia and elsewhere.

Nothing, however, was so spectacular as the violence in Venezuela that turned his visit into a commando operation. Riots in Lima had been a menacing prelude, but it was the murderous attacks in Caracas that provided an urgent, split-second test of Nixon's brainpower, backbone and luck. He handled it with the deliberate coolness of a battlefront strategist who looks to the future as well as the present.

Caracas was the last stop on the 1958 Nixon tour of eight Latin American countries. It was also the most important. The tough core of Venezuela's Communist organization had survived suspiciously well under the Pérez Jiménez dictatorship, and after the January 23, 1958, revolution, it burst like a spore and its influence spread in all directions, particularly through the press, the university and the wobbly and inexperienced ruling junta. While always touchy about possible Communist domination of any hemisphere neighbor, Washington was doubly so about Venezuela for ample commercial, strategic and political reasons.

Thus Nixon's visit was really a specific mission to bolster the junta's prestige and stability and privately convince the new rulers that their benign attitude toward the Communists would ultimately bring grief to Venezuela and perhaps both American continents.

Nixon was invited to Caracas on March 14 after a United States diplomat hinted to the Venezuelan Foreign Minister at a reception that the Vice-President might come in mid-May if asked. The junta and Cabinet happened to be meeting at the time, and a note was rushed to Admiral Wolfgang Larrazabal, the President, who announced immediately that Venezuela would "greatly welcome" a Nixon visit.

The Communists reacted instantly. With aid from most of the non-Communist newspapers they revived and expanded upon the most damning anti-Yankee propaganda: the charge of long and profitable intimacy between the United States and the ex-dictator as "proved" by a medal President Eisenhower awarded him, the Secretary of State's high praise for his regime and the luxurious asylum afforded him in Miami.

Within a week the Labor Minister suggested that Nixon not risk a meeting with labor union leaders. By mid-April the ferment engulfed the university. Student groups passed Stay-Away-Nixon resolutions, all stemming from a common source. By April 24 Ambassador Edward J. Sparks told a junta member he was becoming disturbed. Venezuelan authorities summoned political party and student organization leaders, including the Communists, to a secret meeting April 29. Each of them solemnly pledged "to cooperate in not disgracing Venezuela by doing dishonor to a distinguished visitor." That night Ambassador Sparks was assured officially that "all elements of danger had been counteracted."

While that assurance was being conveyed, Communist party officials were instructing their high school and university subchieftains to accelerate the anti-American drive. Two days afterward the Vice-President was the star, *in absentia,* of the May Day parade in Caracas. Placards and slogans portrayed him as a world villain *sans pareil* and the symbol of North America's lust for war and profits at the expense of downtrodden Venezuelan workers. *Tribuna Popular,* the official Communist newspaper in Caracas, proclaimed the party's battle cry—NIXON, NO!—in huge red letters atop page one on May 3, and sidewalks, walls and fences blossomed overnight with NIXON, NO! in red.

The Vice-President's advance Secret Service agent came to Caracas the next day to review the schedules, travel routes, precautionary arrangements and other details.[1] The seasoned Caracas policemen had been killed or dismissed in the revolution; the new force was not only green and untried, but it was also the target of a psychological campaign. The Communists tried to instill an attitude of softness toward mobs in the new force by reminding individual policemen repeatedly about the fate of their duty-conscious predecessors. But Army officers supervised each unit and vouched for their discipline,

[1] The overseas host country was always responsible for Nixon's safety. But two Secret Servicemen normally accompanied his party, and one preceded it to doublecheck arrangements and served as a contact with local security agents. Twelve Secret Servicemen were on the Latin American assignment. After an assassination report all were ordered to Caracas as part of the routine emergency procedure. This saved Nixon's life. Each agent was later commended by President Eisenhower and awarded an Exceptional Civilian Service Medal.

and Nixon's advance agent found few flaws in the plans outlined by the Venezuelan and American embassy people.

On May 6 Nixon's roundtable session at the university was
canceled at the request of two prominent Venezuelans. They
said the "peaceful demonstration" being cooked up by students might not unduly disturb the Vice-President but would
reflect on Venezuela's good name. The press then quickened
the tempo of agitation: One publication featured a picture of
a Negro being lynched, entitled "American Way of Life."
Another "exposed" Nixon as a friend of dictator Pérez Jiménez. Dominating page one of the *Tribuna Popular* on May 10
was a large photograph expertly altered to picture Nixon as
a snarling beast with sharp fangs for teeth. It was labeled
"Tricky Dick." As May 13 approached, slogans previously
plastered all over the city were systematically altered. An "M"
was painted over an "F" so that "Fuera [go home] Nixon"
became "Muera [death to] Nixon." Rumblings in the slum and
university precincts intensified. Youngsters gossiped excitedly
about their plans and flippantly ignored the shushing of their
elders.

Non-Communist newspapers that had parroted the *Tribuna
Popular*'s line and even featured articles by well-known Communists seemed suddenly shocked by their own power to in-
flame. They sobered up with last-minute appeals for calm in
the city, while the government junta flooded radio and television air waves with spot announcements pleading that the
distinguished guest be treated courteously or Venezuela would
be dishonored.

The government also ordered the commander of the Caracas
army garrison to review and oversee all security precautions.
His first major change involved the Nixon motorcade. It
would form in the street beyond the airport terminal rather
than at the customary place on the flight line, he decreed,
since the line of sleek limousines might otherwise detract
from the splendor of the honor guard.

Caracas, a city of ultra-twentieth-century skyscrapers and
neolithic hovels, and 1,200,000 people, many of them desti-
tute, throbbed with activity on the evening of Nixon's coming.
High-school children paraded downtown breaking windows
and street lights. University plotters bragged openly about

their pending heroics. American security agents hurriedly changed Nixon's route in the city to avoid streets within shooting range of the huge campus, and the Vice-President's schedule of activities was whittled down. A visit with the Municipal Council of Caracas was canceled when the councilmen pleaded they could not be responsible for "events" if the Vice-President appeared at a public session, as planned. Nixon's stroll through Plaza Bolivar to chat with the people and shake their hands also was scratched, and a hush-hush tip about a poison plot created panic in the nation's high echelons. The report was that the murder potion was to be served at the junta's welcoming luncheon for the Vice-President. This affair was hardly subject to cancellation, so the crisis was solved by firing the caterer.

A coded message from the State Department warned of an assassination scheme unrelated to the one Secret Service headquarters in Washington had announced. Venezuelan security chieftains noted the message and declared their grand strategy would cope with every possible situation. Wherever Nixon went, the streets and buildings around him would be so saturated with security agents that every fourth hand he shook would belong to a plain-clothesman, they said.

At nightfall on May 12 the junta notified the American embassy that "everything is under control—all is well." At three the next morning—eight hours before the Vice-President was to land—that assurance was repeated, and the embassy conveyed it by radio to the Vice-President in Bogotá and the President and Secretary of State in Washington.

The deputy American ambassador in Caracas flew to Bogotá with a dispatch case of up-to-the-minute information and briefed the Vice-President during the 640-mile flight over the Andes from Colombia to Venezuela.

"I stressed the strong probability or even certainty of unfriendly demonstrations," the diplomat wrote later in a memorandum to the Secretary of State. "I spoke of the increased activity of the Communists in Venezuela during recent weeks; I said that the two points on which the agitation was almost certain to be based were the presence of Pérez Jiménez and Pedro Estrada [the former secret police chief] in the United States and our restrictions on imports of petroleum. I also showed the Vice-President aboard the airplane a copy of *Tribuna Popular,* May 10, which contained unrestrained propaganda against Nixon. I said, however, that on the basis of reports we've received from responsible Venezuelan authorities, both directly from members of the junta and the Foreign Office, and through the Secret Service representatives in Caracas and [U.S. intelligence agents], we were satisfied that any attempt at violence could be effectively disposed of."

Two hours before Nixon was to land, a swarm of people descended on the airport, snapping to life the hot, listless terminal building. Adolescents, soldiers, government officials, reporters, photographers and policemen were in the melee. The soldiers came in trucks; the boys and girls and their middle-aged leaders in buses; the United States government officials in nine black limousines rented from a mortician for the Nixon motorcades; the United States press corps in a chartered Panagra airplane.

The sight of press photographers set off the airport activities long ahead of schedule. When the cameras pointed at the mob on the terminal balconies, adults gave a signal and their flock of 500 boys and girls unfurled the anti-Nixon banners and proceeded to shake fists and shout insults at the open air. A thousand soldiers then fixed bayonets and formed ranks in four battalions, and policemen scurried to posts atop and around the terminal building, with carbines at the ready. Once they had started, the demonstrators would not stop. Their frenzied screaming, stomping and banner-flailing continued after the photographers pointedly put away cameras.

When the Nixon airplane landed and the Vice-President and Mrs. Nixon emerged, smiling and waving, the mass screech rose several octaves to a pitch that drowned out a Venezuelan Army band and a battery of 105-mm. artillery firing a 19-gun salute.

"I was very surprised in one respect," Nixon said afterward. "I expected placards, but I was surprised that they allowed the airport to be completely dominated by the Commies and their stooges. The minute I stepped off the airplane, while getting the salute, I cased the place. (I always do that when I walk out.) I looked it all over and watched the kind of crowd, thinking, Where will I make an unscheduled stop, where will we move out and shake hands and so forth. And as I looked that one over, I just simply saw that here was one place where we would have an altogether different situation than we ever had in any other country I visited. The crowd was all unfriendly. I could see it; I knew it immediately. I whispered to Walters [the interpreter], 'What are they shouting?' I had asked him to check it before we got off the plane. He said, 'Mr. Vice-President, this whole crowd is against us.'

"So we walked down the steps from the airplane, and I quickly made a few mental notes and decisions. As we trooped the line [inspecting the honor guard] I decided not to wave to the crowd, but to ignore it since they were showing disrespect for their flag and their national anthem as well as ours."

A knot of airplane mechanics standing far off beyond the honor guard was the only demonstrably friendly group of nonpolitical Venezuelans Nixon was to see that day or the next. Their shouts of "Welcome" and "Long live United States" broke through an occasional lull in the racket from the terminal, and Nixon wondered if it was a mirage. He shunned protocol to shake their hands before he was formally presented to the local officialdom.

"As we were walking back [to the officials], I turned to Walters and said, 'Look, we're not going to do the mike scene.' " A microphone had been set up, as is customary, and the Vice-President was prepared to tell his hosts: "It is gratifying indeed to know that the Venezuelan people have embarked once again upon the road to democratic government."

Nixon said he "was not going to be put in the position of doing something undignified. It would have been stupid to have tried to speak and be shouted down. I wasn't going to let that happen. And so we walked in."

Thanks to the Venezuelan police and security chiefs, he walked into trouble. The head policeman had refused an embassy attaché's request that the mob be cleared from Nixon's path. "They are harmless," said the police official. "They have a right to demonstrate." The security chief directed the motorcade to form in the street beyond the terminal. Thus the Vice-President and his wife had to push through a hundred yards of agitated humanity instead of boarding their cars in safety on the airport ramp.

The organized spitting and garbage throwing began as the party approached the landing-field side of the terminal. Before they could reach the shelter of an awning, the band once again struck up the Venezuelan national anthem. The Nixons froze at respectful attention, and the mob on a balcony overhead spat down on them.

"I think that was the time when I felt as irritated as at any time on the trip," said Nixon. "I thought, What a really lousy thing this is." Midway in the anthem he reached down to pick up a rubber noisemaker that had bounced off his cheek. "I was tempted to give it back to the guy. But then I figured that they might think I was throwing something at them. You have to be very careful in a situation like that. You have to think all those things through. My first impulse was to throw it back. If I had done that, it would have been a good move, provided it didn't start something. This was an emotional crowd, and they might have thought I was being unfriendly."

Mrs. Nixon also relaxed her rigid attention at one point to reach through a line of soldiers and shake the hand of a girl who had spat and shouted obscene insults at her. The teenager was startled. Tears filled the eyes that had blazed with hate, and she turned away in obvious shame.

Before the end of the anthem, the adult mob leaders hissed, "Go, go, go," to their charges, and the youths melted away from the balcony and formed ranks on the street to block the Yankee visitors when they emerged from the building. Venezuelan authorities watched solemnly. The soldiers stood erect and at perfect attention, fixed bayonets gleaming in the sunlight. Police disappeared. And a few Secret Service agents and United States military officers cleared paths to the cars through spitting, tripping feet, garbage and swinging fists.

A little girl was elbowed by two escorts through the mob to give Mrs. Nixon a flower bouquet. This was the first token of friendship shown the Vice-President's wife since she had landed. Mrs. Nixon hugged and kissed the child and whispered, "Thanks," in her ear, hoping she heard it above the noise.

In the confusion a teenager grabbed Mrs. Nixon's hand and screeched a question about the Vice-President torturing "little black boys" in Little Rock.

Mrs. Nixon and the wife of the Foreign Minister were assigned to the second limousine of the motorcade. Its back seat was spotted with saliva. Mrs. Nixon wiped it away while her Venezuelan hostess expressed mortification. Major James D. Hughes, the Vice-President's military aide, and two Secret Service agents joined the ladies and rolled up the windows as several of the youngsters surrounded the car to spit and kick at it, while the main mob concentrated on Nixon and his number-one car.

Caracas was 12 miles away. Carloads of the demonstrators slipped into the motorcade. Some rode alongside the Vice-President's vehicle, shouting, spitting and throwing things at 40 miles an hour. Motor scooters joined the melee at the city limits. They zigzagged around the Vice-President and Mrs. Nixon's cars, almost colliding with the police escorting the motorcade on motorcycles.

In the lead limousine the Foreign Minister and the Vice-President were on the back seat, Colonel Walters and Agent Sherwood were on the jump seats, and Wade Rodham, the advance Secret Service agent, sat up front with the Venezuelan chauffeur.

"When we left the airport, I had a chat with the Foreign Minister right away," Nixon said. "He wiped the spit off me with his handkerchief and said he was sorry but the people are very expressive because they have not had any freedom for so many years and the new government did not want to suppress freedom. I told him that if his government did not learn how to control the type of people that I saw there at the airport and control the excesses in which they were indulging, there wouldn't be any government, and there wouldn't be any freedom either. I spoke with great feeling because I was disturbed.

" 'These are Communists,' I pointed out. 'I've seen these same signs and placards all over Latin America. These Communists will deny Venezuela the freedom it deserves and should have.' I also pointed out that they wouldn't let me speak or even him, that they denied both of us freedom of speech and shouted throughout their own national anthem as well as ours.

"He told me that I was right. He said he, too, thought they were Communists. 'But I urge you, if the press should ask you about this, I urge you not to say that they are Communists,' he said. 'You see, here in this country we judge freedom differently.' Then he went off into a long rigmarole from which I gathered that the government wanted to get along with the Communists because the Communists had supported them in the revolution. The Foreign Minister was afraid that my identifying these Communists as such would embarrass the government."

The Foreign Minister changed the subject. "This is an interesting highway," he said. They were on the Autopista, a magnificent dual-lane highway built by Dictator Jiménez to connect the airport and Caracas.

While the motorcade neared city limits, an advance party at the Pantheon several miles away tried frantically to warn Nixon, by radio, to stay away. The scouting group, which included the Vice-President's administrative assistant and a Secret Service agent, had seen the mobs waiting at strategic corners on the Avenida Sucre. They had to park two blocks from the Pantheon and "look as anti-American as possible" for their own protection while pushing their way to a place where they could observe what was going on at the shrine. They sent back three separate warning messages, in code, over a prearranged radio network centered at the Caracas police headquarters. None ever reached the Nixon party.

"We got into town," Nixon said. "What concerned me was that I saw no friendly people on the street. The stores were locked and shuttered. I knew then that we were in very serious trouble. Before we reached the first roadblock the rocks began to hit the car. That is a frightening sound, incidentally—the crack of rocks against a closed car."

The barrage came from a crowd waiting on a slope where the Autopista curves into the city and becomes the lower end of the Avenida Sucre, a modern six-lane roadway with a center divider. Its lower end bisects a neighborhood where policemen were torn apart, trampled and set afire in the revolution four months earlier. The Nixon greeters at this gateway to Caracas waved placards with Nazi swastikas alongside the photograph clipped from the Communist newspaper. They also shouted obscenities in English, the mildest of which was "son of a bitch."

The avenida reportedly had been cleared of all traffic an hour before, and the motorcade rolled along at quite a clip— until it became ensnarled in a solid mass of buses, trucks and cars.

A shouting mass of people surrounded the stalled lead cars and performed the long-since customary rites with spit, garbage and rocks. Some tore the crossed Venezuelan and United States flags from the limousines, and kicked the fenders and doors. One hefty fellow threw himself in front of the vice-presidential car, and was tossed aside like a medicine ball by a Secret Service agent. Six agents had leaped from their cars farther back in the motorcade and rushed up to screen the Vice-President. Half the Venezuelan police escort vanished when the attack began; the other half either sat frozen to their motorcycle seats or scurried about making a pathway through the traffic snarl.

The motorcade again clipped along the avenida at a fair pace, until it was stopped short by another tie-up, this one just four blocks from the Pantheon plaza. "Here they come!" someone shouted. Men and women, young and old, poured from a dingy alley a hundred feet away shouting and waving banners, placards, pipes, clubs and bare fists, like a scene from the French Revolution. At least 500 of them swarmed around the Nixon car, the excess overflowing to envelop the other cars. Practically all of the remaining Venezuelan police quickly disappeared.

The agents operated with cool, contrived skill. Even while being hit at and spat upon they avoided any appearance of antagonism or violence that would stampede the frenzied mob. Agent Robert Taylor was knocked flat by a shell casing. He wiped the blood from his head and resumed the job of trying to keep the mob from the Vice-President, using his shoulders, feet and open palms, instead of a fist or a weapon. Without appearing to do so, agents would trip up an attacker in a way to make a dozen fall. They would gently nudge one individual so that he in turn pushed the others away from a door handle, like sweeping away clusters of flies. The car doors were the principal objective of the gang bent on dragging the Vice-President from his limousine to tear him apart —the most degrading death possible, by Venezuelan standards. In the number-one car, agents Sherwood and Rodham unlimbered their pistols, and the Foreign Minister mumbled, "This is terrible," as the attackers hit the windows and doors with clubs, pipes, their fists and their feet.

The onrushing horde reminded Sam Waugh, president of the Export-Import Bank, of a flood in Plattsmouth, Nebraska, when he was a child. "I felt helpless, like I did when the flood rushed down the main street of our community sweeping all before my eyes."

Nixon turned apprehensively to see, through his back window, if his wife was all right, since she was in the limousine behind his. "It was a relief to find that the mob was concentrating against me," he said. "I felt they would continue that way, and therefore she would be all right." He was thankful for that, Nixon added, because "I knew it would be hopeless for me to try anything anyway." Nixon also noticed that the number-two limousine had driven smack up against his and he thought, "That is pretty wise of the driver"—since the maneuver kept attackers away from the back of his car and the front of Mrs. Nixon's.

"I saw the mob descending on us, and I knew that this was planned," Nixon recalled. "I was surprised to see how many teenagers there were, young ones. Then I saw the collection of the old ones, and I saw they were leading it. It was the same story. I just thought, 'How could people do this?' Then when the first window broke, I realized we were in very serious trouble and I began to think, 'Well, now, how do we get out of this situation?' and 'How do we recoup? How do we get back at them?' Nothing much was said in our car. I knew that the important thing was to find a way to go some place where they weren't expecting us. I was thinking that all along."

The attack intensified. A motorcycle policeman threw a tear-gas bomb. It landed aimlessly behind the milling crowd. Some fled, then came right back, throwing dirt and horse dung. Then the mob started rocking the Vice-President's vehicle.

"It looked as though their tactics were to turn the car over and burn it," Nixon said. "I figured that this was what they were going to try. I wasn't concerned about their smashing the windows and getting me out. But I was concerned that they might get hold of the car and smack it over. I also noted that the police had gone, except for a couple of them who weren't doing a thing.

"We just sat there," the Vice-President continued. "I looked right into the face of the guy who was smashing the window on my side with a club. He smashed it and smashed it, and finally busted it. He hit it about ten times before it cracked. It's hard to hit a window like that. You have to hit it with a good crack. It won't cave in with just a nudge.

"What went through my mind was the complete unreasoning hate in their faces—hate, just hate. I'd never seen anything like that before. Never. This mob was a killer mob. They were completely out of hand, and I imagine some were doped up to a certain extent.

"I thought, 'How are they able to stir the people to this pitch?' Then I realized as this was going on that right here was the ruthlessness and determination, the fanaticism of the enemy that we face. That was what I saw in the faces of the mob. This is really Communism as it is. Some people had been telling me, including the Foreign Minister sitting there at my side, that Latin-American Communists were different, that they were 'theoretical Communists' and really nationalists. Well, I figured, they should know better now."

As the window beside Nixon gave way, Sherwood pulled his gun. "Now is the time to get the sons of bitches," he snapped. Rodham drew his gun, too, and said coldly that he and Sherwood would each "get six of them before they get us." The windows on both sides of the car were now being bashed in. Slivers of glass flaked off at each blow and shot back and forth inside the car, making hissing noises. A man tried to poke a pipe at Nixon through a hole in a window.

A large rock hit the window beside Colonel Walters and stuck there. "Are you all right?" Nixon asked. "Yes, except I have a mouthful of glass," replied the interpreter. "Spit it out, you've got interpreting yet to do today," said the Vice-

President. Something smashed the back window, showering the glass over the Foreign Minister. "It's in my eye," he yelled. "This is terrible, this is terrible."

"Spit was dripping off the windshield," Walters recalled. "From where I sat it was like watching a horror movie. I kept thinking that we were going to move on and get away from it. Then I saw this boy with what looked like a shell casing in his hand. I knew he was going to throw it. I hoped it was a shell casing and not a bomb. Frankly, I was prepared in my mind all along that we would be bombed, particularly when we stopped so long. They could roll the bomb underneath. That was the thing. The gasoline tank would have gone up. I watched this boy, and after what seemed like an awfully long time, he finally threw it, and that is what hit the back window and splattered glass in the Foreign Minister's face."

Twelve minutes after the violence had started—and just as it seemed to be reaching a murderous climax—some Venezuelan soldiers showed up. They made a narrow opening in the traffic tie-up, and Nixon's car shot through it. Mrs. Nixon's car followed close behind. Both headed for the Pantheon, but just before reaching it they swerved off to the right into an alley. Nixon had decided in that split second to abandon the wreath-laying ceremony and to head for safe territory where mobs would least expect him to go.

That decision saved his life and Mrs. Nixon's. It also spared his entourage and many of the 8,000 screeching Venezuelans who crammed the plaza. Subsequent investigations showed that two well-disciplined groups were in the plaza crowd. Each had a special mission. Vice-President and Mrs. Nixon were their targets. The largest group of a hundred or more, including high-school and university students, was to barrage the visitors with rocks and fruit. A unit of hardened experts was then to follow through with homemade bombs. Venezuelan investigators discovered the murder plot while searching the home of a female Communist functionary near the plaza. A cache of about 400 Molotov cocktails was found under the steps, stacked neatly and primed for reissue.

The motorcade disintegrated. The two lead cars managed to keep together, however, and stopped near a medical center to take stock. No one in the ladies' limousine was injured. All in the Vice-President's were scratched or cut. No hospital attention seemed necessary, however, and the road ahead was clear, so the Nixons went to the embassy residence atop a steep, easily defensible hill in the city's exclusive Las Lomas section.

Anger boiled inside the Vice-President, but he was outwardly unruffled and composed. "These incidents are against Venezuela," he said to reporters who caught up with him as he entered the Ambassador's house. "No patriotic Venezuelan would have torn down his country's flag as the mob did to the Venezuelan flag and also to ours. I don't feel it at all as a personal offense. If anything, the future relations of the United States and Venezuela will be better than ever." To a university group which hurried up the hill to apologize, he said, "As far as I'm concerned, the incident is closed."

Major Hughes, one of the first jet pilot heroes in Korea, said, "It was a little bit like heaven," when the emotionally exhausted vice-presidential party reached the comparative safety of the Embassy residence. Gin and tonics were waiting. Nixon nodded pleasantly to several guests already there for a luncheon, then walked off by himself to look pensively out a window. He slumped in an easy chair and beckoned to Hughes. "I can risk my own life, but I have no right risking anybody else's," he told his military aide. "We will stay here. Tell my appointments I would be pleased to see them if they would come here." The Nixons were scheduled to stay at the Circulo Militar, the sumptuous military club which Pérez Jiménez had built for $35,000,000 to ensure the devotion of his Army officers. Mrs. Nixon had a two-day schedule filled with visits to orphanages, hospitals and women's organizations. The Vice-President canceled that and all other plans which required movement outside the embassy quarters, technically United States territory. As Hughes took notes, Nixon outlined a completely new operational plan for the hours ahead. The Vice-President was literally wrung-out, so he went to bed. It was Nixon's first afternoon nap in 12 years of public life. He slept for 40 minutes.

As he napped, his staff quietly transformed the Ambassador's house into a fortress and developed a plan for leaving

Caracas the next day. Meantime, Washington began to throb.

A preliminary flash report to the State Department said the mobs were still at large in the city, the security system obviously had broken down and, while no American was seriously injured, the situation was still unclear. Undersecretary of State Christian Herter concluded from this that the Vice-President and his party "were virtually prisoners in the embassy . . . and the situation was gravely serious," so he alerted the Joint Chiefs of Staff. At the White House, President Eisenhower was furious and apprehensive. Nothing like this had ever happened before. It was the worst mob action ever directed against either of the highest-ranking United States officials. John Foster Dulles, just back from Copenhagen, Paris and Minneapolis, rushed to the White House. By now there was alarm in the administration hierarchy because efforts to reach Nixon by telephone and even via an Air Force radio network had failed. At 2:50 P.M. Washington time (3:20 in Caracas) President Eisenhower ordered the Pentagon to prepare for action. The Joint Chiefs of Staff happened to be conferring with Secretary of Defense Neil McElroy on troop-movement problems in small wars when the White House called General Nathan Twining, the chairman. By nightfall America's military might was poised for the liveliest and most bizarre rescue mission of all time. A naval force of six destroyers, a guided-missile cruiser and an aircraft carrier equipped to land Marines by helicopter moved flank speed toward Caracas with orders to stay just beyond sight of the Venezuelan coast until directed to move in by the President. The Air Force alerted jet-bomber, fighter and fighter-bomber units and evolved a plan for instant action which was informally assigned the code name "Operation Poor Richard." And 1,000 picked fighting men—two companies of paratroopers and two companies of Marines—were rushed to bases in Puerto Rico and Cuba, within easy striking distance of Venezuela.

At 6:05 P.M. the Pentagon announced the Marine and paratroop activities. A communiqué stated: "The movement is being undertaken so these troops will be in a position to cooperate with the Venezuelan government if assistance is requested. This is purely a precautionary measure, and there is no indication that such assistance will be required."

The Navy and Air Force activities were kept secret. Nixon would have preferred no public disclosure of the paratroop and Marine movements as well. He learned of the troop movements three hours after the Washington announcement, when a Venezuelan government official came to plead with the Ambassador for a statement denying that it happened.

Rioting mobs were still loose in the city proper. The Vice-President was dubious about the government's ability to keep order or provide his entourage proper protection. But he also knew that, if the situation worsened to the extent that American troops were needed, it was doubtful that they would find any still-living members of the vice-presidential party to protect. Furthermore, he foresaw a terrible propaganda reaction to Washington's sword-rattling and even a possible revolution in which the Communists might take complete control of Venezuela.

(President Eisenhower later defended his action as "the simplest precautionary type of measure in the world." At the time it was taken, he said, "we knew nothing of the facts. We could get no reports from the outside . . . and not knowing what was happening, and not knowing whether the Venezuelan government might not want some aid from us, we simply put it at places where it would be available.")

At 9:15 P.M. Nixon had his ranking diplomatic aide, Assistant Secretary of State Roy R. Rubottom, Jr., call the State Department for an explanation. Rubottom was told that Secretary Dulles had cabled Nixon all the details. (The message was never received.) The Pentagon announcement was read to Rubottom and a secretary in Caracas took it down so that the Vice-President would know at least what had been said officially. "This whole matter will take a lot of undoing," Rubottom informed the State Department.

At the urgent request of Venezuelan authorities, Nixon and Ambassador Sparks then issued a joint statement declaring their faith in the Venezuelan government's power to maintain law and order without outside help and pointing out that the military action announced from Washington was nothing more than a movement of troops between American bases. The statement added that America had no intention of sending those troops to Caracas unless the Venezuelan government requested it—which Venezuela was not expected to do.

Nixon's staff set up a rigid security system at the embassy residence and completed a tightly integrated departure plan for the next day. Sixty American Army, Navy and Air Force men on duty as instructors of the Venezuelan armed forces were mobilized to join the embassy's five Marines and Nixon's 12 Secret Service agents as guards at the vice-presidential residence. A battalion of heavily armed Venezuelan soldiers manned the streets for blocks around. Everything brought to the house by anyone—flowers, packages, even notes—was carefully checked by security men. At the airport 35 United States and Venezuelan guards were stationed around the Nixon airplane and the private aircraft chartered by the American press group.

Meanwhile the Vice-President had a busy afternoon and evening in his fortress. He met with several groups, including the non-Communist Venezuelan political leaders. Dr. Romulo Betancourt, anti-Communist chief of the leftist Acción Democratica party and subsequently the elected President of Venezuela, insisted the asylum given Dictator Pérez Jiménez in the United States was the root of the trouble.

Nixon smilingly recalled that he had heard the same thing from the Pérez regime when the United States gave Betancourt asylum after the uprising which brought Pérez to power, causing Betancourt to flee. All the political moguls insisted they were upset about the morning's violence, but none cared to point a finger at the Communists, whose leader was a colleague on the committee of political chieftains which had an important advisory role in the government. When Nixon outlined evidence that proved the Communists inspired and led the mob attacks, Dr. Rafael Caldera, secretary general of the Christian Socialist party, protested, "But the Communists issued a statement just a while ago saying they were not responsible." Although the official Communist newspaper gloated over each morsel of the violence, the Communist party headquarters indeed issued a communiqué absolving itself and blaming followers of the ex-dictator, known as "Pérez Jimenistas." But Nixon was amazed that any hard-headed political veteran would believe it.

Later the ruling junta and the Venezuelan Cabinet came to pay their respects. Nixon interrupted their flowery apologies to say there would be no ill will, personally or officially, and to suggest that they forget the incident and discuss affairs of state with him. But Admiral Larrazabal, the provisional President, said he was too dispirited to talk. He apologized again and left, and as he rode down the hill his car was stoned. But little damage was done its bulletproof glass and armor-plated hide.

The Vice-President later said that "the most difficult period in one of these incidents is not in handling the situation at the time. The difficult task is with your reactions after it is all over. I get a real letdown after one of these issues. Then I begin to think of what bums they are. You also get the sense that you licked them . . . though they really poured it on. Then you try to catch yourself . . . in statements and actions . . . to be a generous winner, if you have won.

"Most importantly, you must think of what the lasting impression is going to be. You are writing some history here. You are affecting international policy. You must consider the sensibilities of the people. Those are things I thought about before the press conference that evening."

Nixon met the press at six o'clock on the embassy residence veranda surrounded by an army of security agents.

On his overseas tours the Vice-President customarily recognized local reporters ahead of the United States correspondents accompanying him. On this occasion, however, the American contingent led off, and the first question was: "Never before in the history of the United States has one of our important officials suffered the indignities and violence you suffered in this city today. What is your reaction to this horrible and shameful incident?"

His reaction to the obvious first question was, in effect, to turn the other cheek. He reiterated his friendship for the government and people of Venezuela. "The Communist planners of today's outrage were able to gain a great deal of support from students and other groups because of what happened in this country during the past ten years," he said. "What we saw here was the terrible legacy of the dictatorship of Pérez Jiménez. Dictatorship breeds violence, and violence in turn breeds other dictatorships when allowed to go unchecked."

Nixon urged that the nations of North and South America join to "fight and strive in every positive way against the poverty, misery and disease on which dictators of both the right and left feed to gain power." Then he said, "If this day serves no other purpose than to bring clearly to the attention of officials the character and tactics of those who would overthrow freedom, it would serve a useful purpose."

After the press conference three of his staff members sat with the Vice-President and Mrs. Nixon awhile in an upstairs bedroom. In the intimacy of those closest to him, Nixon released the bitter anger that he had submerged during that hard day of frustration and trouble. As is his custom after long periods of public self-control under trying conditions, he opened the safety valve and "blew his top." Once relieved, he went to bed. It was the last night of Richard Nixon's three-week goodwill tour of Latin America.

A report to Washington at seven P.M. said: "It is relatively quiet everywhere. The residence is under full protection."

Elsewhere in the city, junta President Larrazabal had turned over to the Defense Minister complete responsibility for the Vice-President's safety with authority to take any measures he thought necessary. This, in effect, rescinded his directive of a few days before that ordered soldiers and policemen not to shoot at rioters.

The next morning President Eisenhower telephoned at ten o'clock. The whole country was proud of the Nixons, he said, and a great welcome-home ceremony was being arranged. Furthermore, Eisenhower said he would be there with the two Nixon children despite advice from the State Department protocol people that his presence would violate a rule. The President made it clear that he intended to head the welcoming delegation "because of my admiration for [Nixon's] calmness and fortitude and his courage in very trying circumstances."

Prominent Venezuelans apologized to Nixon through advertisements in morning newspapers. One asked, in huge type: "What would happen to Poland if the Poles did to Khrushchev what we did to Nixon?" Delegations came to the embassy residence to pay their respects and express mortification. Twenty-five women representing Venezuela's principal women's organizations brought flowers to Mrs. Nixon and wept with embarrassment.

Nixon's departure plans were secretly set. He was to leave Maiquetía Airport at three o'clock—nine hours ahead of schedule. But he did not want to land in Washington before the airport reception at the following morning—Thursday, May 15—so an overnight visit to Puerto Rico was arranged with Governor Luis Muñoz Marín.

Major Hughes and Colonel Thomas Collins, Nixon's pilot, worked out the intricate evacuation plan in compliance with the Vice-President's wish not to risk another ride through the city. Three sturdy old twin-engine C-47's were flown to a small landing strip near the embassy residence. Nixon and his entourage were to be whisked to the strip by automobile, then flown to the main airport. An Air Force helicopter was brought in for emergency use if the short automobile ride to the landing strip was found to be dangerous. In addition, four large military airliners were flown to the fields a few minutes from Caracas for use should anything happen to the Vice-President's DC-6 or the American press plane at the airport. Two of the stand-by airliners were poised for immediate take-off at Plesman Field in Dutch Curaçao, and two at Maracaibo, the Venezuelan oil city. Shortly before noon the junta invited the Vice-President and his party to lunch at the Circulo Militar. Nixon replied that he would like to lunch with the junta—but at the embassy residence. Eugenio Mendoza, a civilian member of the ruling body, pleaded with him to reconsider or the government would be disgraced, so Nixon relented, and he and Mrs. Nixon were spirited across the city in limousines surrounded by 500 soldiers in buses and trucks. There were no incidents along the way.

The luncheon was a large and outwardly gay affair. All the important Venezuelan officials and their wives had gathered hurriedly for it. Admiral Larrazabal asked if the Vice-Presi-

dent was aware that Pérez Jiménez had escaped via the landing strip from which he meant to leapfrog across the city.
No, he was not, said Nixon. He ordered the landing-strip
operation canceled immediately, and his aides substituted the
helicopter plan. But it was evident as the luncheon dragged
on that the government wanted to prove, with a motorcade
departure, that it could protect foreign visitors. After the
meal Admiral Larrazabal asked Nixon to tour the spacious
military club, obviously to kill time. It was already past three,
and the Vice-President resigned himself to being "kidnaped"
by the provisional President. "I guess they are going to take
us out through the city," Nixon whispered to his military
aide. "I was sweating blood," Major Hughes confided later.

At 4:15 a plump Army colonel intercepted the inspection
party in the club locker room and told Admiral Larrazabal,
"All is ready." This, it developed, was the signal that the city
was secure. The Admiral cut short the tour and led Nixon
outside to a motorcade that resembled an armored column
coiled for attack. There were hundreds of troopers in an array of military vehicles, and five armor-plated, bulletproof
limousines for the dignitaries. Nixon joined the President-
Admiral in car number one. Mrs. Nixon, directed to car number two, almost tripped over a submachine gun, extra clips of
ammunition, and a tear-gas canister as she got in. Major
Hughes pushed the arsenal aside but kept the tear gas handy.
The Venezuelan security chief, sitting with the chauffeur of
Nixon's car, assured the Vice-President that peace had been
restored to Caracas. As the armada started off, however, he
took a pistol from a holster and a tear-gas gun from a pocket,
and kept one in each hand during the 22-mile ride from the
Circulo to the airport.

Without asking for his consent, the government was taking
Nixon out the hard way—via the Avenida Sucre. Its military
might had been deployed along the route during the morning.
Tanks and armored cars were posted at intersections. Soldiers
and police armed with machetes and tear gas lined the sidewalks. Knots of people who hesitated when ordered to disperse were sprayed with tear gas. So were the alleys from
which the mobs had streamed the day before.

The armada whizzed along at 60 miles an hour through

what looked to Nixon like a "ghost city." The few people still on the streets held handkerchiefs over their noses. Nixon thought this was "a new way to express their contempt" until someone explained about the tear gas.

The airport and its terminal building were empty except for the honor guard, the band and the artillery battery which had performed in the previous day's welcoming ceremony. The artillerymen fired a 19-gun salute and the band struck up "The Star-Spangled Banner" as the vice-presidential airplane taxied off. The music and booming that had been swamped by mob screeches the day before now came through loud and clear.

When the airplane soared away from Venezuelan soil "everyone was relieved at once," said the pilot. "There was a completely new attitude in the crew and the official party." It was 5:05 P.M.

At 11 the next morning—May 15, 1958—Nixon got the heartiest homecoming welcome ever staged in Washington for a Vice-President. President Eisenhower was at the airport with the Cabinet and administration leaders. Senate Democratic leader Lyndon B. Johnson headed delegations of Senators and Representatives. Thousands of university students were there, including Latin Americans carrying banners with slogans of friendship and praise.

"Through the entire trip the Vice-President has conducted himself effectively, efficiently and with great dignity," said the President. "There have been some unpleasant incidents, and he and Mrs. Nixon have faced real danger and risk of harm and even worse . . . [but this will] in no way impair the friendship of the United States and our sister republics to the south."

14 ❋ *Moscow Mission, 1959*

A YEAR later another overseas trip by Nixon burst into headlines around the world. The Vice-President arrived in Moscow on July 23, 1959, ostensibly to open the American National Exhibition at Sokolniki Park and to make a goodwill tour of Russia and Siberia. But as the highest ranking American official to visit the Soviet Union since Khrushchev had come to power, his principal mission was to probe for areas of possible East-West agreement, size up the Soviet leaders on their home ground, break the ice for a future exchange of visits between Eisenhower and Khrushchev, and impress the Soviets with America's sincere desire for peace—and its determination to stand firm against threats and bluster in the international arena.

Any Nixon-Khrushchev talks, the Vice-President knew, would place the American in a disadvantageous position. Since he was not the head of state he could not change U.S. policy to fit the circumstances. He could only defend his country's stated policy. On the other hand, the Premier would be able to adjust Soviet policy to suit convenience. Therefore, Nixon determined to do as little talking and as much listening as possible.

At ten o'clock on Nixon's first morning in Moscow he went to the Kremlin to pay a courtesy call on his host. This was supposed to be merely a protocol appearance; no substantive issues would be discussed. But Nixon quickly learned that when it suited Khrushchev's interests he did not play by the rules.

The meeting began amicably: Khrushchev spoke of the pleasant Moscow weather at that time of year and of the joint effort of the two countries during World War II. He praised a speech in which Nixon had welcomed peaceful competition with the Soviet Union. Then suddenly he charged the United States with a serious "provocation" by enacting a Captive Nations Resolution.

Earlier in July the U.S. Congress had called for the President to proclaim a Captive Nations Week during which time Americans would pray for the liberation of "enslaved peoples" and recommit themselves to supporting "the just aspirations" of those behind the Iron Curtain.

According to the unpublished "memorandum of conversation," the Vice-President replied that he admired Khrushchev's frankness, "but at the same time he wanted to point out that this resolution does not represent a new position of Congress, but rather the fact, which cannot be overlooked, that in our country there are citizens with a national background from Europe and Eastern Europe. These people, of course, make their views known, and Mr. Khrushchev may disagree with these views, but actions of Congress reflect public opinion in our country."

Nixon also stated that President Eisenhower had specifically excluded from his proclamation the language in the congressional resolution that referred to territories now forming a part of the USSR. The resolution was not a call to arms.

"This resolution points up an aspect of our American system that might be difficult for you to understand," Nixon told the scowling Khrushchev. "Actions of this type cannot be controlled as far as their timing is concerned, even by the President, because when Congress moves, that is its prerogative. Neither the President nor I would have chosen deliberately to have a resolution of this type passed just before we were to visit the USSR. Nevertheless, the resolution expressed the substantial views of the people of our country."

Khrushchev replied that "any action by an authoritative body such as Congress must have a purpose." He wondered what sinister scheme was behind it. The Soviet government regarded Nixon's visit as "a contact serving the purpose of rapprochement between the United States and the USSR,"

Khrushchev declared. But Congress now had given Nixon a "ticket" to possible difficulties in Russia.

The American government's action was aimed at inciting people against their governments and against the Soviet government and the Soviet people, Khrushchev insisted angrily. The Communist bloc countries—"these so-called captive nations"—do not live by the "mercy of the United States and the United States cannot bring about any change unless it wants to start a war."

"This stupid decision . . . is a frightening thing," Khrushchev continued, "because it indicated the attitude prevailing in Congress, although of course it does not reflect the attitude of the American people. It means your Congress can do anything and can take just about any action including starting a war. Heretofore the Soviet government thought Congress could never adopt a decision to start a war. But now it appears that, although Senator [Joseph] McCarthy is dead, his spirit still lives. For this reason the Soviet Union has to keep its powder dry."

The Soviet leader went on in this vein until Nixon declared finally that if the concept of peaceful competition which Khrushchev supports so eloquently is to prevail, Americans and Soviets must learn to understand each other and to realize that there will always be certain differences. Hence he suggested adoption of the procedure used at the White House for ending long discussions that seem to get nowhere. President Eisenhower breaks them off by announcing: "We have beaten this horse to death; let's change to another."

Khrushchev's scowl became a smile. "I agree with the President's saying that we should not beat one horse too much," he said. But he insisted on a final word. Adopting the Captive Nations Resolution on the eve of Nixon's important State visit reminded him of a saying among Russian peasants that "people should not go to the toilet where they eat."

Nixon commented that Khrushchev appeared to attach too great an importance to the resolution.

"Fresh shit stinks," replied Khrushchev.

The conversation then switched to pleasantries again. Everyone thanked everyone else for coming. And at 11:55 A.M. the American and Soviet leaders left the Kremlin to preview the exhibition at Sokolniki Park—and, incidentally, to engage in the impromptu verbal encounter that became known throughout the world as the "Kitchen Debate."

The famous Khrushchev-Nixon debate happened by accident. As they passed an exhibition of a new type of television tape, the demonstrator asked them to talk into the camera. The Soviet Premier took the opportunity to continue the earlier discussion at the Kremlin, bitterly attacking the Captive Nations Resolution. Nixon, in turn, tried to change the subject and act conciliatory. The end result was that when the tape was broadcast Khrushchev appeared rude, even insulting, while Nixon won praise for keeping his temper. The Vice-President later commented, "I felt like a fighter wearing 16-ounce gloves and bound by Marquis of Queensberry rules, up against a bare-knuckle slugger who had gouged, kneed and kicked."

Two days later the Premier and Vice-President had their principal talk at Khrushchev's luxurious country dacha overlooking the Moscow River 22 miles from the Kremlin.

Vice-President and Mrs. Nixon had spent the night before at the dacha. The American entourage—Dr. Milton Eisenhower, Ambassador Llewellyn Thompson, Jr., Deputy Assistant Secretary of State Foy D. Kohler and Alexander Akalovsky, the interpreter, were on hand early. The Russian party —the Premier's First Deputies Anastas I. Mikoyan and Frol R. Kozlov, and their wives, and Deputy Foreign Minister Vasily V. Kuznetsov and several aides—arrived before noon. Before long the Soviet Union's No. 1 black Zil limousine rolled up with the Premier and his wife.

As a prelude to lunch Khrushchev invited Nixon to skim along the river with him in an outboard motorboat. Dr. Eisenhower, the Ambassador and Khrushchev's associates followed in other boats. Soon Khrushchev was ordering the convoy to stop so he could commune with the swimmers and sunbathers who literally covered the riverbank and much of the river itself that hot summer day.

At each stop the Premier greeted his constituents with an expertness that any American political veteran might admire. "Do you regard yourselves as slaves or captive people?" Invariably the reply was a thunderous chorus of "No, no, no!"

Nixon laughed and joked and acted as if these sallies were not really intended for him. He shook dozens of wet hands extended by those who swam around the boat, and he happily acknowledged shouts of welcome and good wishes from the crowds. Subsequently, when the statesmen returned to the dacha grounds, Mikoyan observed that he had never seen such fine "river rallies." Nixon told Khrushchev, "I must hand it to you. You never miss a chance to make propaganda!" Khrushchev protested, "No, no, I don't make propaganda. I tell the truth."

Before rejoining the ladies, the Soviet chief led the male guests to a shooting gallery much like those at country fairs in the United States.

"You first," said host Khrushchev, handing Nixon a gun.

"I don't shoot," said Nixon, giving the gun to Thompson.

Nonchalantly, the Ambassador fired away—with every shot a bull's-eye.

He returned the gun to Nixon, who gave it Khrushchev, saying, "You're next."

With a grin, the chunky Kremlin boss passed the gun to Mikoyan.

The First Deputy Premier aimed slowly, fired and hit the target—but not the bull's-eye. Everyone laughed loud and good-naturedly.

Lunch was served at a large oblong table in the shade of stately birch and pine trees planted during the reign of Catherine the Great. Seating was strictly according to protocol, with Nixon and Khrushchev directly across from each other. The meal was a convivial, friendly affair. The Premier and Vice-President ribbed each other playfully, and when Mikoyan sought to try his English on Mrs. Nixon, Khrushchev teased him about being a Lochinvar. When Mikoyan persisted, his boss declared, "She is my partner"—then, running his finger down the table between Mrs. Nixon and Mikoyan, he added with a chuckle, "I bring down the iron curtain."

When the dishes were cleared away, Khrushchev, now in the role of courtly host, invited the wives to remain and contribute to the serious talk. (No one, man or woman, left the table from the time the meal started until the conference ended, over five hours later.)

The Premier opened with a discourse on his country's rocket and nuclear advances. Only the day before, he said, Soviet scientists had briefed him on plans for shooting a 100-ton manned vehicle into space. While the project was still in the planning stage, it was achievable without much difficulty, he asserted.

Then Khrushchev told of a stray practice missile that almost hit Alaska. The conversation, in essence, was as follows:

K—The Soviet Union has excellent missiles. But there are still troubles occasionally with delicate mechanisms. Only the week before a malfunction in the cut-off system of an unarmed practice intercontinental missile created concern in the Kremlin. Instead of dropping in the target area, the rocket kept going, and the Soviet government feared it would land in Alaska. Fortunately, it fell in the ocean.

[Khrushchev paused, then continued.]

K—No doubt the United States monitored that shot. In fact, I know you did. The Soviet Union also has facilities to keep posted on American missile activities.

N—It is very difficult these days for any great nation to do things that are not known to the other side.

K—I agree.

N—The United States was pleased to show Andrei N. Tupolev its missile production facilities when [the noted Russian aircraft designer] visited America in June.

K—Tupolev reported he had not seen much, only the final product, not the insides.

N—Kozlov was invited to witness missile launchings at Cape Canaveral and the Vandenberg Base, but didn't accept.

K—That is because the USSR feels the time is not yet ripe for an exchange of this kind. The United States must liquidate its overseas bases, and then the USSR will show Americans its launching sites and missiles.

N—What about your statement to Averell Harriman that the Soviet Union has provided China with missiles to use against Quemoy?

K—That is untrue. What was really said was that large numbers of missiles would be supplied if the United States attacked China. At present, the USSR is furnishing missiles to no one.

N—It is unfortunate that nations find it necessary to spend such large sums on armaments. The money for one missile would buy 153,000 television sets, or endow several universities, or purchase shoes for several million children.

K—United States missiles cost too much. They come cheaper in the USSR. Soviet military experts calculate 30 billion rubles worth of rockets are required to paralyze vital centers in the United States, Europe and Asia. That includes intercontinental and intermediate range missiles.

N—Does the Premier mean the USSR now has that required number of missiles?

K—[After discussing the matter with his associates at the table] The USSR has the capability. Anyway, American officials must know this since they undoubtedly have the "Soviet Operational Plans" just as the Kremlin has gotten possession of "United States Operational Plans," although it is difficult to judge the authenticity of such espionage prizes because they might have been planted by counterintelligence agents.

N—Since the Soviet Union has intercontinental missiles, why does it continue to build bombers?

(Khrushchev interrupted the conversation at this point to toast the health of President Eisenhower, Mrs. Nixon, the Vice-President, Dr. Eisenhower, all other American guests present, as well as friendship between the Soviet and American people. Nixon responded by toasting the health of his Russian hosts. Khrushchev then resumed the conversation where it had been left hanging.)

K—Russian bomber production has almost been halted. Bombers and fighters are being built only as needed to train Soviet air personnel. The Soviet military now relies mostly on missiles which are more accurate and are not subject to human failure or human emotion. Missiles can feel no revulsion at hitting a target regardless of what it is. Furthermore, navies are now obsolete. They are fit only to provide fodder for sharks. The USSR will build no more cruisers and aircraft carriers.

N—What about submarines?

K—We are building as many submarines as we can. [Mikoyan injected, "as many as needed."]

N—Submarines are excellent for launching missiles and their usefulness in that regard would be greatly enhanced when solid fuel had been developed.

K—That is true, but Russian experts believe it is preferable to launch missiles from land than from the sea.

N—That depends on the strategic situation of the nation involved.

K—I want to reveal another secret. We will use submarines to destroy ports, military areas and the navy of the enemy. Destroying the enemy navy would paralyze his sea communications which is of great importance because the Soviet Union's potential enemy would be highly dependent on sea communications. Our submarines would carry ballistic missiles and anti-missile rockets. Their range is now 500 kilometers. It is being increased to 1,000 thousand kilometers, which our scientists say would be entirely sufficient.

N—Fuel is a big problem in the missile field. Further refinements depend largely on the development of solid fuels. What has the USSR achieved on this score?

K—The Soviet Union has had great success with rocket fuels. But being a politician and not a technician, I am not qualified to discuss solid fuels.

(At this, Mrs. Nixon, giving way to an urge she usually represses, observed with a broad smile that she was surprised to hear that Mr. K was not an expert on every subject. The Premier laughed, and bowed in an extravagantly gallant manner. Mikoyan quickly declared that even someone of Mr. K's superior intellect and leadership qualities does not have hands enough to deal with everything in a government as complicated as that of the Soviet Union.

(The serious discussion resumed with Nixon requesting clarification of a recent Khrushchev statement that the USSR would place intermediate missiles in Albania.)

K—That was because the United States made arrangements to station missiles in Italy. The best place for the USSR to paralyze those missiles is from Albania. Italy and Greece could best be hit from Albania and Bulgaria, while Turkey could be covered from bases in the Soviet Union and Bulgaria.

N—Does the Soviet government make a distinction between collective security arrangements, such as NATO, and the individual nations belonging to NATO?

K—Yes. But each individual member nation has to make its own decision about NATO missile bases if it wants to avoid becoming a missile target.

N—You often speak out publicly about missiles and missile targets. This may leave an impression throughout the world that you do not intend. In today's discussion, for instance, you apparently are simply relating an estimate of Soviet strength and how it would be used to resist attack, or to counterattack. Nonetheless, such talk could possibly be interpreted as threats against other countries. As you know, the United States also has considerable power, but hopes never to have to use it. Regardless of who starts it, another war would be disastrous to the entire world because even a sudden blow could not eliminate the retaliatory power of the other side. The United States and the USSR must recognize that both are strong, both have the necessary will, since their people are strong and determined. Neither should look down on the other. If there is mutual respect, the two could create a basis for the negotiations necessary to ease world tensions and bring about a reduction in armed forces, which both sides desire. It would be well if officials of both nations stopped talking of the balance of power between the United States and the USSR and emphasize instead that both are powerful and want a future of peace instead of war.

K—I fully agree with your estimate of the correlation of forces between the two powers. But Soviet leaders have not made statements that the USSR could destroy the United States without suffering losses itself, even though some American generals have said that the United States could wipe out the USSR. I will reveal another secret. You are undoubtedly familiar with Marshal [Konstantin A.] Vershinin's famous interview [which blanketed the front page of *Pravda* on September 8, 1957] on Soviet capabilities of destruction. It was I who dictated that interview. I was on vacation and summoned the Marshal and a secretary in order to dictate that interview. Our government did not want to let pass in silence certain statements by United States generals, and the Presidium considered at what level the reply should be issued. We chose Vershinin because he is chief of the Soviet Air Force.

(In the "interview," Marshal Vershinin was quoted as assuring the Communist world that the Soviet Union was not vulnerable to United States strategic attack, and he warned the West that the Soviets were capable of laying waste its enemies without suffering much loss to itself.

(After commenting additionally on Russian missile power, the Soviet government's displeasure over American bases and the "secret" of how he literally forced former Foreign Minister Molotov to conclude a peace treaty with Austria, Khrushchev charged that the United States wanted to set up bases in Iran.

(Ambassador Thompson insisted that this was not so.)

K—Even though the United States-Iranian argreement is a secret, I have read it and can even give the Vice-President a true copy of that agreement. I know it has no provision for bases as such, but it does provide for American assistance to Iran in case of "indirect aggression." This means that the United States wants to act as a policeman against the Iranian people when they rise against their government.

N—I hope you do not think that the Communist leaders from 51 countries could meet in Moscow, as they did recently, without the United States knowing what they were doing and what instructions they were getting with regard to subversive activities. Furthermore, Mr. Khrushchev, you should recall that you declared openly during your recent trip to Poland that the USSR would support revolution everywhere in the world.

K—The United States should not pay its intelligence agents because they are no good. Only 12 nations met, not 51, and nothing came out of the meeting that was not published in the press. The United States does not understand Communist ideas. Communists are against subversion and terror. The United States still thinks in terms of conspiratorial parties like the anarchists and nihilists in old Czarist Russia, but even then the Marxists disagreed with such an approach. Marxists have always been against individual terror. Such terror never

served a useful purpose. At the same time, where the bour-
geoisie does not surrender its power peacefully, mass uprisings
are a different thing and are favored by Marxists.

Dr. Eisenhower—Is this not interfering in the internal affairs of other countries?

K—Subversion is a vulgar term, not a scientific term. If the
Soviet Union wanted subversion, it would have organized the
strongest possible Communist party in the United States of
America, and the whole course of history would be different.

N—How do the uprisings in northern Iraq fit into your
theories?

K—I know of nothing going on in Iraq and therefore cannot comment.

N—What about Czechoslovakia?

K—That is an interesting example worth examining. The
Communist party in Czechoslovakia had been the only
party which had not surrendered to the Germans. Its prestige
had been much greater than its influence in the postwar government of Czechoslovakia. So when the Communist party
presented demands on behalf of the people, the government
capitulated. There was not one Soviet soldier in the country
at the time. The Czech revolution was like the American
revolution. There was a complete parallel between the two
situations. It was not King George III who had given the
Americans their independence. American independence had
been won as the result of the American Revolution, and the
sympathies of the Russian people had been on the side of the
Americans at that time.

N—Of course everyone can give his own interpretation of
history. But how do you reconcile your claim that Communists disapprove of individual terror with the fact that the
Soviet press and radio incited terrorism against Mrs. Nixon
and myself when we were visiting Latin America?

K—There is a Russian saying, "You are my guest, but
truth is my mother," so I will not evade that. The sympathy
of the people of the USSR was with those who had been
against you, Mr. Vice-President. You were the target of
righteous Russian indignation directed not against you personally, but rather against the policy of the United States.
The Soviet Union regarded your trip as demonstrating the

failure of United States policy. If you had visited those countries as a tourist, no one would have paid attention to you. The violence was directed against American policy.

N—You have a right to your opinion and to sympathize with such acts as those which occurred in Venezuela. But you should remember that what happened in Venezuela might happen in the world between two countries of great power. When military power like that of the Soviet Union is coupled with revolutionary policies, there is grave danger that matters might get out of control. In comparison, the 2,000-kilometer mistake in the missile that almost hit Alaska was a relatively small error. Men like you and President Eisenhower, tough, reasonable men who are not soft or frightened, must approach the big problems on the basis of give and take. You adhere to one single theme: the United States is always wrong, the Soviets never. On that basis it is impossible to reach settlement between two strong nations. The Geneva Conference of Foreign Ministers [then going on] is an example. Secretary of State Herter, representing the President, has made concessions to meet Soviet points of view. But a point can be reached where one side can go no further. Both sides must give.

K—The Vice-President's attitude toward Venezuela smacked of imperialism. The Eisenhower-Dulles policy was to control Venezuela's decisions because the United States thought that country to be of strategic importance. Such policies result in hatred for the United States everywhere. People of other countries will not tolerate America's imperialistic approach.

N—What of the Soviet Union's approach in Hungary, Poland and East Germany?

K—That is an entirely different matter. Regarding "concessions," when peace is at stake no surrender, but only advance, is possible. Soviet proposals are formulated on a global basis to appeal to the entire world, not just the United States. Soviet proposals are well thought out and supported by the entire world because they are for peace. And as for the Geneva Conference, it is a tea party, and makes little or no sense.

N—But you have said you hope for success in Geneva.

K—Yes, otherwise Foreign Minister Gromyko would have been recalled from Geneva. The key problem is liquidation of the state of war with Germany. A solution to this problem would lead to the solution of other problems. Just like a knitted fabric, if one thread is pulled, the whole garment comes apart. Soviet proposals are formulated to make clear that the Soviet Union seeks no advantage for itself. The West has settled with West Germany without regard for Soviet interests. The Soviet right to reparations has been disregarded. Monetary reform has been introduced. And a tri-zonal agreement has been made. The West also has recognized Adenauer's government. Consequently, Soviet moves in East Germany are similar to those of the West in West Germany. The West violated the Potsdam Agreement not to rearm Germany. It permitted Germany's rearmament with atomic weapons. . . .

(Nixon sought to respond, but Khrushchev continued.)

K—Vietnam offers a parallel example. North Vietnam wants elections, while the United States, contrary to agreements reached over three years ago, opposes them. Why? Everybody knows that the West pulls the strings on the rulers of South Vietnam.

N—Who pulls the strings in North Vietnam—the people?

K—Three powers have signed an agreement on the unification of Vietnam. There is no such agreement on Germany. In any case, historical progress is not determined by legal documents. In Russia the Soviet system was established by "decree of their majesty, the people"—the people decide whether Russia should be socialist or bourgeois. Similarly, the German people must decide the question of German reunification, while the great powers must recognize the fact that now there are two Germanys. You have no intention of making war over Germany; neither do we. What you want is that all Germany go capitalist, isn't it?

Dr. Eisenhower—What the United States wants for Germany is what the German people want for themselves.

K—The fact is that a mother cannot control the birth of her child—and a father is even less capable of doing that. So why does not the United States let East Germany be socialist if its people prefer that system?

N—I do not propose to rehash postwar history. The Soviets obviously have their views, and we have ours, and we disagree on what happens in Vietnam and East Germany. However, I want to make two points. First, I am glad to hear that you agree with the principle of free elections. If you are for elections in Vietnam, why are you against elections in Germany?

K—I am not against elections, but simply want the Germans to decide this question for themselves.

N—The people's views must certainly be properly recorded. Yet in Vietnam the Communists created conditions that made a unification election impossible. North Vietnam would not even permit the international control commission to operate in its territory. . . .

K—[interrupting] Another point regarding Germany: the Soviet government is concerned about the question of West Berlin. The prestige of the great powers is involved, and the USSR does not want to be misunderstood in the world. You, a lawyer, should understand that the strictly legal solution would be for the Western powers to pull out of West Berlin and permit it to become a part of East Germany. But the Soviet Union recognizes the fact of West Berlin's existence, realizes that the capitalist system prevails there and wants to find a way to insure that the will of West Berlin's population would not be violated. If the Soviet Union wanted war, it would not be urging the Western powers to pull out the 11,-000 troops they have in West Berlin, but would want the West to have at least 100,000 troops there, because the Soviets could liquidate them in one blow. The thing to do, in order not to embarrass either side, is to apply the brakes to the Berlin situation and have an interim arrangement for West Berlin. The West should tell Adenauer to negotiate with the East Germans. The West should tell Adenauer that the great powers have no intention of quarreling over the Germans and they will accept any arrangement worked out between the two Germanys. That would end the fiction centering around West Berlin.

(As the discussion on Germany continued, Khrushchev declared sarcastically that, while the United States wants to pray for the captives of socialism, the Soviet Union has no intention to pray for the captives of capitalism because they do not need Russian prayers. Then, with a chuckle, he proposed the novel idea that when men fail to agree on international questions, they should appoint their wives to settle the differences. Mrs. Nixon, Mrs. Khrushchev, Mrs. Mikoyan and Mrs. Kozlov smiled at each other, and the Vice-President brought the conversation back to the German question.)

N—The argument over who set up the West German and East German governments could go on endlessly. When you refer to 11,000 troops in West Berlin, the U.S. can point to 18 Soviet divisions in East Germany. Obviously, the two sides have different approaches to the unification problem. Furthermore, it seems you honestly believe unification would not be practical in the foreseeable future, and also you think the Western powers do not want it.

K—That is so.

N—As a student of history, you should realize why reunification is essential for peace. You should know that when a vital and strong nation is divided, seeds are planted for the emergence of a future leader who would seek to accomplish reunification in any way.

K—Let's be frank about this. The West has proposed so-called free elections so it might engulf East Germany and make all of Germany an ally of the West. The German Democratic Republic does not want the West German political system and does not want to become a member of NATO. Would the West want the Soviet Union to overthrow the present regime in East Germany? The USSR could present the same type of demand with regard to West Germany, but it would be absurd. The inexorable fact is that there are two Germanys in existence. If the West is against recognizing the German Democratic Republic, a formula should be found whereby the West would not have to sign a peace treaty with it. But the formula should make it possible for the Soviet Union to sign such a treaty. Then agreement should be reached that the social order in West Berlin should be determined by its population, and access to that city could also be guaranteed. The Soviet Union recognizes that in the present heated atmosphere any document of the type being proposed might be damaging to one side or the other. Therefore there should be provisional arrangements and the great powers should agree on a time when the treaty itself would be signed.

N—Mr. Khrushchev, do you not see the difficulties that could arise when a time limit is placed on negotiation? Do you not see the position in which it would put President Eisenhower?

(The Soviet leader nodded, and said something to the effect that the West also had established a time period of two and a half years. Then, at Nixon's suggestion, Ambassador Thompson reviewed proposals on Berlin that had been made by both sides, and observed that the United States government cannot understand how the Soviets reconcile their forcing of a crisis on the Berlin question with their words about peace. This enraged Khrushchev.)

K—[Raising his voice] The Ambassador should be careful about how he uses the word "peace." His talk sounds like a threat. The Soviets would sign a peace treaty and the West could declare war if it wishes. When peace is at stake, the Soviet Union is very sensitive, and if the West chooses to fight against its peace treaty, everyone would recognize who is to blame. [Then, in calmer tones] If the Soviet Union did not want to negotiate, it would have signed a peace treaty long ago with East Germany. That was its right, and also the right of the States bordering on Germany. I am not stupid, and can understand the real meaning of Ambassador Thompson's words.

Ambassador Thompson—No threat whatever was implied. Forcing a crisis is not a step toward peace. It is the Soviets who are threatening to force a crisis.

K—What in the Soviet proposal is incompatible to Western interests if the West really wants peace?

N—Neither side should confront the other with an impossible situation.

K—We propose only peace—you yourself used the slogan today—what's wrong with it? Mr. Vice-President, you are right that a calm atmosphere is needed. But the United States should not threaten the Soviet Union with war. Apparently the Vice-President did not want to use that sort of language, and had Ambassador Thompson do it.

N—The Ambassador implied nothing more than you have

said, namely that if you were confronted with an impossible situation, you would have the means to do what was necessary about it.

(The conversation continued to focus on Germany, with Mikoyan observing at one point that the German people want "confederation," not unification. Then other issues were brought up.)

N—What do you consider the main purpose for discontinuing nuclear weapons tests?

K—It would lay a basis for disarmament, improve international relations and strengthen peace.

N—Do you regard atomic fallout to be dangerous?

K—Of course, all scientists say so.

N—Why, then, do you not accept the President's proposal for discontinuing atmospheric tests as a first step? This would solve the fallout problem while negotiations on the other stages of the test ban continue.

K—There would still be the question of high altitude tests. The President has proposed to continue tests at altitudes above 50 kilometers, and this would be deceiving public opinion.

N—Is it accurate to characterize the Soviet position on test bans as "all or none"?

K—Yes, all or none. Since the United States has more bombs than the Soviet Union, Soviet leaders cannot understand why the United States wants to continue tests—unless the American bombs are inferior to Soviet bombs.

N—What about the problem of underground tests?

K—The Soviets have not conducted a single underground test and plan to conduct none. Furthermore, the Soviet Union is producing no tactical nuclear weapons, only strategic ones. A tactical bomb with a 100,000-ton yield requires the same amount of nuclear explosives as a strategic weapon with a yield of several million tons. Maybe the United States has money to waste on tactical bombs, but not the Soviets.

N—Is the Soviet Union planning to use "atomic dynamite" for peaceful purposes, such as building canals and harbors?

K—That sort of thing would be a deception designed to continue nuclear weapons tests. TNT is completely adequate for construction purposes.

(Mikoyan interrupted to note that the Soviet Union had agreed in Geneva to permit a limited number of underground explosions for peaceful purposes. Khrushchev acknowledged it, and added it was "a foolish . . . stupid concession.")

N—It is obvious from all that has been said that there are broad possibilities for effective discussions between you and President Eisenhower—or at a meeting of Chiefs of States—provided there is no atmosphere of crisis. There is this important question, Is there room for negotiation in the Soviet position on Germany? Before answering, please imagine that President Eisenhower is sitting across the table . . . and also you should realize that he would not want to come to a meeting if you were not prepared to negotiate.

K—That is a fair question and would be better answered in terms of what the Soviet Union would not accept. President Eisenhower then could form his own judgment as to Soviet willingness to negotiate. The Soviet Union could never accept a perpetuation of the occupation regime in West Berlin, regardless of whether there was a summit meeting or not. The Soviet position is flexible and fluid except on this one point of occupation status. The West may offer any proposals to ensure the present social order in Berlin and access to that city. As for a peace treaty with Germany, it could ensure the status quo of the two Germanys until time liquidates the military blocs. The treaty could include the most liberal provisions, including some for the withdrawal of Soviet troops from East Germany and Poland.

Shortly thereafter—at 8:45 P.M.—the conference was concluded. As the Premier and Vice-President walked toward the house, they discussed briefly the pending, but still secret, exchange of visits between Khrushchev and Eisenhower, and Nixon requested permission to write Khrushchev about the C-130 case.

Thus ended the five-and-a-quarter hour meeting that Nixon would later describe as his "hand-to-hand combat with Khrushchev on the outstanding differences between the United States and the USSR." Yet the climax of their relationship was not revealed until 1967, when both men were no longer in power. Then the former Soviet Premier, speaking from the same dacha, told NBC of a conversation he had had with John F. Kennedy at Vienna in 1961:

"I told him [said Khrushchev], 'The fact that you became President was due to us. We made you President.' He asked me how he should understand that. I said, 'I'll tell you how. You collected 200,000 more votes than Nixon. Nixon asked us for Powers, the U-2 Pilot, to be released [Khrushchev meant the C-13 crew] . . . and if we had done it, he would have received half a million votes just for that—because that would have shown that Nixon could have established better contacts with the Soviet Union. But we guessed his plans. We decided not to give him any answer, and just to give it to you when you moved into the White House. So what do you think of that?' I asked Kennedy. He said, 'I agree with you entirely. If you had not acted the way you did, Nixon would definitely have got his 200,000 votes.' "

15 ❋ *Home Work, 1953–1961*

CHARLES G. DAWES, who was Vice-President of the United States under Calvin Coolidge, remarked during his term that the job he held was "the easiest in the world" because he had only two responsibilities—to listen to Senators give speeches and to check the morning paper for news of the President's health. Indeed, the Constitution specifies nothing more for the Vice-President than that he should preside over the Senate and succeed to the presidency if the office is vacated.

During Nixon's eight years as Vice-President, he was called upon to cast more tie-breaking votes in the Senate than any of his 35 predecessors. But relatively little of his time was spent in the Senate chamber. Rather, it was the many non-constitutional duties he assumed that were to change the concept of the vice-presidency.

Immediately after Eisenhower was nominated in 1952 he called Nixon to his suite at Chicago's Blackstone Hotel. At that time he recalled how President Roosevelt had failed to inform Vice-President Truman on many basic decisions and that this had created a serious situation when Truman was elevated to the presidency in 1945. It was vitally important, General Eisenhower said, that this should never happen again and so, if he became President, he would make sure Nixon participated in all policy-making meetings. Moreover, Nixon would be given assignments to prepare him for the possibility that he might suddenly find himself President.

Eisenhower was true to his word. During his administration Nixon was a member of the Cabinet and presided over 19 meetings; he was a member of the National Security Council and presided over 26 meetings; he attended the weekly meetings with the congressional leadership; he was given access to the most secret security information and read the daily intelligence reports from all over the world; he was made chairman of the president's Commission on Government Contracts and chairman of the Cabinet Committee on Price Stability; and he traveled 160,000 miles to 55 countries as the President's emissary. Nixon also was given the task of taking over some of the ceremonial burdens of the presidency and served as Eisenhower's representative at everything from a golf trophy presentation to a State dinner for the King of Morocco.

On September 3, 1957, President Eisenhower sent Nixon a memorandum which for the first time in history assigned a Vice-President a major role in foreign policy.

"My basic thought is that you might find it possible—and intriguing—to be of even more help in our whole governmental program dealing with affairs abroad than you have been in the past," Eisenhower wrote, in part. "By your extensive travels you have been of inestimable assistance to the Secretary of State and to me. In addition you have gained an understanding of our foreign problems that is both unusual and comprehensive. My belief is that this knowledge and comprehension, supplemented by your special position of having one foot in the executive branch and one foot in the legislative branch, can be advantageously used in helping to lay out advanced programs and schedules. . . ." and for the next page and a half the President outlined additional responsibilities he wanted the Vice-President to assume in helping to shape trade, mutual assistance, technical and direct aid, and monetary and defense policies.

Nixon's increased influence was reflected in the speed with which many of his subsequent proposals for Latin America were carried out. In the six months after his 1958 trip there was more positive action than ever before in United States relations with its southern neighbors. Emphasis was on cultivating increasingly influential elements in universities and labor unions, promoting economic development and pointing the impact of United States information projects and propaganda at the worst sore spots of misunderstanding. The student exchange program was doubled—and then some. Seminars were formed to permit great numbers of Latin American university students at least a month of undergraduate study per year at a North American institution. San Marcos University in Lima, the scene of the first anti-Nixon riot, became the first school in Peru to establish credit courses in North American literature and language. Added status was given labor attachés to maintain closer liaison with workers' organizations in each country. After years of reluctance, the United States joined the international agency for stabilizing coffee prices. The Export-Import Bank was authorized to lend an additional two billion dollars. There was quick approval by several United States monetary agencies of loans throughout the continent, many of which had been pigeonholed for months, including varying sums to settle immigrants from Europe and elsewhere. There were also loans and grants to build technical schools, expand technical assistance and provide drought and disaster relief, particularly in Brazil. Nixon struck at the belief of Latin Americans that the United States encourages dictatorships by stating that the U.S. government hereafter would base its relationships with Latin government officials on this dictum: "For dictators, a formal handshake, nothing more; for free governments, an embrace."

The Vice-President also had another unique opportunity to evaluate a key area of Latin America when, on April 15, 1959, Fidel Castro, who had recently overthrown the Batista dictatorship in Cuba, arrived in the United States for an 11-day speaking tour. Castro's visit was unofficial, so he was not scheduled to meet with President Eisenhower. But on Sunday, April 18, the Cuban Premier in his battle-fatigue uniform and the American Vice-President met alone for three hours in Nixon's office in the Capitol. No staff members or photographers were present.

At the time a large body of opinion leaders in the United States was sympathetic to Castro, who had come to power a little more than three months before. The Cuban revolutionary was actively courting public favor in this country. The lead story on page one of the *New York Times*, April 18, was headlined:

CASTRO DECLARES
REGIME IS FREE
OF RED INFLUENCE

Three days later a *Times* front-page headline read:

CASTRO RULES OUT
ROLE AS NEUTRAL;
OPPOSES THE REDS

"The bearded soldier said that his heart lay with the democracies and that he did not agree with communism," the *Times* story reported Castro as having declared on the "Meet the Press" television program.

In this context, the "rough draft" that Nixon made of his session with Castro, which was sent to the CIA, the State Department and the White House, makes especially interesting reading today.

"When Castro arrived for the conference he seemed somewhat nervous and tense [Nixon began]. He apparently felt that he had not done as well on 'Meet the Press' as he had hoped. . . . I reassured him that 'Meet the Press' was one of the most difficult programs a public official could go on and that he had done extremely well—particularly having in mind the fact that he had the courage to go on in English rather than to speak through a translator."

(Getting down to substantive issues, Nixon continued.)

"I suggested that while I understood that some reasonable time might elapse before it would be feasible to have elections [in Cuba], it would nevertheless be much better from his viewpoint if he were not to state so categorically that it would be as long as four years before elections would be held. . . . He went into considerable detail as he had in public with regard to the reasons for not holding elections, emphasizing that 'the people did not want elections because the elections in the past had produced bad government.' . . . I pointed out that it might be very possible that the people of Cuba were completely disillusioned as far as elections and representative government were concerned, but that this placed an even greater responsibility on him to see that elections were held at the very earliest date and thereby to restore the faith of the people in democratic processes. Otherwise the inevitable result would be the same dictatorship against which he and his followers had fought so gallantly. I used the same argument with regard to freedom of press, the right to a fair trial before an impartial court, judge and jury, and on other issues which came up during the course of the conversation. In every instance he justified his departure from democratic principles on the ground that he was following the will of the people. I, in my turn, tried to impress upon him the fact that while we believe in majority rule that even a majority can be tyrannous and that there are certain individual rights which a majority should never have the power to destroy."

(Nixon here commented, "I frankly doubt that I made too much impression upon him." The conversation then turned to what Nixon judged to be Castro's "primary concern"—economic development.)

"It was apparent that while Castro paid lip service to such institutions as freedom of speech, press and religion, that his primary concern was with developing programs for economic progress. He said over and over that a man who worked in the sugar cane fields for three months a year and starved the rest of the year wanted a job, something to eat, a house and some clothing, and didn't care a whit about whether he had freedom along with it. I, of course, tried to emphasize that here again as a leader of his people he should try to develop support for policies which could assure progress with freedom rather than without it.

"We had a rather extended discussion of how Cuba could get the investment capital it needed for economic progress. He insisted that what Cuba primarily needed and what he wanted was not private capital but government capital. He gave me some rather confused arguments as to why plants that were licensed and/or owned and operated by the government would serve the best interests of Cuba better than privately owned enterprises. I told him quite bluntly that his best hope as far as the U.S. was concerned was not in getting more government capital but in attracting private capital. I explained that government capital was limited because of the many demands upon it and the budget problems we presently confronted. I pointed out that private capital, on the other hand, was expansible and that he would be serving the interests of Cuba far better by adopting policies which would attract it. . . .

"I tried tactfully to suggest to Castro that [Governor Luis] Muñoz Marín had done a remarkable job in Puerto Rico in attracting private capital and in generally raising the standard of living of his people and that Castro might well send one of his top economic advisers to Puerto Rico to have a conference with Muñoz Marín. He took a very dim view of this suggestion, pointing out that the Cuban people were 'very nationalistic' and would look with suspicion on any programs initiated in what they would consider to be a 'colony' of the United States. . . . I am inclined to think that the real reason for his attitude is simply that he disagrees with Muñoz' firm position as an advocate of private enterprise and does not want to get any advice which might divert him from his course of leading Cuba toward more socialism of its economy."

(Castro then "bitterly assailed" the U.S. press and Nixon "tried to explain that speaking from some personal experience that it was necessary to expect and to learn to take criticism both fair and unfair." Next Castro spoke of "a very disturbing attitude" on the part of the American people generally: "Every place I go you seem to be afraid—afraid of Communism, afraid that if Cuba has land reform it will grow a little rice and the market for your rice will be reduced. . . .")

Nixon answered "that we welcomed the industrialization and development of Latin America, that one of our best customers was Canada, for example, which was highly industrialized and that as economic conditions improved in any country this was not only good for that country but good for us as well. I also tried to put our attitude toward Communism in context by pointing out that Communism was something more than just an idea but that its agents were dangerously effective in their ability to grasp power and to set up dictatorships. I also emphasized, however, that we realized that being against Communism was not enough—that it was even more important that we convince people every place that we want to help them achieve economic progress in a climate of freedom."

(After several other subjects were discussed, "but none

worth noting" in Nixon's opinion, the Vice-President came to the heart of his report.)

"My own appraisal of Castro as a man [Nixon concluded] is somewhat mixed. The one fact we can be sure of is that he has those indefinable qualities which make him a leader of men. Whatever we may think of him, he is going to be a great factor in the development of Cuba and very possibly in Latin American affairs generally. He seems to be sincere, he is either incredibly naïve about Communism or under Communist discipline. . . ." Even after leaving office Nixon did not reveal more than the barest facts about what was in this confidential memorandum on Castro (although none of its information was classified). But in his memoirs, he did write rather ruefully, "My position was a minority of one within the administration and particularly so within the Latin American branch of the State Department."

When President Eisenhower established by Executive Order in 1953 the Committee on Government Contracts, assigning it the task of "improving and making more effective the non-discrimination provisions of government contracts," it was appropriate that he appointed Vice-President Nixon as the group's chairman. For Nixon always had been on record as a strong supporter of civil rights. During his years in the House of Representatives he voted for the Anti-Poll Tax Bill and the Fair Employment Practices Act. And, although no civil rights measures were before the Senate during Nixon's tenure, as Vice-President he was to make a key ruling that would clear the way for passage of the 1957 Civil Rights Act.

The Committee on Government Contracts consisted of several prominent businessmen, such as Fred Lazarus, Jr., of the Federated Department Stores, union leaders George Meany and Walter Reuther, Howard University President James Nabrit, Jr., and representatives of government agencies (Department of Defense and the General Services Administration, for example) that were most actively involved in awarding contracts. But the group was given no enforcement powers and its accomplishments were solely dependent on its powers of persuasion and pressure.

For the first few years the Nixon committee concentrated on putting out educational material, holding conferences of contractors, churchmen and other civic leaders, and helping businesses to formulate nondiscriminatory personnel policies. Some notable gains were made, especially in the District of Columbia, where agreements were secured from the public transportation and telephone companies to integrate their work forces.

But by early 1959 Nixon decided that the time had come for a new emphasis. It was not enough, he felt, to get an employer to agree to hire solely on the basis of qualification and then sit back and hope that a qualified Negro would apply. What now was needed, in Nixon's opinion, were specific commitments from contractors that a definite number of qualified Negroes would be employed within a given period of time in jobs from which they were traditionally barred.

Staff director Irving Ferman geared the committee's administrative machinery to get these hard and fast commitments. One example of the committee's work involved an International Latex plant on Delaware's Delmarva Peninsula, an area of considerable racist sentiment. While the company had attempted to hire Negroes in the past, all efforts were unsuccessful because of employee resistance. After negotiations with the Nixon committee, however, the company hired Negroes for clerical, laboratory and production positions, and also made arrangements to use the facilities of the predominantly Negro Delaware State College to provide advanced training for its white laboratory technicians.

Nixon's "new emphasis" was not just on more jobs, but on those jobs that demanded greater skills. As early as 1956, for the first time in American history, clerical, technical and professional jobs exceeded the number of "blue collar" jobs. "Nixon insisted," Irving Ferman now recalls, "that the disadvantaged minority groups must be educated to provide the work force required by the new technological orientation of our economy." But simultaneous with better job education, Nixon argued, there must be concrete evidence of job opportunities for Negroes in these higher-skilled categories. For these reasons, the committee began to concentrate on white collar jobs.

In its seven years in operation the Nixon committee received 1,042 complaints and processed 851 of them. It received awards from such organizations as the National Conference of Christians and Jews, Freedoms Foundation, the National Newspaper Publishers Association and the American Jewish Committee. It also received commendation from a lady who was usually one of the chairman's severest critics: Mrs. Eleanor Roosevelt, on August 11, 1960, wrote in her newspaper column, "This committee, headed by Vice President Richard Nixon, has done a very good job on elimination of discrimination on work done under government contracts."

Nixon was given a second important chairmanship by Eisenhower when the President created a Cabinet Committee on Price Stability for Economic Growth in 1959. For executive vice-chairman—the group's top professional—Nixon chose W. Allen Wallis, a towering redhead, who was then dean of the University of Chicago's Graduate School of Business. (He is now president of the University of Rochester.) The Cabinet representatives ranged in economic viewpoint from Postmaster General Arthur Summerfield on the right to Secretary of Labor James Mitchell on the left. In the committee's deliberations, as in other activities within the Cabinet and the administration, Nixon generally sided with the Mitchell faction.

With outside help from such leading economists as Arthur F. Burns, Joseph Pechman, Herbert Stein and George Shultz, the committee produced a series of statements in no-nonsense prose on price stability, economic growth and other topics. They came down hard on the threat of inflation, whose effects, they said, "inflict unjust hardships on the many families whose incomes are fixed in dollars or do not rise in proportion to prices, violate our standard of fair play by harming families whose incomes are average or below-average more than families whose incomes are above average, [and] contradict promises implied when people put aside income in insurance, government bonds, retirement funds and other forms of saving; for when the money is returned it fails to buy the goods and services that people were led to expect when they put the income aside." Yet the committee refused to take the line, then fashionable in some administration circles, that inflation was simply due to the wickedness and selfishness of unions and monopolists.

Under Dean Wallis' tutelage, the Vice-President was given, in effect, a cram course in applied economics. One result was a committee statement on the aims of U.S. economic policy, which read, in part:

What we really want is an ever freer, richer, better life for everyone.

Our economy must provide conditions that develop the mind and the spirit, as well as an abundance of material comforts and mechanical marvels. It must provide expanding opportunities for every individual to realize his own potentialities to the utmost and to open wider vistas for his children. It must encourage initiative, independence and integrity. It must preserve and enlarge the dignity and moral worth of the individual. Our economy must, in short, strengthen the basic ideals and traditions of American life.

Our ways of working and of consuming constitute a large part of our whole way of life, and are closely intertwined with nearly all the rest. The goods and services provided by our economy, and growth in the economy, provide the means for preserving and enlarging the dignity of the individual. They make it possible to approach more closely our ideals of personal freedom, justice and fair play, broad and equal opportunity, the rule of law, and mutual respect and charity. Those very ideals and traditions are themselves responsible above all else for the unparalleled economic progress which our country has experienced under our Constitution.

The committee's statements were widely reprinted for use in colleges, adult education courses and in-plant programs. Much of its work, however, was consultative within the administration, trying to see that each agency took into account not only its primary mission, but all the effects of its policies in promoting or impeding economic growth. In the spring of 1960, for instance, Wallis began to work behind-the-scenes with Nixon's encouragement to get a loosening in Federal Reserve policy; the change was finally made in summer and may have been a major reason why the slight recession of 1960 bottomed out by February of 1961.[1]

The question of whether Nixon could put into practice his views on economic policy and inflation was given a very real test by the steel strike of 1959.

The 116-day strike, longest since World War II, began on July 15. On October 9 President Eisenhower invoked provisions of the Taft-Hartley Act, but it was not until November 7 that the Supreme Court upheld the injunction that directed the steelworkers to go back to the mills for an 80-day cooling-off period. By this time, besides affecting the half-million members of the United Steelworkers of America, the strike had idled an additional half-million workers in allied industries, while the loss in wages and production in the steel industry alone amounted to over six million dollars.

At first the thought of a strike had not been popular with the workers and their families. Times were good and their memories long. Most could still recall the hardships of long walkouts in 1946, 1952 and 1956. A. H. Raskin, the labor expert of the *New York Times,* thought the strike might have been averted if initially the companies had put as little as a nickel on the bargaining table. Industry, however, made a serious miscalculation during the prestrike negotiations. It made encyclopedic demands for abolishing work rules, scrapping jobs and changing seniority classifications. The objective, it said, was to end manpower waste. But for the union members it looked suspiciously like management was trying to return them to "industrial slavery."

Thus with industry intrepid and union chief David McDonald now fully backed by his rank-and-file, it was clear by mid-December that negotiations were hopelessly deadlocked with a resumption of the strike set for January 26, 1960. This then was the situation when Vice-President Nixon entered the picture.

[1] If imitation is the highest form of flattery, Nixon could take some satisfaction from President Johnson's 1968 economic message in which he announced plans to appoint a Cabinet Committee on Price Stability whose assignment and proposed method of operating was to parallel closely that of the Nixon committee.

The night before President Eisenhower left for an 11-nation tour in early December he asked Nixon and Secretary of Labor Mitchell to see if they could actively help settle the strike. This idea met with approval from both union and management leaders. So began a series of secret meetings at Nixon's Washington home, which he was later to categorize as "eight days and nights of the most intensive discussions I have ever participated in."

"At the beginning of these negotiations," Nixon recalled, "the possibilities of settlement seemed hopeless. The companies' offer was for a wage-benefit package which the companies estimated would add 31 cents to their costs over a period of 30 months. In addition, the companies asked for revision of Section 2B of the contract so that management would have more control over local work practices which they felt was essential for increased efficiency.

"The unions," Nixon continued, "completely opposed any changes in the work practice provision of the contract. On the economic side, Mr. McDonald at our first meeting bluntly stated, 'I cannot settle with the steel companies for less than the amount that I received from can and aluminum [companies] without a strike.' "

The union figured its contract with the can and aluminum companies had increased wage-benefit costs by 52 cents over a 30-month period. Therefore the union was asking the steel industry for 52 cents; management was offering 31 cents.

It was at this point that Nixon asked Roger Blough, president of U.S. Steel, and McDonald whether they would like him to recommend an amount in between their two positions. Both sides agreed. Two days later Nixon came up with an acceptable figure of 41 cents and the work practices issue was referred to a study commission.

Nixon's main argument in breaking the log jam was to convince industry that if it did not settle the strike now the issues would be settled for it by an election-year Congress that was dominated by members elected with union support.

Some sources attacked the Nixon settlement as inflationary, but the Vice-President argued that "it was less than half of the postwar pattern in wage-benefit increases in the steel industry" (41 cents as compared with 81 cents) and that "this was the first contract since the war in which the increase was such that the companies did not find it necessary to increase prices at the time the contract went into force."

The most widely held conclusion, as expressed by columnist James Reston, was that "the steel strike settlement was definitely inflationary in at least one important respect: It has greatly inflated Vice President Nixon's political stock."

Nearly 30 years ago there was a Vice-President named Alexander Throttlebottom. He had been invented for a Broadway musical, *Of Thee I Sing,* in which nobody could remember his name, his face or what he did. In one scene, Vice-President Throttlebottom wanted to withdraw from the ticket because, as he put it, "What if my mother were to find out?" But the political bosses assured him that his mother would never hear about his candidacy and, besides, he would have forgotten it himself in three months.

During the Eisenhower administration, with a mandate from the President, Richard Nixon removed the Throttlebottom concept of the vice-presidency from the lexicon of American public life. Never again would the office be without responsibility and importance.

16 ✼ *Presidential Campaign, 1960*

BY the time Nixon gave Leonard Hall and J. Clifford Folger the go-ahead signal to begin organizing his campaign for the 1960 Republican presidential nomination, it is likely that there was already no way the prize could have been denied him. The date of the Nixon-Hall-Folger meeting was November 7, 1958.[1] As early as the previous March, Nixon was reported to be the favorite of 64 percent of the nation's Republicans, a two-years-before-the-convention rating that was unmatched by any other prospective nominee in the history of the Gallup Poll.

But a possible stumbling block to the Vice-President's ambition was Nelson Rockefeller, whose election as Governor of New York provided the G.O.P. with one of its few bright spots in the 1958 elections. However, on December 26, 1959, after having taken extensive soundings around the country, Rockefeller declared, "I believe . . . that the great majority of those who will control the Republican convention stand opposed to any contest for the nomination. . . . My conclusion, therefore, is that I am not, and will not be a candidate for the nomination for the presidency. This decision is definite and final."

Yet by mid-May Rockefeller was letting it be known that he

[1] Hall would be Nixon's campaign chairman; Folger, a Washington investment banker and Ambassador to Belgium, was to head the finance committee. They would be joined in running the Nixon organization by Robert H. Finch, a 35-year-old California lawyer, who had been G.O.P. chairman of Los Angeles. Finch's title was to be campaign director.

would be receptive to a presidential draft and on June 8 he issued a blast at Nixon and "those now assuming control of the Republican party." Since the Associated Press on May 24 confirmed, in detail, the fact that Nixon already had more than enough delegates to get the nomination, Rockefeller's renewed activities posed a threat only in so far as they might weaken the Vice-President's chances in November.

On Friday, July 22, Nixon decided to fly to New York to meet with Rockefeller at the Governor's triplex apartment on Fifth Avenue. Meantime, in Suite 808 of Chicago's Sheraton-Blackstone Hotel, Charles Percy, chairman of the Republican Platform Committee, was awaiting the last of eight subcommittee reports. Eight secretaries were standing by to cut stencils of the draft platform so that the full committee could begin its final deliberations at nine A.M. the next morning. But the real work of platform-drafting was over—so thought those in the chairman's suite. Then around 10:30 P.M. Chuck Percy received an unexpected telephone call.

Nixon and Rockefeller were on the line and wished to discuss a number of issues, notably national defense and civil rights. In Suite 808 there were three phone extensions: Percy was on one; Roswell Perkins, Rockefeller's representative, was on a second; and on the third, at different times during the nearly four-hour conversation, were Gabriel Hague, the New York banker who was executive secretary of the Platform Committee; Congressman Melvin Laird, the committee's vice-chairman; Research Director William Prendergast of the Republican National Committee; Robert Merriam and Stephen Hess, White House aides; and others. As the subjects were being ticked off—economic growth, foreign policy, medical care for the aged—the phone suddenly went dead. The hotel switchboard operator, having finished her day's work, pulled the plugs and went home, thereby disconnecting the Vice-President of the United States and the Governor of New York. It took 15 minutes to get the call going again.

The outcome of the Nixon-Rockefeller meeting, which became known as "the Compact of Fifth Avenue," changed relatively little of the proposed platform that Percy was about to submit to his committee. In fact, the wording of some of the 14 points that Nixon and Rockefeller publicly agreed upon actually came from the Platform Committee's draft as read to them over the phone. On the key national defense plank, for instance, the "Compact of Fifth Avenue" added only 62 words to the 540 in the original draft.

NATIONAL DEFENSE PLANK

Before the "Compact of Fifth Avenue"	After the "Compact of Fifth Avenue" (Italics indicate changes)
The future of freedom depends heavily upon America's military might and that of her Allies. Under the Eisenhower-Nixon administration, our military might has been forged into a power second to none. This strength, tailored to serve the needs of national policy, has deterred and must continue to deter aggression and encourage the growth of freedom in the world. This is the only sure way to a world at peace.	SAME
We have checked aggression. We ended the war in Korea. We have joined with free nations in creating strong defenses. The Republican party is pledged to making certain that our arms, and our will to use them, remain superior to all threats. We have, and will continue to have, the defenses we need to protect our freedom.	We have checked aggression. We ended the war in Korea. We have joined with free nations in creating strong defenses. *Swift technological change and the warning signs of Soviet aggressiveness make clear that intensified and courageous efforts are necessary, for the new problems of the 1960's will of course demand new efforts on the part of our entire nation.* The Republican party is pledged to

making certain that our arms, and our will to use them, remain superior to all threats. We have, and will continue to have, the defenses we need to protect our freedom.

The strategic imperatives of our national defense policy are these:

SAME

—A second-strike capability, that is, a nuclear retaliatory power that can survive surprise attack, strike back and destroy any possible enemy.

SAME

—Highly mobile and versatile forces, including forces deployed, to deter or check local aggressions and "brush fire wars" which might bring on all-out nuclear war.

SAME

—National determination to employ all necessary military capabilities so as to render any level of aggression unprofitable. Deterrence of war since Korea, specifically, has been the result of our firm statement that we will never again permit a potential aggressor to set the ground rules for his aggression; that we will respond to aggression with the full means and weapons best suited to the situation.

SAME

Maintenance of these imperatives require these actions:

SAME

—Unremitting moderniza-
tion of our retaliatory
forces, continued development of the manned bomber
well into the missile age,
with necessary numbers of
these bombers protected
through dispersal and air-
borne alert.

SAME

—Development and produc-
tion of new strategic weapons without ever again neg-
lecting them as intercon-
tinental missile development
was neglected between the
end of World War II and
1953.

—Development and pro-
duction of new strategic
weapons, *such as the Po-
laris submarine and ballistic
missile.* Never again will
they be neglected, as intercontinental missile development was neglected between
the end of World War II
and 1953.

—Continued top-priority development of hardening, mobility and dispersal programs
for long-range missiles and
the speedy perfection of new
and advanced generations of
missiles and anti-missile missiles.

—*Accelerate as necessary,*
development of hardening,
mobility and *production*
programs for long-range
missiles and the speedy perfection of new and ad-
vanced generations of missiles and anti-missile missiles.

—Intensified development of
active civil defense to enable
our people to protect themselves against the deadly
hazards of atomic attack,
particularly fallout; and to
develop a new program to
build a reserve of storable
food, adequate to the needs
of the population after an
atomic attack.

SAME

—Constant intelligence operations regarding Commu-
nist military preparations, to

SAME

prevent another Pearl Harbor.

—A military establishment organized in accord with a national strategy which enables the unified commands in Europe, the Pacific and this continent to continue to respond promptly to any kind of aggression.

SAME

—Strengthening of the military might of the free-world nations in such ways as to encourage them to assume increasing responsibility for regional security.

SAME

—Continuation of the "long pull" preparedness policies which, as inaugurated under the Eisenhower-Nixon administration, have avoided the perilous peaks and slumps of defense spending and planning which marked earlier administrations.

SAME

There is no price ceiling on America's security. The United States can and must provide whatever is necessary to insure its own security and that of the free world and to guarantee the opportunity to fulfill the hopes of men of good will everywhere. To provide more would be wasteful. To provide less would be catastrophic. Our defense posture must remain steadfast, confident and superior to all potential foes.

There is no price ceiling on America's security. The United States can and must provide whatever is necessary to insure its own security and that of the free world *and to provide any necessary increased expenditures to meet new situations,* to guarantee the opportunity to fulfill the hopes of men of good will everywhere. To provide more would be wasteful. To provide less would be catastrophic. Our defense pos-

ture must remain steadfast,
confident and superior to all
potential foes.

Barry Goldwater, the conservative leader, immediately
branded the Nixon-Rockefeller agreement a "surrender" and
the "Munich of the Republican party." In retrospect, however, it is not so apparent who was surrendering to whom or
if there was really any surrender at all. One of Rockefeller's
most strongly stated views was that the United States must
"work toward an annual rate of growth of 5 to 6 percent."
As translated into the "Compact of Fifth Avenue," this read:
"The rate of our economic growth must, as promptly as possible, be accelerated by policies and programs stimulating our
free enterprise system—to allow us to meet the demands of
national defense and the growing social needs and a higher
standard of living for our growing population. As the Vice-
President [Nixon] pointed out in a speech in 1958, the achievement of a 5 percent rate of growth would produce an additional ten billion dollars of tax revenue in 1962." Was this
then a Rockefeller surrender, a Nixon surrender, or had the
two agreed all along? Or on national defense policy, where
Rockefeller had been repeatedly calling for an additional three
billion dollars in appropriations, no specific figure appeared
in the "Compact." The platform plank, as we have seen, spoke
only of "any necessary increased expenditures to meet new
situations."

Nevertheless, the "Compact" started the most violent platform committee fight in Republican annals. There were probably three reasons behind the committee's strenuous response
to the Nixon-Rockefeller meeting.

First, it threatened the committee's image of itself. Histori-
cally, platform committees do not write platforms, they approve them. Any group of over 100 members is too unwieldy
to perform the detailed drafting required in the several days
in which it is in session. However, this had not been spelled
out to the 1960 Republican Platform Committee. On the contrary, Chairman Percy—a businessman of good will, but limited political experience at the time—worked hard at making
his committee feel engaged in the platform-making process.
And this comradely gesture was to prove counterproductive

to the job at hand—getting a document adopted. For when on Saturday morning, July 23, it was made vividly apparent that the platform was being "dictated" from 1,000 miles away, the committee, oversold on its own importance, thrashed out at the force that was crushing its collective ego.

Second, the committee was more conservative than the party's probable presidential nominee. Nixon had taken no part in, or paid particular attention to, the selection of the Platform Committee members. Thus, by a process of natural selection, membership on the committee was often a reward for long service or financial support to the party. Many of the committee members would have been less than happy with a *Nixon* platform; when told that what they were being asked to approve was a *Rockefeller* platform, it was like waving a red cape in front of a bull.

Third, and probably most important, Nixon had underestimated or been unaware of how the public and the party would perceive the *symbolic* aspects of the "Compact"—such things as his having gone to Rockefeller, rather than Rockefeller having come to him; the "Compact" having been released by Rockefeller, not Nixon; and the wording of the "Compact" (it began, "The Vice-President and I met today at my home in New York City. The meeting took place at the Vice-President's request. . . .") Nixon felt their joint statement faithfully reflected his views; he was "genuinely surprised," he said, when it was greeted in Chicago as a "surrender." But the American people were not analyzing parallel texts. It *looked* like a surrender. And the Platform Committee members, who were prepared to make Nixon President despite some of his views, suddenly felt ashamed and angered for themselves and their candidate.

Before the fight was over, the committee had been in continuous session for 11 hours and in session for over 36 hours in a three-day period. Finally Nixon came to Chicago, and, "meeting groups of delegates on virtually a round-the-clock basis," put down the rebellion.

Then the convention quickly transacted most of its business in one four-hour meeting on Wednesday, July 27. The platform was approved and Nixon was unanimously nominated for President. Later that night the newly chosen presidential nominee called a meeting of 32 party leaders, and, after listening to their opinions, selected Henry Cabot Lodge as his running mate. Through the televised debates at the United Nations, Ambassador Lodge had become a popular figure across the country; as the vice-presidential candidate, Nixon felt, he would underscore the foreign policy experience of the Republican ticket.

The next day Rockefeller introduced the convention to its standard-bearer, "a man of courage . . . a man of vision and of judgment . . . Richard E. Nixon." Despite bobbling the middle initial, it was a graceful statement and Nixon responded with a speech which he would recall as "a high point of my campaign." As the formal kickoff of his bid for the presidency, the Republican leader told the assembled delegates:

> One hundred years ago, in this very city, Abraham Lincoln was nominated for President. . . . The question then was freedom for the slaves and survival of the nation. The question now is freedom for all mankind and the survival of civilization.
>
> We shall build a better America . . . in which we shall see the realization of the dreams of millions of people not only in America but throughout the world—for a fuller, freer, richer life than men have ever known in the history of mankind.
>
> What we must do is wage the battles for peace and freedom with the same . . . dedication with which we wage battles in war. . . . The only answer to a strategy of victory for the Communist world is a strategy of victory for the free world. Let the victory we seek . . . be the victory of freedom over tyranny, of plenty over hunger, of health over disease, in every country of the world.
>
> When Mr. Khrushchev says our grandchildren will live under Communism, let us say his grandchildren will live in freedom.
>
> Our answer to the threat of Communist revolution is renewed devotion to the great ideals of the American Revolution . . . that still live in the minds and hearts of people everywhere.
>
> I believe in the American dream, because I have seen it come true in my own life.

Abraham Lincoln was asked during the dark days of the tragic War between the States whether he thought God was on his side. His answer was, "My concern is not whether God is on our side, but whether we are on God's side." My fellow Americans, may that ever be our prayer for our country. And in that spirit—with faith in America, with faith in her ideals and in her people, I accept your nomination for President of the United States.

The *New York Times*'s banner headline proclaimed: NIXON ASKS THAT FIGHT AGAINST COMMUNISM BE WAGED ON SOCIAL AND ECONOMIC FRONTS. Less newsworthy that day—yet destined to play a major role in shaping the course of the presidential election—was another event that was reported far down the *Times*'s page. "In Hyannis Port, Mass., Senator John F. Kennedy accepted an invitation by the National Broadcasting Company to appear on eight one-hour programs with his opponent." The article went on to say that Herbert G. Klein, Nixon's press secretary, expressed the Vice-President's willingness to debate. The debate proposal was quickly picked up by the other TV networks, who offered free time to the Democrats and Republicans if Congress would suspend the rule that required giving equal time to all candidates, including those of minor parties and the crackpots who always get their names on ballots in some states. The rule suspension passed Congress during its post-convention session and was signed by President Eisenhower on August 24.

The first Gallup Poll taken after the Republican convention showed Nixon leading Kennedy, 51 to 49.

In his acceptance speech at the convention Nixon had promised that "I, personally, will carry this campaign into every one of the 50 states of this nation between now and November 8." To keep this 50-state-campaign pledge, Nixon got off to a fast start, visiting Nevada, California, Hawaii, Washington and Maine between August 2 and 13. Nixon's design was to use the month of August for appearances in a number of states that were either difficult to reach (Hawaii and Alaska) or politically predictable (Maine, Vermont, New Hampshire, Mississippi and Louisiana). This plan had to be temporarily altered when in Greensboro, North Carolina, on August 17, Nixon cracked his knee on a car door, the knee became seriously infected and the Republican campaigner was sent to Walter Reed Hospital (August 29–September 9).

The two-week enforced absence from the campaign trail gave Nixon an excuse to renege on the 50-state pledge and concentrate instead on those vote-rich industrial areas where he knew the election would be won or lost. Top advisers pleaded with him to do this. He rejected their advice with the result that in order to make up for lost time he had to intensify a campaign that already promised to be the most intense in presidential election history. Nixon's first week of campaigning after he left the hospital covered 14 states and more than 9,000 air miles. By that Sunday, he later confessed, "I could hardly pull myself out of bed." And each week thereafter the pace increased. But when Nixon flew to Alaska (three electoral votes) on the Sunday before election day, he could say that he had kept his promise—he had become the first presidential candidate to speak in every state in the union.

Some pundits would salute his stamina while questioning his wisdom. For part of the drawn and tired appearance that Nixon was to project over TV could be attributable to the frantic pace that he forced on himself. Yet ironically, as Princeton University professor Stanley Kelley, Jr., has shown, Nixon and Kennedy spent exactly the same percentage of their time in the 24 doubtful states (74 percent) and the same amount of time in those states during the last three weeks of the campaign (88 percent).[2]

From the organizational and statistical standpoint, any Democrat should have overwhelmed any Republican in the 1960 national election. Across the country, there were three registered Democrats for every two Republicans. Democrats controlled all the major power centers—the governorships, both Senate seats, all the congressmen and both houses of the legislature—in 11 states, while the Republicans enjoyed that amount of power in only one, New Hampshire. Thirty-

[2] The main difference in distribution of candidates' time, according to the Kelley study, is that Democratic vice-presidential candidate Lyndon B. Johnson spent 43.4 percent of his time in the South (where his party was to do well), while the Republican vice-presidential candidate Henry Cabot Lodge spent 47 percent of his time in the Northeast (where his party was to do poorly).

four governors were Democrats to 16 Republicans. In Congress, the Democratic majorities were 66–34 in the Senate and 280–152 in the House. Democrats dominated the legislatures in 29 states, the Republicans in seven. In 128 of the nation's 177 cities the mayors were Democrats.

It was hardly surprising then that Nixon, who had to capture five to six million Democratic votes in order to win, generally began his set speech with a "vote the man, not the party" message. In a typical example of this approach, he told an audience in Portland, Oregon, on September 13:

> . . . I am not going to begin by saying to those who are Republicans in this audience, "Vote for me because I'm a Republican and you're a Republican."
>
> I believe that when we select a President of the United States that our history tells us that the American people look not just to party labels. They look behind them. They look to the man. They look to what he stands for, and they try to determine what kind of leadership America needs, and they say, "Will this man provide the leadership America needs, and does he stand for the positions that I believe in?"

Kennedy's set speech, on the other hand, would include a phrase such as: "No Democratic candidate for the President has ever run and said, 'Parties don't matter,' because we are proud of our record. We want to be identified with it. We want to follow it." (Buffalo, September 28)[3]

Nixon's main theme was "experience." As he put it at Grand Forks, North Dakota, on September 14:

> I realize that the experience of the candidates, when you vote for President and Vice-President, will have a lot to

[3] A confidential memorandum circulated among key Democratic figures by the party's National Committee noted: "Nixon's clear association in the people's minds with the Republican party makes it of utmost importance to strengthen that association. At the beginning of 1960 the Democratic party was still close to its 1958 popularity peak. To close the three–two advantage which Democrats enjoy, Nixon must create an 'above the party' image. Democrats can prevent this by continually linking him to the unpopular policies (pro-big business, anti-farmer) of the Republican party. . . . The new Nixon must be constantly made a Republican, big-business Nixon."

do with your decision. It would not be appropriate for me to talk about my experience as compared with that of my opponent; it is appropriate for me to talk about the experience of my running mate. And I would say that I am proud that he is on the ticket with me; I would further say that I don't know of any man in the world today who has done a better job of standing up against the men of the Kremlin and representing the cause of peace and freedom than he has. . . .

The Vice-President had to defend the record of the Eisenhower administration—"when we came into office in 1953 the United States was at war. We have ended one war; we have avoided other wars; and today we do have peace and have it without surrender of principle or territory"—while pointing out that a record "is not something to stand on; it is something to build on."

But Kennedy, as the candidate of the out-party, was free to attack:

The Republican orators are fond of saying that experience in foreign policy is a major issue in this campaign. I agree. But the issue is not merely experience of the candidates. It is the experience which the whole nation has gone through in the last eight years. . . . Never before have we experienced such arrogant treatment at the hands of our enemy. Never before have we experienced such a critical decline in our prestige, driving our friends to neutralism, and neutrals to outright hostility. . . . [Alexandria, Virginia, August 24]

Over and over again the Democratic nominee repeated, "I say we can do better. . . . I say it is time to get this country moving again."

The most difficult issue for both candidates was raised by Kennedy's religion. On September 7 a Protestant group, led by the prominent clergyman Norman Vincent Peale, issued a statement charging that a Catholic President would be under "extreme pressure" from his Church's hierarchy. Five days later, during an appearance on "Meet the Press," Nixon stated that "it would be tragic . . . for this election to be determined primarily, or even substantially, on religious grounds" and that he had "issued orders to all of the people in my campaign not to discuss religion, not to raise it, not to allow anybody to participate in the campaign who does so on that ground, and as far as I am concerned, I will decline to discuss religion. . . ." [4] The next day Kennedy made his now-famous speech before the Houston Ministerial Association in which he told of his belief "in an America where the separation of Church and state is absolute. . . ."

But full and honorable statements on their positions by both candidates did not end the so-called religious issue. Part of the reason was that the bigots could not be turned off—the Fair Campaign Practices Committee reported in November that nearly 200 scurrilous anti-Catholic publications had been circulated anonymously during the campaign; and part of the reason was based on the political logic of the "Bailey-Sorensen Report."

When Kennedy had sought the Democratic vice-presidential nomination in 1956, two of his principal associates (John Bailey and Theodore Sorensen) prepared a memorandum to convince the delegates that the addition of a Catholic to the national ticket would be sound politics. "The Catholic vote," they wrote, "is far more important than its numbers—about one out of every four voters who turn out—because of its concentration in the key states and cities of the North. These are the pivotal states with large electoral votes. . . ." They concluded: "If he [Kennedy] brought into the Democratic fold only those normally Democratic Catholics who voted for Ike, he would probably swing New York, Massachusetts,

---

[4] On August 16, 1960, a memorandum was issued by Len Hall and Bob Finch, at the direction of Nixon, laying down the following guidelines:

"1. No person or organization *conditioning their support on religious grounds* will be recognized in this campaign.

"2. There should be no discussion of the 'religious issue' in any literature prepared by any volunteer group or party organization supporting the Vice-President, and no literature of this kind from any source should be made available at campaign headquarters or otherwise distributed.

"3. Staff and volunteer workers should avoid discussing the 'religious issue,' either informally or casually, since this might be construed as some kind of deliberate campaign."

Rhode Island, Connecticut, Pennsylvania and Illinois—for 132 electoral votes. If he also wins the votes of Catholics who shifted to the Republicans in 1948 or earlier, he could also swing New Jersey, Minnesota, Michigan, California, Wisconsin, Ohio, Maryland, Montana and maybe even New Hampshire—for a total of 265 electoral votes (needed to win: 266)."

Apparently still following this line of reasoning in 1960, the Democratic candidate's brother and campaign manager, Robert Kennedy, repeatedly put the question, "Did they ask my brother Joe whether he was a Catholic before he was shot down [during World War II]?"—thus inspiring such headlines as: BOB KENNEDY SCORES STRESS ON RELIGION (Cleveland *Plain Dealer*) and CREED ISSUE MUST BE MET, BOB KENNEDY SAYS HERE (Cincinnati *Enquirer*). More blatantly, Harlem Congressman Adam Clayton Powell was saying, "The Klan is riding again and . . . all bigots will vote for Nixon and all right-thinking Christian and Jews will vote for Kennedy rather than be found in the ranks of the Klan-minded." Faced with this form of "reverse bigotry," Nixon maintained silence but, as he would say later, his opponent had a "heads I win, tails you lose" proposition going for him.

On September 14 the Gallup Poll showed Kennedy had pulled into the lead, 51 to 49.

The first of the four Kennedy-Nixon television debates was held on September 26. The rules of practical politics dictated that the Vice-President should not have agreed to meet his opponent: he was the better known and he would have to be on the defensive as a representative of the party in power. "He [Nixon] had no reason to help build up an audience for Kennedy," Sorensen wrote. The explanation Nixon later gave for his action was that "the pressures for joint appearances in some form or other were irresistible" and he could not decline "to participate in a program which the majority of the American people, regardless of party, wanted to see." But there seems to us to be another, perhaps overpowering, reason why Nixon chose to debate, namely, *he was convinced he could win.* Nixon's whole career led him to this conclusion—he had been elected to Congress by outdebating his opponent in 1946; he had stayed on the ticket in 1952 by his effective use of television; he reached his highest popularity after the "Kitchen Debate" with Khrushchev in 1959. Now by combining debating and television he could impress millions of Democrats and independents (whom he could not otherwise reach) and put the election on ice.

One of the debates was to be devoted exclusively to domestic issues and one exclusively to foreign policy. Nixon, of course, wished foreign policy to have the biggest audience. He calculated that this would be the final debate and so agreed to lead off with a discussion of the domestic, an area in which the Democratic party traditionally proposes more elaborate programs than the Republican. But as the ratings would show, millions more people watched the first debate than any of the subsequent ones. Therefore, Nixon had allowed Kennedy to expose his most appealing wares to the largest audience. Yet this distinction may have been more apparent than real, for, although the candidates debated such domestic matters as the farm program, minimum wage legislation, financing of school construction and medical care for the aged, they often turned to the international ramifications of domestic questions.

Careful reading of the text of the first debate shows that neither candidate really said much or scored any clearly distinctive points. There were, however, two notable differences between them. First, as Theodore H. White has pointed out, "Mr Nixon was debating with Mr. Kennedy as if a board of judges were scoring points; he rebutted and refuted, as he went, the inconsistencies or errors of his opponent. Nixon was addressing himself to Kennedy—but Kennedy was addressing himself to the audience that was the nation." Second, there was the contrast between how the candidates looked—the handsome, healthy Kennedy and Nixon, who appeared, wrote the Baltimore *Sun*'s Thomas O'Neill, "like a picture on a post office bulletin board." The Vice-President's problem was partly technical, having to do with lighting and new tubes in the TV cameras; partly his perpetual "five o'clock shadow," which is evident even five minutes after he has shaved; and partly because he had lost ten pounds during the campaign. (Make-up and four milk shakes a day improved his appearance for the rest of the debates.) But Kennedy had done more than just present an attractive image; merely by holding his own in the verbal give-and-take he had undercut Nixon's key "experience" argument.

Aside from the effect this had on voters, the really telling impact of the first joint appearance was on the candidates, their entourages and Republican and Democratic partisans across the country. Before September 26, the Nixon camp was riding high. Huge, enthusiastic crowds were turning out for the Republican candidate, even in the Deep South, and the Nixon campaign organization was full of zest. The Kennedy campaign, on the other hand, had not yet got off the ground. At Detroit's annual Labor Day rally in Cadillac Square, the combined efforts of United Auto Workers president Walter Reuther and the other labor leaders could hardly turn out a respectable crowd for Kennedy; people everywhere seemed to have a lackadaisical attitude toward their standard-bearer and his cause.

But the candidates and their followers underwent an immediate change after the first debate. Now the Kennedy camp was jubilant, while the Nixon camp became grim and nervous and could talk only of "recouping." The next day and for days afterward, crowds turned out to see the handsome figure of the Democratic candidate in the flesh, while Republican officials descended on Nixon to see for themselves if he was as "sick" as he had appeared on the television screens. At one point, Press Secretary Herbert Klein found it necessary to issue a statement: "Mr. Nixon is in excellent health and looks good in person."

The other three debates (October 7, 13 and 21) were "won" by Nixon, according to most public opinion polls. But the rating surveys indicated that many millions of Americans only watched the first debate.[5] As Nixon's pollster, Claude Robinson, reported to him after the final confrontation be-

[5] The television industry reported that 75,000,000 people watched the first debate, while the candidates' pollsters reported privately that the figure was close to 70,000,000. On the second debate the industry figure was 62,500,000, the politicians' figure was 51,000,-000; in the third, the figure was 60,000,000, according to the industry, and 48,000,000 according to political pollsters; and on the fourth debate the spread between the industry and political pulse-takers was 70,000,000 and 48,000,000.

tween the candidates, "Voters give Nixon a little the better in stating his case in the fourth debate. . . . Kennedy, however started the campaign as the less well-known candidate and with many of his adherents wondering about his maturity. He has done a good job of dissipating the immaturity label. . . ."

Substantively, the TV debates raised no lasting issues, although two foreign policy differences were thoroughly aired. One concerned the islands of Quemoy and Matsu off the China coast. Kennedy at first called them strategically worthless and indefensible. Nixon countered: "It's the principle involved. These two islands are in the area of freedom. The [Chinese] Nationalists have these two islands. We should not force our Nationalist allies to get off them and give them to the Communists." On the second issue—Cuba—Kennedy proposed strengthening the "anti-Castro forces in exile, and in Cuba itself, who offer hope of overthrowing Castro." This, of course, was exactly what the CIA secretly was doing. Since CIA Director Allen Dulles had briefed Kennedy, Nixon assumed his opponent had no excuse for endangering a covert operation by turning it into a campaign issue. "For the first and only time in the campaign," Nixon was to write, "I got mad at Kennedy personally." (Several months after the election, Dulles said his briefing of Kennedy had included Cuba but not the training program for Cuban exiles.) To protect the rebel forces, Nixon felt he had to "go to the other extreme" and attack Kennedy's proposal as "dangerously irresponsible" and "an open invitation for Mr. Khrushchev . . . to come into Latin America. . . ." Ironically, Nixon, the strongest foe of Castro in the Eisenhower administration, was applauded by "liberal" columnists and commentators for criticizing Kennedy's proposal.

The last week in October a traffic violation arrest in Georgia created a stir in the presidential campaign. The accused, jailed for a relatively minor infraction, was the Rev. Martin Luther King, Jr. John Kennedy immediately called the civil rights leader's wife to express sympathy and concern, and Robert Kennedy dramatically inquired into King's right to bail. For his part, Nixon asked the White House to have the Justice Department determine whether King's constitutional rights had been infringed. This was done privately, without fanfare. Thus Nixon appeared mute. Kennedy campaigners, especially in Negro communities, charged Nixon with lack of interest—and worse.[6] King's father, an Atlanta clergyman, announced he would switch to Kennedy and suggested that other Republican-inclined Negroes do likewise. (The King incident may have tipped the balance in several states, including South Carolina, of all places, where a solid bloc for Kennedy in Negro precincts accounted for his 9500-vote majority.)

Earlier in the campaign Nixon refused an opportunity to generate anti-Kennedy sentiment among Negroes (and possibly ensure Republican victory in Illinois). Without Nixon's knowledge, members of his campaign organization in Chicago planned and secretly financed mass demonstrations at the Merchandise Mart to protest job discrimination in that huge business complex owned by the Kennedy family. But when Nixon got wind of that ploy he vetoed it with the comment he was running against John Kennedy and not his father or brother-in-law who operated the Chicago enterprise.

The Nixon cause, however, received a boost in the last eight days of the campaign when President Eisenhower took to the hustings. The Eisenhower-Nixon relationship had been the subject of much speculation since a presidential press conference on August 24. Eisenhower had been asked "to give us an example of a major idea of his [Nixon's] that you adopted. . . ." He replied, "If you give me a week, I might think of one." The remark was gleefully picked up by the Democrats as a graphic rejoinder to Nixon's "experience" claim. (Actually, Eisenhower's statement came at the end of the press conference when he was anxious to bring it to a close. It was supposed to mean, so he thought: "I'll

[6] According to Bruce L. Felknor of the Fair Campaign Practices Committee, "some bigoted Democrats . . . peddled, never officially, but rather widely in white communities where the tactic would clearly pay off, a flier displaying three photographs of Nixon in various poses of affection and affinity with Negroes. Some were Americans in business suits and some Africans in tribal regalia. The caption presented the devastating fact: Nixon had been a member of, and a contributor to, the NAACP for ten years."

meet with you again next week and will give you the answer then." But it was hardly surprising that his words were given a less innocent meaning.) Then Eisenhower's failure to speak out for his Vice-President during September and October caused more raised eyebrows. One psychological explanation, propounded by Theodore White and others, was that Nixon was rebelling against Ike, the father-figure—"the Nixon people," wrote White, "and Nixon himself, who had been treated like boys for so many years by the Eisenhower people, now apparently itched to operate on their own. . . ."

On October 31 Nixon went to the White House to discuss the President's participation in the closing phase of the canvass. The Democratic presidential candidate promptly accused Nixon of trying to get Eisenhower to rescue his sinking campaign. "If he can't stand up to the American people alone," Kennedy taunted on November 1, "how is he going to stand up to Mr. Khrushchev?"

What actually happened at the White House luncheon meeting on October 31 would have been sensational news at the time. Eisenhower himself, dismayed by Nixon's refusal that day to permit him to make an all-out campaign effort, learned the whole story long afterward. Neither he nor Nixon ever enlightened campaign chairman Len Hall or other Republican moguls who had expected that Monday afternoon to agree upon a victory-clinching strategy—but instead had been disappointed and angered by the strange performance of their candidate. Some, including Hall, never forgave Nixon. And eight years later Hall privately listed his peculiar surprise that climactic day at the White House among reasons for opposing the former Vice-President's 1968 bid for the Republican nomination.

The lunch started on a note of high optimism. Eisenhower, in a bouncy mood, declared he now was a soldier in the ranks, ready and willing to undertake any assignment the new commander (Nixon) proposed. Hall cheerfully acknowledged that was the kind of news he hoped to hear. Others chimed in. The country would be reassured and its morale lifted by a dramatic display of the Ike and Dick team fighting shoulder-to-shoulder, as always, suggested one strategist. Another stated the people everywhere were aching to show they still liked Ike, and thus the projected Eisenhower tour would stun the "commentators and politicians" who so fervently wanted the Eisenhower-Nixon administration repudiated. Finally campaign director Hall took from his briefcase the carefully prepared plan for intensive Eisenhower campaigning and proposed, with a chuckle, that "we get down to business" in order to uphold the reputation for political sagacity of all those around the table who had just made victory predictions. But as Hall proceeded to review the projected Eisenhower itinerary, Nixon asked if he might interrupt. Quietly, he expressed gratitude for all Eisenhower already had done in his behalf, said he believed the American people were well aware of his role as the President's associate and deputy for eight years and the continuing closeness of the Eisenhower-Nixon team, and suggested the President now could be most helpful by concentrating during the remaining campaign days on a couple of previously scheduled appearances and an election-eve broadcast to the nation. As virtually everyone in the room gasped, Nixon added that he had given considerable thought to the idea of a massive politicking drive by Eisenhower and concluded it might not be proper for the President. Nixon said he and all his associates appreciated beyond words Eisenhower's willingness to barnstorm the country for the Nixon-Lodge ticket, especially since no one knew better than the President how exhausting that sort of intensive campaigning would be. It was difficult to resist Eisenhower's offer, Nixon concluded, but on reflection he felt (and hoped) the President and his other friends in the room would appreciate Nixon's decision.

But what about Chicago? asked Eisenhower's principal political deputy, explaining that Illinois Republican leaders had been pleading for a speech there. More questions popped up. What about Detroit?—Los Angeles?—Buffalo? Nixon, responding in a near-whisper, repeated that he thought it would be unwise for the President to barnstorm. Eisenhower already had done as much as had been asked of him, he added, and the few speeches set for the concluding campaign days—especially the election-eve broadcast—should have just the impact the Republican ticket desired.

The White House session which had begun with such

enthusiasm and ebullient optimism ended in an aura of gloom. When Nixon left, Eisenhower beckoned Hall to one side and asked what was "disturbing" the Vice-President. Hall, irked to the point of despair, shrugged. Eisenhower, clearly puzzled and upset, wondered whether his Vice-President wanted to become President badly enough.

Eisenhower and Hall were unaware, of course, of a conversation Nixon had had earlier that morning with Major General Howard McC. Snyder, the President's physician, and a telephone call very late the night before from Mrs. Eisenhower to Mrs. Nixon. Mamie Eisenhower confided to Pat Nixon that she was concerned about Ike's physical condition and that she hoped the Vice-President would restrain her husband's eagerness for a vigorous campaign swing. Early the next day Snyder called Nixon to request a private visit before the White House luncheon. The doctor told Nixon that Eisenhower had not been sleeping well. A sudden surge of physical activity, like an aggressive campaign schedule, might be disastrous, in his opinion. Dr. Snyder then joined Mamie Eisenhower in asking Nixon's cooperation for the sake of Eisenhower's health and perhaps his life.

Although he was more anxious than anyone for the lift an Eisenhower campaign swing would give his election chances, Nixon had decided immediately after the Mamie Eisenhower call that the President's barnstorming plans would be nullified. And as he entered the White House that midday the biggest problem on Nixon's mind was how to dissuade the President gracefully. Secretary of Interior Fred Seaton, who was "in" on the secret, recalls Nixon well knew that Eisenhower's all-out assistance would be invaluable and perhaps even decisive, yet the Vice-President did not hesitate in making a decision not to endanger Eisenhower's life.[7]

On election eve, Dwight D. Eisenhower, speaking from a studio of the Columbia Broadcasting System in Washington,

[7] Six years later the fact of Mrs. Eisenhower's telephone call to Mrs. Nixon was revealed, in part, by Ted Lewis of the New York *Daily News*. Wrote Washington columnist Lewis in 1966: "Now at last, we know the truth. Nixon preferred to lose rather than jeopardize Ike's health."

told his countrymen, "I shall exercise my right [to vote] tomorrow, as I hope you will, also. For myself, because of my firsthand knowledge of their capacity, dedication and character, I shall vote for Richard M. Nixon and Henry Cabot Lodge, as again I hope you will." The next day, Tuesday, November 8, 1960, 68,883,341 Americans went to the polls to vote for President. It was the largest turnout in history—both in absolute figures and in percentage of potential voters. According to the recorded returns, Richard M. Nixon received 34,107,646, or 49.55 percent of the total vote; John F. Kennedy received 34,227,096, or 49.71 percent of the total vote. Thus Nixon lost by the narrowest percentage margin of any man who had ever sought the presidency.

Like so much in that election which still is subject to debate and analysis, Tom Wicker, Washington Bureau Chief of the *New York Times,* contends the result in Alabama raises doubts about which candidate really won a popular vote. "Nixon clearly got 237,981 popular votes in that unaccountable state [Alabama]," writes Wicker. "Depending on how one finally counts those Alabamians who voted for something called 'Unpledged Electors,' Kennedy got 324,050 or 318,303 or 147,295. Using the first two Kennedy totals would have given him a national popular vote plurality of either 118,000 or 113,000 (the figure usually cited); but using the lowest of the three totals—which the Democratic National Committee did in 1964 in determining the size of the Alabama delegation to the National Convention—would have given Richard Nixon a national popular vote plurality of 58,181 votes."

Nixon carried 26 states with an electoral vote of 219. Kennedy received 303 electoral votes from 23 states. The Republicans made a net gain of 21 seats in the House of Representatives and two in the Senate. In the 359 districts in which there were Republican House candidates, Nixon ran ahead of 235, or about two-thirds of the total. (On the Democratic side, 303 House candidates pulled more votes than Kennedy.) In the 34 states where there were Senate races, Nixon's percentage of the vote was higher in 27; in the 26 gubernatorial elections, Nixon ran ahead of the Republican candidate in 19 states. Over all, Nixon ran approximately 5.5 million votes ahead of the Republican party in the nation.

Len Hall's glum reaction on reading the state-by-state returns was: "But for less than 12,000 votes, *we* would have been the heroes, and *they* would have been the bums." Republican Manager Hall's exasperation was over the fact that a shift of just 11,424 in the 7,294,910 votes recorded in five states would have decided the election in Nixon's favor.

When a candidate such as Nixon loses by two-tenths of 1 percent of the total vote, dozens of theories spring up to explain the cause of defeat. And all of them, of course, could be right—or wrong.

Robert Finch, Nixon's able campaign director, said: "Conceding the worst on everything else, we still would have won if 400,000 people had not become unemployed during the last 30 days of the campaign."

President Kennedy and those intimate with his campaign were certain that the paramount factor in his victory was the television debates, especially the first one. Press Secretary Pierre Salinger told us long after the election that the Kennedy circle was surprised Nixon agreed to the joint appearances. Impressive evidence for their analysis has come from Elmo Roper, the highly respected pollster, who found in a post-election survey that 57 percent of the voters said they had been influenced to an extent by the debates, 6 percent of them— some 4,000,000 voters—decided how to cast their ballots on the basis of the television performances, and their verdict was three to one for Kennedy.

Whether the "religious issue" helped or hurt Nixon is still a matter of dispute. However, it is provable that the most pronounced switch among any identifiable group of voters occurred among Catholics, while Protestants appeared to show no marked change. According to the Gallup Poll, the Republican presidential vote among Catholics in 1960 fell 27 percentage points below the 1956 level. Just as the Theodore Sorensen–John Bailey Memorandum had claimed regarding the potential advantage of Kennedy's religion, the "swing" was most pronounced among normally Democratic Catholics in the "pivotal states" listed by Sorensen and Bailey. That "swing" provided Kennedy's winning margin in at least six of those major states which he carried by less than 1 percent of the vote. Those six states gave the Democratic ticket 106 electoral votes, nearly half the winning majority. On the other hand, the Survey Research Center of the University of Michigan estimated that Kennedy's Catholicism caused him a net loss of 1,500,000 popular votes, yet its study did not pinpoint the relationship between popular and electoral votes, and its researchers admitted at a press conference that Kennedy's religion may have helped him win the Electoral College. A report for the Republican National Committee, prepared by Stephen D. Pfleiderer, concluded: "Anti-Catholicism certainly cost Kennedy large numbers of votes. But it probably cut most deeply in states that are not among the giants in the electoral college and in one-party states in which a Democratic candidate can suffer a substantial vote loss without losing the state. If many Catholics voted for President Kennedy in order to end a custom which seemed to bar one of their faith from the highest office in the United States, their action was understandable. . . . Now that the barrier has been removed, we can expect that a false issue has been eliminated from the political arena, and that we shall never again go through a campaign like that of 1960." [8]

No election in history has been so diagnosed, reviewed and hypothesized about by so many. Why Kennedy won and Nixon lost—and the genesis of the microscopic margin of votes by which one became the victor and the other the vanquished—has been pinpointed, explained, interpreted and speculated about in an incredible variety of ways, ranging from the plausible to the ridiculous. Rehashing extraordinary campaigns and elections—the Monday-after quarterbacking of politics—is an interesting exercise that is often instructive and generally harmless. But among the collection of solutions to 1960 is one

[8] Whether Catholics voted for or against Nixon, many of them were grateful to him for the way he conducted his campaign. Richard Cardinal Cushing, Catholic Archbishop of Boston and intimate of the Kennedy family for many years, in a Baltimore speech on January 13, 1961, declared: "If I were asked to name the Goodwill Man of 1960, I would unhesitatingly give the accolade to Richard Nixon . . . During the recent campaign, which tested and taxed all his powers, physical and mental, he never exploited the religious or any other issue that would tend to divide the American people."

serious case that is certain to excite more investigative fever among future historians than it has among contemporaries. In essence there was substantial evidence of ballot-box chicanery in several states, especially in Texas and Illinois, which the Democratic ticket won by hairbreadth margins. Without the electoral votes of Texas and Illinois, Kennedy would have lost decisively and Nixon would have won.

Significantly, even in the heat of the post-election fuss about the frauds during November and December, 1960, no informed or responsible individual on either side associated John Kennedy with the skulduggery, not even by implication.

A tantalizing aspect of both the Illinois (Chicago) and the Texas cases, in fact, is that Kennedy probably benefited indirectly simply because he was a Democratic candidate on the Democratic line of voting machines and ballots. In Chicago, for instance, the prime target of Mayor Daley's powerful Democratic machine was a Republican prosecuting attorney whose aggressiveness in local law enforcement gravely threatened the Democratic machine's survival. The Daley organization's all-out efforts—employing virtually every time-proven big-city trick, from voting tombstones and floaters to spoiling Republican ballots and tallying the "votes" of those who once had lived on streets evacuated for superhighways—was a marked success. The Democratic candidate, a reliable man by the Daley machine standards, was elected prosecuting attorney and the troublesome Republican was ousted. And incidentally, the bloated Democratic majority produced so effectively in Chicago enabled the presidential ticket to win the state of Illinois by 8,858 votes (out of 4,757,409).

The Texas story differed only in terms of reference. The inspiration for its massive vote juggling was at a much higher level than local prosecuting attorney. He was Senate Majority Leader Lyndon B. Johnson, the most powerful Democrat in Washington and the most awesome politician in overwhelmingly Democratic Texas, and on the ballot in 1960, as candidate for Vice-President, on the Kennedy ticket. Organization Democrats were in command of every gear in the Lone Star State's election machinery, from precinct tally clerk to state Board of Canvassers. The state board, which ran the whole election operation in Texas and was also court of last resort on the vote tallies, was made up of three party stalwarts, two of whom happened to be managers of the Democratic campaign in Texas. Under that board's eagle eye, the election shenanigans ranged from ballot-box stuffing and jamming the Republican column on voting machines to misreading ballots cast for Republicans and double counting those for Democrats. Typical was the result in Precinct 27, Angelina County, where 86 individuals cast ballots and the officially reported vote was 148 for Kennedy-Johnson, 24 for Nixon-Lodge. That remarkable tally and thousands of others somewhat like it were approved without apparent question by the Democratic campaign managers sitting as the state's election Board of Canvassers. As officially recorded, 2,311,084 votes were cast and counted in Texas that November day, and the Kennedy-Johnson ticket was declared victorious by 46,257.

New York Times man Tom Wicker makes a noteworthy point regarding vote frauds in the foreword to Neal R. Peirce's superb book on the Electoral College, *The People's President,* published in 1968. "A shift of only 4,480 popular votes from Kennedy to Nixon in Illinois, where there were *highly plausible charges of fraud* [emphasis supplied] and 4,491 in Missouri would have given neither man an electoral majority and thrown the decision into the House of Representatives," writes Wicker. "If an additional 1,148 votes had been counted for Nixon in New Mexico, 58 from Hawaii, and 1,247 in Nevada he would have won an outright majority in the electoral college." And Wicker adds: "Any experienced reporter or politician knows that that few votes can easily be 'swung' in any state by fraud or honest error."

In a post-election report following the Kennedy-Nixon race, Richard Wilson, the veteran Washington correspondent and columnist, wrote in *Look* magazine: "For the first time, many thousands of Americans suddenly realized that elections can be stolen. They only half-believed it before 1960, as part of our historical lore. . . . Many, many thousands of voters and civic-minded people in several leading states no longer take the easygoing attitude toward election frauds." The article was entitled "How to Steal an Election."

The New York *Herald Tribune* had reached a similar conclusion earlier, on the basis of investigation by its national political correspondent.[9]

A week after the election, the *Herald Tribune* correspondent went to Austin to give a lecture at the University of Texas. While there he talked to some old friends in the Texas press corps. Never before had he seen Texas political reporters so furious—and insulting. They wanted to know, damnit, why you "self-righteous" and "overpaid" *national* political correspondents were ignoring what went on in their state. The paper's correspondent conceded he had seen handouts from Republicans hollering "fraud." But that is standard operating procedure for losers of exceedingly close elections—and usually the facts, as offered back in Washington, hardly justified the allegations. But at the prodding of his Texas colleagues, the New York newspaperman agreed to stay awhile and look around.

The Lone Star State had a poll tax. In effect, this meant a total reregistration of voters before every election. Thus the Texas enrollment books had a minimum of dead wood and floaters, and anyone could determine precisely how many were eligible to vote in each precinct, community and county just by counting names on the poll tax list.

Approximately half of the votes cast in Texas were on paper ballots. Under Texas law, there operates what is known as the "negative ballot." Voters are supposed to strike out all the candidates they do not want instead of merely checking the ones they favor. In addition to Democratic and Republican candidates, the Texas ballot in 1960 listed standard-bearers for the Prohibition and Constitution parties. It was obvious to anyone who checked them as the New York reporter did that ballots on which voters had failed to scratch out the minor party candidates were more likely to be thrown out in areas that went for Nixon than in Kennedy territory. There were the cases in Fort Bend County, for instance. In Precinct One, which recorded 458 votes for Nixon-Lodge and 350 for Kennedy-Johnson, there were 182 votes voided, while none was voided in Precinct Two, where the vote was 68-to-one for the Democrats.

An exercise in elementary arithmetic—adding and subtract-

[9] Earl Mazo, the co-author of this book.

ing—indicated that a minimum of 100,000 votes officially tallied for the Kennedy-Johnson ticket simply were non-existent. The Democrats had carried Texas by a margin of 46,000 votes, slightly less than one two-hundredths of 1 percent of all the votes counted.

In Chicago the chicanery, while old-fashioned, was more sophisticated. Mountains of sworn affadavits by poll watchers and disgruntled voters reported such incidents as these:

—Ward 4, Precinct 77: "Democratic precinct captain [name listed] voted twice, giving his name first time as James L. Williams, 4640 Drexel (signature card No. 256). This observer saw Democratic precinct captain [name listed] handing money outside the polling place."

—Ward 5, Precinct 22: "One voter [named] put six paper ballots in box."

—Ward 6, Precinct 38: "At about 10:15 A.M. the [voting machine] indicator indicated 121 votes [had been cast] after 43 persons had voted."

—Ward 4, Precinct 6: "From their behavior it is quite evident all judges in this precinct are really from the Democratic organization. One judge [named], who was classified as a Republican, told a voter to whom she was giving assistance that he must vote Democratic, even though he clearly stated that he wished to vote Republican."

—Ward 4, Precinct 6: "The name Estes Hemphill did not appear on the printed precinct register. . . . However, an Estes Hemphill was permitted to vote. [The man calling himself] Estes Hemphill stated at the polling place that he had moved from 4140 South Berkeley to 1042 East 41st Place. On a recanvass made Nov. 12, no Estes Hemphill could be located at either address. In fact, no such address as 1042 East 41st Place could be found."

Early in December, after four articles on Texas and Chicago had appeared in the *Herald Tribune,* the Vice-President invited the paper's correspondent to drop over. The writer was well aware that Nixon's office had been deluged with much more evidence and many more facts than a journalist could possibly unearth, and he assumed the Vice-President finally had resolved to take legal action in the interest of recounts and a thorough, Federally instituted investigation. But as it turned out, that was not Nixon's decision at all. In a memorandum for his personal records, which he prepared immediately after the visit with the Vice-President, the correspondent noted:

"Right off, as we shook hands, he said, 'Earl, those are interesting articles you are writing—but no one steals the presidency of the United States.'

"I thought he might be kidding. But never was a man more deadly serious. We chatted for an hour or two about the campaign, the odd vote patterns in various places, and this and that. Then, continent-by-continent, he enumerated potential international crises that could be dealt with only by the President of a united country, and not a nation torn by the kind of partisan bitterness and chaos that inevitably would result from an official challenge of the election result."

At one point Nixon said, calmly as though talking to himself: "Our country can't afford the agony of a constitutional crisis—and I damn well will not be a party to creating one just to become President or anything else." (The *Herald Tribune* series on election frauds was to have consisted of twelve articles, but Nixon successfully pleaded that it be discontinued for the sake of national unity.)

State laws governing elections vary considerably, and few are so written as to encourage election recounts. Generally, the penalty clauses provide for punishing those found guilty of participating in frauds, but the corollary remedy—that is, overturning an officially declared presidential vote count—is almost nonexistent.

It would have taken at least a year and a half to get a recount in Cook County, Illinois, and there was no procedure whatever for a losing candidate to get a recount in Texas. The odds that Nixon could have reversed the results or thrown the election into the House of Representatives were extremely long. However, the pressure on Nixon, as party leader, to make a case that the Republicans could carry into the 1962 and 1964 elections was formidable. But Nixon's mind was made up.

Both Vice-President Nixon and President-elect Kennedy took Florida vacations after the grueling campaign. (Nixon had traveled 65,000 miles through 50 states; Kennedy had

traveled 44,000 miles in 45 states.) On November 14 they
met at Nixon's hotel on Key Biscayne. Because of the closeness of the election, Kennedy said, he planned to put some
Republicans in his administration. Perhaps Nixon might wish
to undertake a foreign assignment on a temporary basis?
Nixon declined. "I sensed that he was considerably relieved
when I answered his suggestion in this way," Nixon recalled.
"He readily dropped the subject."

Nixon's last official duty as Vice-President was to preside
with Speaker Rayburn over a joint session of Congress on
January 6, 1961, and announce the results of the Electoral
College.

> Mr. Speaker [said Nixon] . . . This is the first time in
> 100 years that a candidate for the presidency announced
> the result of an election in which he was defeated and
> announced the victory of his opponent. I do not think we
> could have a more striking and eloquent example of the
> stability of our constitutional system and of the proud tra-
> dition of the American people of developing, respecting
> and honoring institutions of self-government.
>
> In our campaigns, no matter how hard fought they may
> be, no matter how close the election may turn out to be,
> those who lose accept the verdict, and support those who
> win. And I would like to add that, having served now in
> government for 14 years . . . as I complete that period it
> is indeed a very great honor to me to extend to my col-
> leagues in the House and Senate on both sides of the aisle
> who have been elected—to extend to John F. Kennedy and
> Lyndon Johnson, who have been elected President and
> Vice-President of the United States, my heartfelt best
> wishes, as all of you work in a cause that is bigger than
> any man's ambition, greater than any party. It is the cause
> of freedom, of justice and peace for all mankind.
>
> It is in that spirit that I now declare that John F. Ken-
> nedy has been elected President of the United States, and
> Lyndon B. Johnson, Vice-President of the United States.

17 ❊ *Private Citizen, 1961*

AT midday on January 20, 1961, Vice-President Nixon became a private citizen, without public office or responsibility, for the first time in 14 years.

He drove to the inauguration ceremony with his successor, Lyndon Johnson, and Mrs. Nixon with hers, Mrs. Johnson. There was a spirit of good will in both limousines. Mrs. Johnson spoke of what a great responsibility she was undertaking and said she would have to call Mrs. Nixon for some pointers; Mrs. Nixon replied that she would be happy to oblige. Both women were well aware that no calls would ever be made by either, in the opinion of another occupant of the limousine.

On the platform in front of the Capitol Nixon heard his recent rival tell the American people, "Let us begin," and when the ceremonies ended he was the first to shake hands with the new President and wish him well. Then, as the gay, victorious Democrats queued up for the gala parade to the White House, Mr. and Mrs. Eisenhower and Mr. and Mrs. Nixon went off to a farewell luncheon at a private club on F Street. The next day the Nixons left for a vacation in the Bahamas. They had often talked about taking a long, lazy vacation someday. Now the "day" had come—but the vacation ended abruptly in less than two weeks because Nixon simply could not stand the idleness.

The first decision that the unemployed former Vice-President was going to have to make was how would he earn a living. The offers were numerous. Universities and colleges, foundations and businesses asked him to become their president. One offer to head a large business enterprise included the lure of over a half-million dollars in gilt-edged securities. But after canvassing the opportunities, Nixon concluded that if he were to have the time and freedom to participate in public affairs, the practice of law gave him most latitude.

So in March he joined the Los Angeles firm of Adams, Duque & Hazeltine, whose senior partner, Earl C. Adams, had originally offered Nixon a position in 1946 and who had been a contributor to the famous fund that became an issue in the 1952 presidential election. The law firm's clients included such corporate giants as the American Express Company, Rexall Drug, Metropolitan Life Insurance and the Prudential Insurance Company. Rather than become a partner, however, Nixon's position was to be "of counsel," which meant that he could choose his own clients and apportion his time as he saw fit.

The greatest advantage of private life, Nixon felt, was that he would have more time to spend with his family. Only a few close friends knew what a blow the 1960 election had been to the candidate's two children. Julie, then 12, had looked forward with all the passion of her heart to a triumph for her father, yet the last month of the campaign was an unending torture. A few classmates taunted her with the most virulent political attacks on the father she adored. She put up a brave front at school, then at home she wept as though her heart would break. Tricia was enduring a somewhat similar ordeal in her class and so was seldom in a mood to be sympathetic with her younger sister.

The Nixons' move west was made at the end of the school year. Their English Tudor house in Washington was sold—for $101,000, the same amount they had put into it—and they sublet another English Tudor in Los Angeles from movie director Walter Lang until construction was completed on a house they were building in Trousdale Estates, overlooking Beverly Hills. The Lang house had a large swimming pool and Dick Nixon learned to his chagrin that both his teen-age daughters could beat him in a race across it.

After the disastrous Bay of Pigs landing in April, the White House phoned Nixon's home to invite him to meet with the President. The Republican leader was out; when he returned, there was a note on his desk from Tricia: "Dear Daddy, I knew it would happen! JFK called and wants you to come down to see him. I knew he would have to come begging for your help." At the 75-minute meeting, Kennedy asked Nixon, "What would you do now in Cuba?" "I would find a proper legal cover and I would go in," Nixon answered. He then suggested to the President three possible legal justifications for taking such action: "One, a new definition of aggression, based on the premise that Soviet-bloc equipment was used by the Castro forces, and that we had an obligation to see that the Freedom Forces were at least equally supplied; second, send American forces in under our treaty right because of the potential threat to Guantánamo; third, send American forces in to protect the lives and rights of the several thousand American citizens still living in Cuba." (Years later Nixon wrote that there were two major lessons to be learned from the Bay of Pigs: "First, when a decision has been made to commit American prestige, we must be prepared to commit an adequate amount of American power. . . . Second, American foreign policy must always be directed by the security interests of the United States, and not by some vague concept of 'world public opinion.' ")

Nixon withheld his public comments on the new administration for the traditional 100-day honeymoon period. Then in May he made his first speaking tour since the election with stops in Chicago, Detroit, Des Moines, Columbus and Oklahoma City. He called for a summit meeting between Kennedy and Khrushchev and sharply criticized Democratic farm programs and the so-called Tractors-for-Cubans deal, which he said was not only morally wrong, but would establish a bad precedent—"If we go down this road with Castro, every tinhorn dictator in the world is going to be encouraged to shake down the United States by asking ransom for political prisoners he now has or may acquire."

He also told the Republican Citizens League of Illinois that "there is no question in my mind that a majority of the voters actually would have supported us [Nixon-Lodge in 1960] if we had had an organization equal to that of our opponents in the key states and in the big cities. Such an organization in the future will assure victory for our cause." As the titular leader, the meaningless title given to a party's last presidential candidate, Nixon was obviously anxious to apply his talent to rebuilding the G.O.P.'s fortunes. But his speaking tour illustrated a problem. He told the Executives' Club of Chicago that the members of his party who hold elective offices understandably believe that they, rather than he, should speak for the party. "I shall speak," Nixon said, "as a private citizen." Yet, as he interpolated in his Des Moines text, "This country has an investment in me, an investment in my experience on which I'll owe interest the rest of my life." This then was Nixon's dilemma: Could he maintain a meaningful leadership role without a meaningful leadership position? The question would haunt him in the months ahead.

Although the size and enthusiasm of the crowds that greeted him in May were amazing, for private citizen Nixon the trip was in sharp contrast to the way he had once traveled as presidential candidate Nixon or Vice-President Nixon. Instead of Air Force planes or chartered flights, he now flew commercial; no advance men smoothed his way through the masses of well-wishers; no Secret Service men held back the autograph-seekers. For the most part, Nixon had to fend for himself. Alan Otten, of the *Wall Street Journal,* when interviewing him in his suite at the Savery Hotel in Des Moines, noted that on the wall behind the Republican leader hung a large, colored picture of John F. Kennedy. "In this and an infinite number of other ways, some subtle and some blunt," Otten reported, "Mr. Nixon is reminded constantly of the power and the glory he so narrowly missed."

Besides those he might reach through public speaking, another avenue to potential influence opened up for Nixon that May when he signed a contract to become a newspaper columnist. The Los Angeles Times-Mirror Syndicate agreed to pay $40,000 for ten articles. (Ultimately Nixon wrote an eleventh as a "bonus.") These columns, which appeared in major newspapers around the country between June 20, 1961, and April 6, 1962, illuminated Nixon's views and, also importantly, the various roles he saw himself playing in the polity.

The first column, headlined NIXON WARNS U.S. NOT TO FALTER IN FIRM STAND ON BERLIN, was aimed at an audience of one—John F. Kennedy. Nixon was worried that speeches by Democratic Senate leaders in favor of making Berlin a "free city" were meant to be an administration trial balloon. Thus Nixon was using his new forum to say to the President, in effect, if you accept this proposal I will do my best to mobilize public opinion against you. The next month, when Kennedy issued a stern warning to Khrushchev on Berlin, the Republican leader put out a statement calling for its support by "all Americans regardless of party."

In his second column, Nixon used his newspaper space to back Kennedy in an area that has always had relatively little popular appeal—long-range funding of foreign aid. "A year-to-year basis is inadequate, inefficient and outmoded," Nixon argued. "Long-range programs are necessary to insure more efficient and adequate planning, to obtain better qualified personnel to administer the programs, and to enable our negotiators to compete on more equal terms with the Communists who have no inhibitions whatever when it comes to promising aid over a multi-year period." Nixon had some disagreement with the Democratic administration on this issue, but basically, he concluded, "If we continue to treat the [foreign aid] program as a stepchild of diplomacy, it will never really be effective. We must begin to view foreign aid as a respected arm of our nation's power."

Three days later columnist Nixon returned to his role as leader of the opposition party and gave Kennedy a terrific lashing for his actions in Laos and Cuba and for what he called "a Hamlet-like psychosis which seems to paralyze" the administration in the field of foreign policy.

Other columns, reflecting Nixon's primary interest in international relations, were devoted to the debate over the admission of Communist China to the United Nations ("The United States is not responsible for keeping Red China out of the UN. The Red Chinese government, by its own words and deeds, has disqualified itself for membership in an organization of peace-loving nations. . . . Communist China, by any yardstick of measure, is an unrepentant aggressor nation. As such, it does not meet the charter requirements for membership in the UN"); the fighting in the Congo (proposing a federation of the Tshombe, Adoula and Gizenga governments as "a workable, logical first step in bringing peace and stable government to the Congo"); East-West trade ("Trading with the Communists is like playing cards with a stacked deck. Almost everything that the Soviets sell to our allies is available or can be produced in the free world. The reverse is not true. The Communists are far more dependent on what they can buy from us than [the free world is on] what our allies get from them"); the financial crisis in the United Nations ("The UN is financially sick today because many countries refuse to pay their share for operations that they oppose, such as in the Congo and the Middle East. This is like a child saying that if you won't play my game I'll take my marbles and go home. . . . The UN is a club and morally it should act like a club. In any club a member who is in arrears is posted and loses his right to vote. A club member always has the right to withdraw from the club, but not to refuse payment for duly-approved assessments. . . . The United Nations is not Utopia, but it is worth saving"); and what Nixon called "moral neutralism" (". . . we are fed to the teeth with some neutral leaders . . . who try to blackmail us by threatening that if we don't give them everything they want they will turn to the Communists . . . being perhaps painfully blunt, if it weren't for the military strength of the United States and our allies, no nation in the world could be neutral today. They would all be Communist. Neutralism is a luxury that someone must be strong enough to defend against the predatory raids of Communist aggressors").

As Nixon's personal involvement in California politics mounted, his newspaper writings turned more to domestic affairs. In a column devoted to the John Birch Society he accused Robert Welch, its founder, of "irresponsible tactics . . . [that] have hurt the fight against Communism" and called Welsh "a would-be dictator." In another column, which Nixon viewed as the other side of the same question, he proposed "a responsible attack upon Communism and Communist influence within the United States."

Writing, he found, was strangely fascinating; difficult, yet satisfying. In June, 1961, novelist Adela Rogers St. John persuaded him to do a book. Mrs. St. John had been a friend and booster of Nixon's since he was her grocery boy in Whittier. The project was not planned as the conventional politician's memoirs, but would be an analysis of six crises in which he was a major participant—the Hiss Case, the fund episode during the 1952 presidential campaign, President Eisenhower's illnesses, the mob attacks during the Vice-President's 1958 trip to Latin America, the "Kitchen Debate" with Khrushchev in Moscow and his race for the presidency.

Nixon's book-writing technique was unique. He never went near a typewriter. Rather he scribbled notes and phrases on large, yellow lawyer's pads; then dictated the finished product into a machine. Even with the assistance of researcher Alvin Moscow, *Six Crises* took seven months to complete, nearly twice as long as Nixon expected. On several occasions he secluded himself in the desert town of Apple Valley or at Trancus Beach in order to concentrate completely on the book. This was productive, but often hazardous. Twice he forgot his key and had to climb a fence to get into his cottage; another time he lost Checkers while walking along the beach at night and ran for about a mile before finding his famous dog, sitting at the water's edge, waiting.

When *Six Crises* was published in late March, 1962, it became an immediate best-seller, as expected. The finished product—460 large pages—was part autobiography, part exposition on current political issues and part an effort "to distill out of my experience a few general principles on the 'crisis syndrome.'" Putting the highlights of Nixon's career in a crisis context was something of a gimmick and not very useful, but the success of Nixon writing about Nixon was another matter and hotly debated by reviewers. Tom Wicker in the *New York Times* thought *Six Crises* "a remarkably readable book," but felt "it offers almost no answer at all to the question that has hung from the beginning over his [Nixon's] head: what kind of a man is he?" In Wicker's opinion, "The book's great lack . . . is any significant disclosures about Nixon the man, what he really felt, thought, believed, what he really was." Yet reading the same book, radio reporter William Costello, who had authored a hostile biography of Nixon, said in the *New Republic* that it was "a stark revelation of the restless, frustrated diffident psyche of the protagonist." The former Vice-President, to Costello, "wraps himself in a cloak of masochism" and "is never unaware of nameless, faceless enemies waiting to pounce."

Generally though, reviewers agreed with David Rees, who stated in the *Spectator* (London) that Nixon's opus was "both a well-written book of memoirs and an indispensable and interesting source for anyone concerned with the climacterics of American politics between 1948 and the election of 1960." Probably the most accurate up-close assessment was made by Dr. Alexander Heard, then of the University of North Carolina. "Like its author," he wrote in *Political Science Quarterly,* "*Six Crises* is complex and interesting, a lot more so than most autobiographies written by defeated candidates."

Describing the state that Richard Nixon returned to in 1961, Lord Bryce once said, "California, more than any other part of the Union, is a country by itself." Its hundred million acres were compressed within natural boundaries—forests on the north, desert on the south, water on the west, mountains on the east. Its land mass stretched the equivalent of from Boston to Charleston, South Carolina, or from Amsterdam to Rome. In gross national product it exceeded all but eight nations in the world.

Every minute California's population increased by one new resident; 1,460 new Californians a day; enough new citizens each year to fill a city the size of Oakland or San Diego. It would become the nation's most populous state by the end of 1962; by the end of the century, so said the California Department of Health, its population would be 50 million.

If California could have been one nation, it also could have been two states, divided east to west, at the Tehachapis. The state was a study in contrasts. Geographically, it contained both the highest and lowest points in the continental United States. It had some of the flavor of Western rugged individualism while accepting 20 cents of every federal dollar spent on defense contracts. It had burgeoning cities and lonely ghost towns, such as Bodie, which once maintained two burying grounds, one for "decent folk," the other, much larger, for the rest.

The majority of Californians lived in the southern third of the state. The population of Los Angeles County alone exceeded that of 42 of the 50 states. As a rule of thumb, southern California was considered Republican and northern California Democratic, but above all, California voters were fickle and unpredictable.

Governing such a state under any circumstances would have been a challenge. But what made the job infinitely more painful were the "reforms" that Hiram Johnson put through at the beginning of the century. Elected Governor in 1910, he devoted his two terms to scrambling party lines and instituting a series of structural changes designed to insure that future Californians would be uncorrupted by meaningful political parties. The Johnson program included: the direct primary, with a prohibition on preprimary endorsements by political parties; the referendum, initiative and recall; nonpartisan local elections; the almost complete elimination of patronage; and cross-filing, which, as we have seen, permitted a candidate to enter the primaries of both parties at the same time and was finally abolished in 1958.

Under this nonparty system, there sprang up in California a type of politics that was based, to a large extent, on individual personalities—on men who, in a sense, were parties unto themselves. Foremost of these figures was Earl Warren, who was elected Governor in 1942, won both party nominations for re-election in 1946 and in 1950 captured 65 percent of the vote to become the only three-term Governor in California history.

Also in 1950 Goodwin J. Knight, once a hard-rock miner, was re-elected lieutenant governor after abandoning plans to oppose Warren, whom he considered too liberal. Congressman Nixon was elevated to the U.S. Senate that year, where he joined Senator William F. Knowland of the conservative Oakland *Tribune* family, who had been appointed in 1945 by Warren. The only Democrat in the whole state to hold major office was Attorney General Edmund G. (Pat) Brown.

When Nixon was elected Vice-President in 1952, his Senate seat was filled by State Controller Thomas H. Kuchel, a Warren protégé; and, when Warren was made Chief Justice of the United States in 1953, Goodie Knight stepped into the Governor's chair, proving, once in power, to be even more liberal than his predecessor. Knowland, Knight, Nixon and Kuchel were all re-elected between 1952 and 1956. The Republican party was in the presumably happy position of an impresario with too many stars.

But when Knowland came charging home from Washington in 1958, intent on wresting the governorship from Knight as a launching pad for his presidential ambitions, he triggered a chain reaction of seriocomic catastrophes: Knowland bumped Knight into the Senate primary, where Knight bumped San Francisco Mayor George Christopher. Then both Knowland and Knight were mauled in the general election, helped by a divisive right-to-work law on the ballot. Pat Brown, the inoffensive son of a poker-parlor operator, became Governor by a million votes; Democrats gained control of the legislature for the first time since 1888 and their popular vote margin was the largest won by either party since 1883.

Thus were California Republicans, dispirited and divided, contemplating another gubernatorial election when Richard Nixon returned to his home state, which he had carried against Kennedy by 35,000 votes. To many party officials and legislators, the former Vice-President was the logical choice to head their ticket. As Murray Chotiner said in early July, "There is a very definite, strong feeling on the part of most informed people [in the California Republican party] that he should run for Governor. He is our strongest candidate and in politics you run your strongest candidate." Pressures on Nixon increased as the election year drew closer.

Nixon, however, did not want to run. "I do not look on the governorship of California as an office I want or need as an ego-builder, or as a steppingstone to the presidency," he said. Private life had some real attractions. In setting up arrangements for his income taxes he suddenly realized that he would earn more during his first year out of office than his total earnings during 14 years as Vice-President, Senator and Representative. Besides his handsome new four-bedroom home, the swimming pool, the sleek Starfire Oldsmobile convertible with all the "extras" (including air conditioning), Nixon's post-Washington year had produced an unexpected satisfaction—he shot a hole in one! (Not an avid golfer, Nixon made this memorable shot with a No. 5 iron on the 155-yard third hole at the Bel Air Country Club.) He knew that a race against Pat Brown would not be easy, although those around him tended to deprecate the Governor as a wishy-washy bumbler. Early summer polls showed Nixon leading Brown by 53 to 37 with 10 percent undecided, yet the Democrats held a 1.3-million advantage in voter registration. Then, too, Nixon's personal tastes were oriented away from state issues; it was the national and international arena that he found most stimulating. But this had nothing to do with status or prestige. While some of his friends questioned whether the former Vice-President should "step down in class," Nixon never bothered himself with this notion.

His decision, Nixon told state party leaders, would be made by the end of September. This early announcement would give other contenders plenty of time to make their case if he should decide against the running.

Combined with the growing pressure from California Republicans, Nixon was being counseled to run by many national leaders. General Eisenhower urged him to make the race as a matter of duty; he said that the polls clearly indicated a majority of Californians wanted an opportunity to choose between him and Brown. Others, such as Len Hall and Barry Goldwater, told him that his influence would wane without a public office. Chotiner, in an interview with David S. Broder, of the Washington *Star,* said he doubted Nixon could stay in the forefront of Republican affairs "unless he runs for Governor or does something else to keep himself before the public. Making speeches, writing articles and publishing a book aren't enough." [1]

Moreover, if Nixon was to continue to have a national influence, he would have to have an office staff to handle the mounting mail and to provide other logistical support. But Nixon did not have the personal wealth necessary to underwrite such an operation and his major 1960 money-raisers told him that it would be impossible to get contributions for a noncandidate.

Possibly the most important factor in Nixon's painful decision was what James Bassett, of the Los Angeles *Times,* called

[1] Senator Hugh Scott, of Pennsylvania, recalls that Nixon held a meeting of 21 political friends and asked them if he should run. Twenty-one, including Scott, said he should.

"1961's most popular political syllogism." As the astute Bassett put it:

> He needs a forum if he is to retain any semblance of national party leadership.
> California's governorship is such a forum.
> But this would eliminate him from the '64 GOP nomination—by his own admission.
> Since President Kennedy's re-election seems fairly predictable at this juncture, that wouldn't be too hard to renounce, anyhow.
> And if Nixon were re-elected governor [in 1966], in 1968 with Mr. Kennedy finally out of the picture, he'd be a prime national candidate and still in his politically vigorous mid-50's.
> Of course, any such reasoning requires counting a great many chickens for which the eggs haven't yet been laid, much less hatched.

If Nixon was thinking along these lines, which seems likely, the grand irony of the 1962 gubernatorial race, as we shall see, may have been that while the Democrats were successfully attacking him for trying to use Sacramento as a vehicle for a second confrontation with Kennedy in 1964, this was exactly what Nixon was trying to avoid.

Nixon's rule is never to make an important decision before it is necessary. He announced his decision about the Governor's race on Wednesday, September 27, 1961. The night before, Nixon went to dinner at a Los Angeles fish restaurant with some close friends. Those at his table felt Nixon had not finally resolved what to do. When informally polled, three of his dinner companions thought he would run and two felt he would not.

Later that night Nixon called a family council. He outlined the pros and cons. Mrs. Nixon said she would go along with whatever he wanted to do; Julie said she would also; and Tricia, 15, snapped, "Let's show them, Daddy—let's run."

Upon taking his daughter's advice, Nixon started to figure out whom to notify ahead of the formal announcement. When the "must" list of friends approached the 100 mark, he felt it would be impossible to call any without calling all and resolved to notify personally only General Eisenhower and Kyle Palmer, a retired newspaperman, who was one of his oldest friends and was critically ill. Nixon had some fun outlining his position to Eisenhower in terms of his recent hole-in-one. "I told him I made it by not thinking about the last hole [meaning the 1960 election] nor the next [the 1964 election]. But by concentrating on the one immediately ahead I put together a perfect swing—and that's exactly what I am going to do in 1962."

Later, in making his decision public, Nixon said, in part:

I shall be a candidate for Governor of the State of California in 1962.

In making this announcement, I base it on several circumstances, a few of which I would like to share with this group tonight.

First, there is a selfish reason: I often hear it said that it is a sacrifice for men or women to serve in public life. For me, I have found it to be the other way around. On my return to private life, I have found that, from a salary standpoint, the income has been beyond anything I could ever have dreamed. And I have found, of course, other things in private life that are very attractive.

But after 14 years as a congressman, as a Senator and as Vice-President of the United States, I find that my heart is not there—it is in public service. I want to be in public service.

And I have concluded that, as far as my present opportunities are concerned, the most challenging, the most exciting position that I can seek, and in which I could serve, next to being President of the United States, is to be Governor of what will be the first state in the nation.

Commenting on Nixon's return to the political battlefield, columnist James Reston wrote, "Savage or not, politics is like booze and women: dangerous but incomparably exciting. . . ."

18 ✵ *Gubernatorial Campaign, 1962*

HARDLY had Nixon thrown his hat in the ring than Democrats and Republicans began taking pot shots at it. Said State Attorney General Stanley Mosk, a Democrat: "Californians will hardly be flattered to have their governorship considered Nixon's consolation prize, a vehicle to satisfy his personal ambitions." Said Assembly Minority Leader Joseph Shell, a Republican: "Nixon has no working knowledge of the governorship because he has been occupied with national and international affairs since 1952."

Mosk's statement was predictable and could be brushed aside by a seasoned campaigner like Nixon. But Shell posed an entirely new problem—a serious revolt from the conservatives within Nixon's own party.

Joe Shell would be Nixon's main opponent in the Republican primary election of June 5, 1962. Although Hearst columnist Bob Considine dismissed him as "somewhat to the right of William McKinley politically," Shell had some important attributes as a candidate. He was a blond, ruggedly handsome, former Rose Bowl football star, who flew his own plane to political rallies. Moreover, his father-in-law was an oil tycoon: he would not falter for lack of money.

Nixon's strategy during the next eight months was to ignore Shell and direct all his fire at Governor Brown. "It has always been my belief that the best way for a candidate to prove that he is worthy of his party's nomination," Nixon said, "is by demonstrating how well he can campaign against the man he will have to beat in November—rather than by attacking a fellow Republican."

But what Shell represented was a very real threat to Nixon's ultimate success even if Shell himself was not. The former Vice-President had been one of the first Republican leaders to speak out against the John Birch Society. In March, 1962, he told the convention of an important political organization: "The California Republican Assembly, acting in the great tradition of our party for individual liberties and civil rights, should use this opportunity to repudiate, once and for all, Robert Welch and those who accept his leadership and viewpoints." Then, too, Nixon had joined Pat Brown in urging defeat of the Francis Amendment, a ballot proposition which was designed "to combat the Communist menace in California" and which allowed a wide assortment of groups and individuals to designate who was a "subversive." Nixon thought the right-wing-sponsored measure was clearly unconstitutional and did not hesitate to say so. Suddenly, Nixon, whose national career was initially based on his investigation of Alger Hiss and who had been the American Communist party's favorite target for years, found himself being branded as "soft on Communism." He even had to issue a statement defending his membership in the Council on Foreign Relations! Nixon, however, was hardly in a mood to laugh at the irony. For it is a rule of thumb in California politics that a Republican can win statewide office only by holding 90 percent of his own party's registered voters and gaining 20 percent of the Democratic vote. This meant Nixon would need the almost unanimous support of ideological conservatives to defeat Brown.

In the June primary Nixon won over Shell by a two-to-one margin, but as his research staff told him, he would have to get 75 percent of the Shell vote to capture the governorship. So, in an attempt to woo the right flank of his party, Nixon proposed a "responsible" program to deal with internal Communism. For example, in a statewide radio broadcast entitled "Twelve Goals for Californians," which Nixon delivered on October 28, he listed Goal Number Eight as "Fighting Communism":

Especially at a time when the Communists have stepped up their activities abroad—in Cuba, Berlin and Southeast

Asia—our goal in California must be to intensify our opposition to Communism at home.

We owe our young people the best education in the
nation on the meaning and tactics of Communism and the
alternatives of freedom.

I also believe that we should not dignify Communists
with a forum on the campuses of our tax-supported colleges
and universities. It is a Communist tactic to lie to further
his cause, just as Khrushchev and Gromyko lied to our
President about the Soviet missile build-up in Cuba. A free
educational system, dedicated to the truth, should have no
place for speakers who vow to overthrow our Constitution
by any means that serve their ends.

For this reason, I favor barring from our state campuses
any individuals who refuse to testify before a legislative
committee investigating Communism or who refuse to
comply with the Subversive Activities Control Act of 1951,
the basic anti-Communist law of the land, which I helped
to write.

Nixon had reason to believe that this was an appealing issue
to stress. A private survey of 1,000—a good-sized sampling
for a state poll—concluded, "Especially in California, there
is a very strong feeling that America is threatened from
within by Communism as much as from outside." (Eighty-
one percent agreed with this proposition, 15 percent disagreed, and agreement was even higher among Republicans.)
"Nixon's audiences, indifferent when he talks about lumber,
fish and game, or other so-called state issues, come to life
when he discusses Communism," wrote Peter Kaye, who covered the Republican candidate for the San Diego *Union*. This
may have been the way it looked to Nixon at the time, but
in retrospect, his proposals failed to mollify the extreme right,
while they had quite another effect on many independents,
who viewed Nixon's emphasis on fighting Communism as a
scarcely credible issue for a state candidate. (Communist
party functionary Dorothy R. Healey later wrote, "The campaign cry of 'soft on Communism' did as much for Nixon in
1962 as 'Rum, Romanism and Rebellion' did for Blaine in
1884!")

Unlike the presidential race in which Nixon had to defend the administration, he was now free to attack, to exploit the weak spots in the incumbent's record. What he found, however, was that while Pat Brown may have been an inconsequential man, he was a very adequate Governor. His record was good in education and highways, superb in solving the state's complex water problem. During three years in office he had laid the basis for constructing a huge system to carry water from the mountains in the north, through the San Joaquin Valley, over the Tehachapis, to the parched metropolitan areas in the south. Furthermore, the Brown administration had been virtually scandal-free. The best example of shenanigans that the Republicans could find was a contract to a "political crony" of the Governor's to operate Squaw Valley State Park, which, in the opinion of GOP Chairman John Krehbiel, resulted "in the taxpayers taking a $900,000 beating."

Therefore, Nixon, instead of going into the campaign with a dramatic, blockbuster issue, had to base his attack on a cluster of smaller issues, which he hoped could be made to add up to one big issue. Nixon's basic campaign speech declared:

> In the next four years my goal is to make California the first state in crime prevention; first in waste-free, low-tax government; first in jobs. . . .
> What is the record of the present state administration?
> Instead of being first in crime prevention, California is now first in crimes committed. Today, according to the FBI, there are more major crimes in California than in New York, Pennsylvania and New Jersey together—states whose combined population is twice as large as California's.
> Instead of being first in waste-free, low-tax government, California is now first in the cost of government, which has forced upon our people the heaviest tax burden in the nation. The present state administration has given California the greatest tax increase in history—nearly one billion dollars in four years.
> Instead of being first in jobs, unemployment in California rose 44.8 percent in the past three years. Our state now has

the worst record of business failures of all the major industrial states and the worst record of bankruptcies in the nation.

All of which, Nixon reminded his audiences, created a "leadership gap" in Sacramento.

Because the Democrats were counterattacking Nixon for not being familiar with state problems, he felt it necessary to go well beyond the purview of most gubernatorial candidates in spelling out a detailed platform. By election day he had proposed 21 "Programs for a Greater California," ranging in scope from freeway construction and rapid transit to revitalizing the motion picture industry, from saving $27 million on welfare costs to setting up an organization to use retired persons to help train school dropouts, from agriculture to drug addiction, from traffic safety to government reorganization.

At the same time, Nixon tried to turn his years in Washington into an advantage. "I want to meet head-on tonight the charge that because of my experience in national and international affairs I am somehow or other less qualified to run for Governor of California," he told a meeting of precinct workers in Sacramento. "I want to plead guilty to my experience in national and international affairs."

> California no longer stands on the shores of the Pacific in isolation [Nixon continued]. The decisions made in Washington, in London, in Paris and in Moscow influence the welfare of the people of California—sometimes indirectly and sometimes directly—and I think the people of California want a Governor who has knowledge of what is going on in the world, beyond the borders of our state. . . .

He talked of missile and aircraft production, of the tariff and federal welfare programs, and reminded listeners that there is no better training ground than Washington, D.C., for an awareness of the "urgent need to return power and responsibility [to] where they belong in a free society—to the states and cities and private citizens."

A poll taken by Belden Associates of Dallas in mid-1962 showed that when Californians were asked for whom they voted in 1960, 42 percent said Kennedy, 37 percent said

Nixon. *But Nixon had carried the state.* As the poll pointed out, "This involves neither an error in sampling, or a deliberate falsehood on the part of the respondent[s]; rather, it demonstrates a desire for rapport with 'the winner.'" Pat Brown's private polls contained similar results. When Californians were asked to choose between Nixon and Kennedy in 1964, the President was the overwhelming winner. "There is no doubt," concluded the polling organization of Louis Harris and Associates, "that as long as Richard Nixon is unable to shake himself loose from appearing to be Kennedy's 1964 opponent for the presidency, a direct Kennedy-Nixon comparison will invariably put Nixon in one of his most unfavorable lights." This report, based on 1,002 interviews made in August, bears special attention because of the degree to which its recommendations coincided with the Democratic strategy. Here is the heart of the Harris proposals to Brown:

> . . . the charge that Nixon is interested in running for Governor to use that office solely as a steppingstone for the presidency has a resiliency and effectiveness. It adds up to an indirect charge that Nixon is not sincere as a person, but it gears it to a specific act on his part, namely his race for Governor. It also allows the Democrats to charge that Nixon is not interested in California and the problems of the state. It also allows Brown to maneuver Nixon into making the 1962 gubernatorial election a rerun of the 1960 presidential election, except that this time Kennedy holds a 62–38 percent lead.

We specifically tested this proposition in this survey. We asked voters if they thought Nixon were primarily interested in serving as Governor of California or in preparing another run for the White House. Here is what we found:

NIXON'S PRIME INTERESTS

	Total Voters %
Serving as Governor of California	36
Running for President	64
Not sure	(15)

By a clear 64–36 percent count, the voters have not been sold at all on the proposition that Richard Nixon is genuinely interested in the state or the job of Governor. Part of the reason is that he has been so widely identified with national and international problems that this part of his reputation is today fighting his efforts to identify with California issues, as the following table indicates:

NIXON'S GENUINE INTERESTS

	Total Voters
	%
California problems	37
National and international problems	63
Not sure	(19)

Here the margin only varies by one percentage point. Clearly, Nixon is not thought to be interested primarily in California problems.

The three sets of facts all check out with remarkable uniformity. Nixon is really using the governorship as a stepping-stone, he is not really interested in state problems and he is not really interested in serving as Governor of the state.

What they add up to is that Richard Nixon is out for himself, trying to get the voters of the state to allow themselves to be used for his own ambition and his own schemes of achieving power. This charge can be made by top Democratic party spokesmen first, and then should be picked up late in the campaign by Governor Brown, especially when he is campaigning with President Kennedy. Brown should turn to Kennedy on the platform and say that Nixon's real aim is not to serve as a Governor of California and to meet the very real problems facing the people of the state, but rather to run against this man, John F. Kennedy. Brown can then ask the voters who they would choose in such a case today, and that the way to stop such a calloused power play is to reject the Nixon bid for Governor in 1962.

President Kennedy had to cancel his October trip to California because of the Cuban missile crisis, so we will never know whether this scenario would have been acted out. But the Governor's basic line of attack was almost identical with the one proposed by the Harris organization.

Nixon did everything in his power to slam the door on presidential speculation. As he announced on a national television program:

> Not only will I not seek the presidency in 1964, not only will I not accept a draft, I will see to it that there is no draft, through this method: The nominee of the Republican party in 1964 I believe should be selected by the voters of California—selected in our primary. I will not be a candidate in that primary. There will be no native son delegation. And I am going to invite Governor Rockefeller, Senator Goldwater, Mr. Romney, if he becomes Governor and wants to be a candidate, and any others, to come in, and whoever wins that primary will have my support for the presidency.
>
> Now, I think after that statement nobody can question the honesty of something I have been trying to get across for months, that in running for Governor I think this state needs a four-year Governor. I want to be a four-year Governor, and I cannot therefore run for President in 1964.

But as Harris told the Democrats, no one took Nixon's protestations seriously.

Most California political campaigns are conducted on two levels—the formal level on which the candidate is the chief spokesman and the issues are generally legitimate and germane; and an underground level, usually conducted by zealots and cranks of both left and right, who have given the state a well-earned reputation for having the dirtiest politics in the country. In 1962 the underground was working overtime.

The first underground work to surface was a 36-page booklet called *California Dynasty of Communism,* written by Karl Prussion, a self-styled "former FBI counterspy within the Communist conspiracy"—the Communist press called him "a stool pigeon." Prussion asserted, "Governor Pat Brown, over the years, has established an unchallengeable record of collaborating with and appeasing communists from 'top to bottom.'" His evidence included such facts as Brown, when California attorney general, "prohibited the usage of the Bible for religious purposes in public schools," Brown had worked with the American Civil Liberties Union, "the defensive armor-plate of the communist conspiracy," and Brown "appeared publicly on the platform with Communist-fronter Martin Luther King." Prussion's booklet also used a photograph that appeared to show Brown bowing to Khrushchev. In fact, the Brown pose was cropped from a picture of a Laotian girl teaching the Governor how farewell is said in her country. The Democrats promptly printed posters:

EXPOSED!
GOP Red Smear against Gov. Brown . . .
Distributed by Nixon-GOP Slate Headquarters
EXPOSED!

Apparently some of the booklets had been on sale at a Republican headquarters in Beverly Hills. When questioned about this on "Meet the Press," Nixon replied, "I think that kind of a pamphlet is disgraceful. I repudiate it. If I had known that anybody [connected with the Republican campaign] was distributing it, I would have stopped it instantly."

The Nixon camp, in turn, got a court order to prevent the Democrats from distributing two leaflets, "Questions Nixon Won't Answer about the $205,000 Hughes Tool Co. Loan" and "Want This Kind of Governor in California?" The latter dealt with a land deed Nixon had signed in 1951 in Washington which contained a restrictive covenant. (Such clauses had been declared unconstitutional by the U.S. Supreme Court and so lawyer Nixon had not bothered to have it deleted.) The Hughes loan was prominently aired during the only joint appearance of Nixon and Brown. At a national meeting of United Press International editors and publishers in San Francisco on October 1, the question was raised by a California publisher who was also a Brown-appointee on the state Board of Education.

MR. BRADEN: My name is Tom Braden and I am from the Oceanside *Blade Tribune* and I am going to ask you about the Hughes Tool Company loan of $205,000.

I wanted to ask you whether you as Vice-President, or as a candidate for Governor, think it proper for a candidate for Governor, morally and ethically, to permit his family to receive a secret loan from a major defense contractor in the United States?

CHAIRMAN O. PRESTON ROBINSON (Salt Lake City *Deseret News & Telegram*): Mr. Nixon, you don't need to answer that question if you don't want to. I would rule it out on the basis that it is outside the issues of this campaign.

MR. NIXON: As a matter of fact, Dr. Robinson, I insist on answering it.

CHAIRMAN ROBINSON: All right, fine.

MR. NIXON: I welcome the opportunity of answering it.

Six years ago, my brother was in deep financial trouble. He borrowed $205,000 from the Hughes Tool Company. My mother put up as security for that loan practically everything she had—a piece of property, which, to her, was fabulously wealthy and which now is producing an income of $10,000 a year to the creditor.

My brother went bankrupt six years ago. My mother turned over the property to the Hughes Tool Company. Two years ago at the presidential election, President Kennedy refused to make a political issue out of my brother's difficulties and out of my mother's problems, just as I refused to make a political issue out of any of the charges made against the members of his family.

I had no part or interest in my brother's business. I had no part whatever in the negotiation of this loan. I was never asked to do anything by the Hughes Tool Company and never did anything for them. And yet, despite President Kennedy refusing to use this as an issue, Mr. Brown, privately, in talking to some of the newsmen here in this audience, and his hatchetmen have been constantly saying that I must have gotten some of the money—that I did something wrong.

Now it is time to have this out. I was in government for 14 years as a congressman, as a Senator, as Vice-President. I went to Washington with a car and a house and a mortgage. I came back with a car and a house and a bigger mortgage.

I have made mistakes, but I am an honest man. And if the Governor of this state has any evidence pointing up that I did anything wrong in this case, that I did anything for the Hughes Tool Company, that I asked them for this loan, then instead of doing it privately, doing it slyly, the way he has—and he cannot deny it—because newsmen in this audience have told me that he has said, "We are going to make a big issue out of the Hughes Tool Company loan."

Now, he has a chance. All the people of California are listening on television. The people of this audience are listening. Governor Brown has a chance to stand up as a man and charge me with misconduct. Do it, sir!

GOVERNOR BROWN: Mr. Nixon, in connection with the Hughes note, I have said nothing about it to anyone whatsoever, other than to ask some people as to why your campaign manager, when the note was first disclosed, stated that the note was made by someone else, and I wanted to know the facts in connection with that situation.

That's the only question that I have asked of anyone in connection with this campaign, and I have no comment to make, other than that single fact—the fact that during the presidential campaign some question was asked of you, I can't remember what it was, and someone brought that information to me. As a matter of fact, a member of the Republican party. And I did pursue it and I did read the story in the *Reporter* magazine, but until this moment I never said anything about it other than in casual conversation from time to time, in connection with reading a story in the *Reporter* magazine.

CHAIRMAN ROBINSON: Thank you, Governor Brown.

This undoubtedly was the high point of the campaign for Nixon. When polled immediately afterward, most reporters agreed with the estimation of the San Jose *Mercury*'s Harry Farrell: "I think Nixon won the debate on the basis of the Hughes Tool Company answer."

Other underground issues were used by enthusiasts of both candidates. One way in which the Republicans were able to ascertain the anti-Nixon whispering campaigns was by a content analysis of the questions that listeners called in to the telethons they ran in different parts of the state. A memorandum prepared for Nixon by his research staff stated in part:

The third largest category [of questions about education] related to a current campaign in educational circles which charges RN with favoring a 6-day school week. Most of the questions were similar to this: "Is it true that if you are elected, schoolchildren will have to go to school on Saturday?" The proposal is favored by a small minority of educators, and is generally extremely unpopular among both teachers, parents and students. These questions were almost solely from San Diego and San Francisco. [Nixon never favored such a proposal.]

. . . the fact that 40 out of 70 labor questions in San Diego were on right-to-work—a disproportionate amount, judging from the other telethons—might indicate that there was some organized activity here. Most of the questioners who implied a stand appeared opposed to such laws, and seemed to be of the belief that RN favored them, either overtly or covertly. [Nixon opposed a right-to-work law in California.] [1]

Interest in welfare was also uniform, but strongest in Fresno, where the issue ranked first. . . . A large number of questions implied a belief that RN would cut pensions and welfare checks, or cut needy persons off the welfare rolls." [Nixon had stated that he would not take such actions.]

. . . Many of the questions reflected a belief that RN was prejudiced or had a bad voting record on civil rights. Sample: "Why have you consistently opposed equal rights for minorities?" "Is it true that you signed a restrictive covenant on your home in Washington?" [Nixon's votes in Congress had been down the line for civil rights.]

As the campaign moved into the most crucial period in late October, Nixon felt, even without a blockbuster issue, that his chances were on the rise. Key workers had joined his organization from outside the state—Nick Ruwe from Detroit, John Ehrlichmann from Seattle, John Nidecker and Victor Lasky from New York; experienced secretaries and researchers, such as Rose Mary Woods, Loie Gaunt, Jane Dannenhauer, Doris Jones, Betty McVey, and Agnes Wal-

[1] The lead article in *People's World* of September 29, 1962, began: "The law firm with which Richard M. Nixon is now associated was one of the largest single contributors to the 1957 campaign for a 'right to work' law in California." Nixon, of course, joined the firm in 1961.

dron, were holdovers from his vice-presidential office; campaign manager Bob Haldeman, Los Angeles vice-president of the J. Walter Thompson advertising agency, had been Nixon's chief advance man during the presidential race; and Herb Klein was again on leave from his post as editor of the San Diego *Union* to serve as press secretary. Immediately after the election, Bob Finch, who could not join the staff full time because of a serious illness in his family, wrote us, "I have been closely associated over the past 18 years with many political campaigns, ranging from the state legislature to the presidency. I can say categorically that I have never seen a campaign where the money—dollar for dollar—was more effectively raised, controlled and spent than the one just past. I can also say that I have never seen a campaign team—volunteers and staff—so competently balanced and totally dedicated as was the case this fall."

On Friday, October 19, Nixon concluded a highly successful three days of whistle stops down the coast with rear-platform remarks in Santa Cruz, Watsonville, Salinas, King City, Paso Robles, San Luis Obispo, Santa Maria, Pico Rivera, Fullerton, Anaheim, Orange, Santa Ana, San Juan Capistrano, Oceanside, Del Mar, San Diego and an off-train rally at Santa Barbara. An old-fashioned campaign train had become enough of a novelty to provide an air of gaiety to the electioneering. A large press corps, both state and national, were aboard the *Win With Nixon* Special. Newspaper polls that had shown Nixon trailing by 48–42 in September now had him narrowing the gap to 46–43.

Then on Monday, October 22, Nixon sat in his room at the Edgewater Inn in Oakland and watched President Kennedy announce that the Soviets had deployed missiles 90 miles off our shore in Cuba. Nixon turned to an aide and said that he had just lost the race for Governor of California. His reason was that Californians, along with the rest of the world, would be glued to these critical international developments. No one could be expected to pay attention to the state issues on which he was basing his campaign. His momentum had stopped and could not be recaptured, though he would try every wile he had learned over 14 years, including another Checkers speech. The election, in Nixon's opinion, was settled, even if he could not announce it publicly.[2] Having said this, Nixon went out to meet the press.

As one who has urged for several months that stronger action be taken in Cuba [Nixon said], I fully support the actions that the President has taken today.

There are obvious risks in this action. But the risks of inaction are immensely greater. In my view, this action will not lead to war. As in Quemoy and Matsu and Lebanon, in dealing with Communist aggression, strong action actually decreases the possibilities of war.

From traveling throughout California and talking to thousands of people I am sure that an overwhelming majority of the people in the first state in the union will support the President's actions.

Although the nation is in the midst of a political campaign, I know that whenever our peace and freedom is threatened, Democrats and Republicans alike will think of America first, rather than party first.

Nearly 5,930,000 Californians went to the polls on November 5. For the first time in history there were more votes cast in California than in any other state. Of the major party vote, the Republican candidate received 47.4 percent. Thus Richard M. Nixon had lost, as he privately predicted he would and as the polls publicly predicted. It was therefore all the more surprising when at 10:20 on the morning after the

---

[2] Why then did other Republican gubernatorial candidates, such as George Romney in Michigan, win? On October 25, three days after the Kennedy speech, Market Opinion Research conducted a telephone survey for Romney in Detroit. It concluded that the Cuban missile crisis did not affect the race for Governor, but that the Republican candidate for congressman-at-large had been adversely affected and probably would be defeated (as he was), although up to that point he had been shown in a favorable position by the Detroit *News* Poll. Apparently the voters correctly perceived the international crisis as being more relevant to contests for federal office than for state office. In California, however, Nixon was a candidate for *state* office whose background had turned *international* affairs into a broad issue. Therefore, the Cuban missile crisis well may have been the determining factor in the election for reasons other than Nixon's belief that it cut off debate on strictly California questions.

election, he strode into a press conference at the Beverly Hilton Hotel where Herb Klein was formally conceding his defeat. This is what Nixon told the 100 startled newsmen:

Good morning, gentlemen. Now that Mr. Klein has made his statement, and now that all the members of the press are so delighted that I have lost, I'd like to make a statement of my own.

I appreciate the press coverage in this campaign. I think each of you covered it the way you saw it. You had to write it in the way according to your belief on how it would go. I don't believe publishers should tell reporters to write one way or another. . . .

I have no complaints about the press coverage. I think each of you was writing it as you believed it.

I congratulate Governor Brown, as Herb Klein has already indicated, for his victory. He has, I think, the greatest honor and the greatest responsibility of any Governor in the United States. . . .

I wish him well. I wish him well not only from the personal standpoint, because there were never on my part any personal considerations.

I believe Governor Brown has a heart, even though he believes I do not.

I believe he is a good American, even though he feels I am not.

And therefore I wish him well because he is the Governor of the first state. He won and I want this state to be led with courage. I want it to be led decisively and I want it to be led, certainly, with the assurance that the man who lost the campaign never during the course of the campaign raised a personal consideration against his opponent—never allowed any words indicating that his opponent was motivated by lack of heart or lack of patriotism to pass his lips.

I am proud of the fact that I defended my opponent's patriotism.

You gentlemen didn't report it, but I am proud that I did that. I am proud also that I defended the fact that he was a man of good motive, a man that I disagreed with very strongly, but a man of good motive.

I want that—for once, gentlemen—I would appreciate

if you would write what I say, in that respect. I think it's very important that you write it—in the lead—in the lead.

Now, I don't mean by that, incidentally, all of you. . . . One reporter, Carl Greenberg [of the Los Angeles *Times*] . . . wrote every word that I said. He wrote it fairly. He wrote it objectively.

I don't mean that others didn't have a right to do it differently. But Carl, despite whatever feelings he had, felt that he had an obligation to report the facts as he saw them. . . .

Now, above everything else, I want to express my appreciation to our volunteer workers.

It was a magnificent group. Five hundred thousand dollars was spent [by the Democrats], according to *Newsweek* magazine, to get out the vote on Election Day. They had a right to do that if they could get the money. We didn't have that kind of money. But believe me, we had wonderful spirit.

And our 100,000 volunteer workers I was proud of. I think they did a magnificent job. I only wish they could have gotten out a few more votes in the key precincts, but because they didn't Mr. Brown has won and I have lost the election.

I'd like to say a word nationally. I know that some of you are interested in that. I have not been able to appraise the results for the Congress because not enough of them are in. . . .

Well, the most significant result of this election was what happened in four major states: Rockefeller's victory in New York, Scranton's victory in Pennsylvania, Rhodes's victory in Ohio, Romney's victory in Michigan—means that in 1964 the Republican party will be revitalized.

Now, it will be revitalized, of course, provided the Republicans in California also can [find] new leadership—not mine—because I have fought the fight and now it's up to others to take this responsibility of leadership, and I don't say this with any bitterness, because I just feel that that's the way it should be.

But the Republican party under new leadership in California needs a new birth of spirit, a new birth of unity, because we must carry California in '64, if we are to carry the nation.

But when you look at New York and Pennsylvania, Ohio and Michigan and the solid Republican Midwest, 1964 is a horse race. . . .

One last thing: What are my plans? Well, my plans are to go home. I'm going to get acquainted with my family again. And my plans, incidentally, are, from a political standpoint, of course, to take a holiday. It will be a long holiday. I don't say this with any sadness. I couldn't feel, frankly, more, well, frankly, proud of my staff for the campaign they helped me to put on. We campaigned against great odds. We fought a good fight. We didn't win. And I take the responsibility for any mistakes. As far as they're concerned, they're magnificent people, and I hope whoever next runs in California will look at my staff and take some of these people—use them—because they are—they're great political properties, shall we say, putting it in the—in a very materialistic way.

One last thing: People say, What about the past? What about losing in '60 and losing in '62? I remember somebody on my last television program said, "Mr. Nixon, isn't it a comedown, having run for President, and almost made it, to run for Governor?" And the answer is I'm proud to have run for Governor. Now, I would have liked to have won. But not having won, the main thing was that I battled—battled for the things I believed in.

I did not win. I have no hard feelings against anybody, against my opponent and least of all the people of California. We got our message through as well as we could. The Cuban thing did not enable us to get it through in the two critical weeks that we wanted to, but nevertheless, we got it through, and it is the people's choice.

They have chosen Mr. Brown. They have chosen his leadership, and I can only hope that that leadership will now become more decisive, that it will move California ahead, and so that America can move ahead—economically, morally and spiritually—so that we can have character and self-reliance in this country. This is what we need. This is what we need to move forward.

One last thing. At the outset I said a couple of things with regard to the press that I noticed some of you looked a little irritated about. And my philosophy with regard to the press has never really gotten through. And I want it to get through.

This cannot be said for any other American political figure today, I guess. Never in my 16 years of campaigning have I complained to a publisher, to an editor, about the coverage of a reporter. I believe a reporter has got a right to write it as he feels it. I believe if a reporter believes that one man ought to win rather than the other, whether it's on television or radio or the like, he ought to say so. I will say to the reporter sometimes that I think well, look, I wish you'd give my opponent the same going over that you give me.

And as I leave the press, all I can say is this: For 16 years, ever since the Hiss case, you've had a lot of—a lot of fun—that you've had an opportunity to attack me and I think I've given as good as I've taken. It was carried right up to the last day.

I made a talk on television, a talk in which I made a flub—one of the few that I make, not because I'm so good on television but because I've done it a long time. I made a flub in which I said I was running for Governor of the United States. The Los Angeles *Times* dutifully reported that.

Mr. Brown the last day made a flub—a flub, incidentally, to the great credit of television that was reported—I don't say this bitterly—in which he said, "I hope everybody wins. You vote the straight Democratic ticket, including Senator Kuchel." I was glad to hear him say it, because I was for Kuchel all the way. The Los Angeles *Times* did not report it.

I think that it's time that our great newspapers have at least the same objectivity, the same fullness of coverage, that television has. And I can only say thank God for television and radio for keeping the newspapers a little more honest.

Now, some newspapers don't fall in the category to which I have spoken, but I can only say that the great metropolitan newspapers in this field, they have a right to take every position they want on the editorial page, but on the news page they also have a right to have reporters cover men who have strong feelings whether they're for or against a candidate. But the responsibility also is to put a few Greenbergs on, on the candidate they happen to be against, whether they're against him on the editorial page or just philosophically deep down, a fellow who at least will report what the man says. . . .

I leave you gentlemen now and you will now write it. You will interpret it. That's your right. But as I leave you I want you to know—just think how much you're going to be missing.

You won't have Nixon to kick around any more, because, gentlemen, this is my last press conference and it will be one in which I have welcomed the opportunity to test wits with you. I have always respected you. I have sometimes disagreed with you.

But unlike some people, I've never canceled a subscription to a paper and also I never will.

I believe in reading what my opponents say and I hope that what I have said today will at least make television, radio and the press first recognize the great responsibility they have to report all the news and, second, recognize that they have a right and a responsibility, if they're against a candidate, to give him the shaft, but also recognize if they give him the shaft, put one lonely reporter on the campaign who will report what the candidate says now and then.

Thank you, gentlemen, and good day.

Later Nixon would dismiss the so-called "last press conference." "There had been some reporting errors, some deliberately prejudicial," he said. "I took a lot of it in 14 years. I owed it to myself to say what I felt about it. Now I can take it another 14 years." Pat Brown, who was watching his defeated opponent on television, said, "Nixon is going to regret all his life that he made that speech. The press will never let him forget it."

19 ✳ *Wall Street Lawyer, 1963–1968*

IT is a place and a symbol.

The place was the uppermost limit of what is now New York City during the early colonial years. There the Dutch built a wooden palisade to protect settlers from Indian attack, thus giving it a name—Wall Street.

As it has been since 1697, Wall Street is buttressed at its western end by Trinity church, burial ground for Alexander Hamilton. The Continental Congress met at the corner of Wall and Broad; close by in Federal Hall the first Congress under the Constitution counted the electoral votes and announced the unanimous election of George Washington.

The symbol is nearly as old as the place. "Pitchfork Ben" Tillman, the fiery Senator from South Carolina, for example, designed a cartoon in the 1896 election of a giant cow straddling the United States—her head was being fed by the farmers of the West and a Wall Street capitalist milked her in the East.

But Wall Street and the adjacent avenues that comprise the symbol—Broad, Nassau, Exchange Place—hold not just the venerable House of Morgan, the Chase Manhattan and the other great financial institutions. For the leading edge of Wall Street's work is often performed by a special breed of lawyer, who can be found in the offices of 50 or so large law firms.

In 1963 one of these law firms—known as Mudge, Stern, Baldwin & Todd—had its offices on the upper floors of 20 Broad Street, a skyscraper that hugs the austere New York Stock Exchange. Across the street is Federal Hall, now a national monument. Mudge, Stern had 22 partners, 35 associates, for a total of 57 lawyers, and a prestigious history that went back nearly a century. The third-ranking partner, Roger Baldwin, had been a founder of the American Civil Liberties Union. But of the firm's original founders, three were dead and the other was semi-retired. In the opinion of some Wall Street lawyers, Mudge, Stern needed an infusion of new life and energy.

On May 2, in the year after Richard Nixon was defeated for Governor of California, a typed announcement from the former Vice-President was passed out to reporters waiting in the lobby of the Waldorf-Astoria Towers. It read:

> On June 1, 1963, I shall move my residence to New York City and shall become counsel to the firm of Mudge, Stern, Baldwin & Todd.
>
> After I have met the six months' residence requirement of the New York law, I shall apply for admission to the New York bar. When admitted to the bar, I shall become a general partner in the firm.
>
> Pending my admission to the New York bar, I shall engage principally in matters relating to the Washington and Paris offices of the firm.

In Sacramento, Governor Pat Brown said that Nixon's move "confirms my view, which I repeated often during the campaign, that he regarded California primarily as a stepping-stone on a path that would lead him back to the East."

"Many have tried to read into [my move to New York] some dark and sinister motive," Nixon was later to tell Peter Kihss of the *New York Times*. Wrote Joseph Alsop: "The Rockefeller strategists, along with a good many who are pretty intimate with Nixon in California, are now convinced that presidential ambition was a prime, though temporary, motive for Nixon's California-to-New-York migration."

Politics—presidential variety or otherwise—however, had nothing to do with Nixon's move, other perhaps than the desire to escape the bitter struggle over the remains of the California G.O.P. after the 1962 election. Nixon came to New York because he was convinced that he was through in elective politics. He had made this point rather distinctly at his "last press conference." He came because New York for a lawyer is "the center, the hub." It is where his professional opportunities are "greater than any place in the United States, in the world," in Nixon's opinion.

He readily admitted that "from the standpoint of a place to live, day in, day out, I don't think anything can surpass California, for climate, for cleanliness, for general over-all spirit, a very gracious way of life, the outdoor way of life." Yet New York offered Nixon something that—after the defeats of 1960 and 1962—he needed more than sunshine. "New York is very cold and very ruthless and very exciting and, therefore, an interesting place to live," he observed to Robert J. Donovan of the Los Angeles *Times*. "It has many great disadvantages but also many advantages. The main thing, it is a place where you can't slow down—a fast track. Any person tends to vegetate unless he is moving on a fast track. New York is a very challenging place to live. You have to bone up to keep alive in the competition here."

After the California campaign Nixon mentioned his "fast track" theory to Elmer H. Bobst, board chairman of Warner-Lambert Pharmaceutical Company, a college dropout who had earned millions and the sobriquet "Vitamin King." Bobst was then in his late seventies. He had been one of the chief suppliers of money for Nixon's political expeditions and had developed an almost paternal affection for the young politician. Bobst, in turn, mentioned his conversation with Nixon to his own lawyers—Mudge, Stern, Baldwin & Todd. At the same time, Donald M. Kendall, president of Pepsi Co., Inc., advised his friend Nixon that his company would have need of his legal services if he practiced law on the East Coast. Now fortified with the prospect of being able to carry his "own weight," Nixon reached a satisfactory understanding with the New York law firm.

Admission to the New York bar, as in other states, is generally by sitting for an examination which runs several days. Nixon, however, was entitled to admittance without taking the examination, a privilege known as reciprocity, which is extended to any applicant who is a practicing lawyer in another jurisdiction, as Nixon was in California.

New York's principal requirement for reciprocal admission is a 500-word statement discussing "What do you believe the principles underlying the form of government of the United States to be?" Nixon routinely complied without doing any special research or polishing his draft. Therefore he was surprised when Lowell C. Wadmond, the chairman of the Committee on Character and Fitness (for admission to practice), described the Nixon analysis as the "finest" he had graded in 28 years. Lowell requested permission from the state judiciary to make the essay public, an entirely unorthodox procedure. The high court divided over whether to release it, but finally decided that the statement's value as an article of public information outweighed precedent and that they themselves would announce it. In December, at Nixon's formal swearing-in ceremony in Albany, Presiding Justice Bernard Botein read the statement to those assembled:

The principles underlying the government of the United States are decentralization of power, separation of power and maintaining a balance between freedom and order.

Above all else, the framers of the Constitution were fearful of the concentration of power in either individuals or government. The genius of their solution in this respect is that they were able to maintain a very definite but delicate balance between the federal government and the state government, on the one hand, and between the executive, legislative and judicial branches of the federal government, on the other hand.

By contrast, in the British system, the Parliament is supreme. In the present French system the primary power resides in the executive, and in some older civilizations the judges were predominant. Throughout American history there have been times when one or the other branches of government would seem to have gained a dominant position, but the pendulum has always swung back and the balance over the long haul maintained.

The concept of decentralization of power is maintained by what we call the federal system. But the principle is much broader in practice. Putting it most simply, the American ideal is that private or individual enterprise should be allowed and encouraged to undertake all functions which it is capable to perform. Only when private enterprise cannot or will not do what needs to be done should government step in. When government action is required, it should be undertaken if possible by that unit of government closest to the people. For example, the progression should be from local, to state, to federal government in that order. In other words, the federal government should step in only when the function to be performed is too big for the state or local government to undertake.

Shortly thereafter the name of Mudge, Stern, Baldwin & Todd was officially changed to Nixon, Mudge, Rose, Guthrie & Alexander.[1] A number of Nixon's new partners were Democrats. Before he joined the firm none of them knew him except as a public personality, and it was a personality that some of them did not like. Yet in a surprisingly short time Nixon won over the skeptics—not only because of his ability and his capacity for hard work, but because as one close associate put it, "I never get the feeling it's embarrassing to state a contrary view" to Nixon. "He is a great leveler in meetings," partner John Mitchell comments. "He gets people closer together, breaks through the ice between them and gets right to the heart of things. He can throw the chaff out and find the wheat quicker than any man I've ever seen."

Under Nixon's leadership the firm has grown to 105 lawyers. At least five partners are Jewish. There are Negro associates. Clients of Nixon, Mudge now include General Precision Equipment Corporation, Irving Trust Company, Stone & Webster Engineering, Blair & Company, Cargill, Hornblower & Weeks, Studebaker-Worthington, Mutual of New York, Investors Diversified Services, General Cigar, National Bulk Carriers, Eversharp-Schick, Matsui of Japan and a half-dozen railroads.

Viewing this remarkable growth, two young lawyer-writers, William M. Treadwell and Joel M. Fisher, have concluded, "Nixon himself is not solely responsible for this resurgence. An extremely capable combination of men have been at work. For a Wall Street law firm is like an odd assortment of even numbers. Everybody is equal. Yet some are more equal than

[1] A sixth name was later added—Mitchell—when the Nixon firm merged with a smaller office that specialized in municipal law and whose senior partner was John Mitchell.

others, and someone must see to it that the equals jell . . .
nevertheless [Nixon is] *the* chief partner in the firm. As
such he is their pace-setter. He sets the tone and style, and
furnishes the central image, both within and without. Main
directions are of his choosing. The others will follow his lead.
He attracts a certain body of clientele, and his associates
must render them the bulk of the necessary legal service they
seek. Or, his partners bring in a type of business in which
they specialize, and he must be the all-important generalist.
He is a catalyst in other words, melding together the disparate
ambitions and conflicts of a variety of men, giving them order,
cohesion and forward thrust."

Much of Nixon's own legal work has involved negotiating
with foreign governments on behalf of his clients, particularly
Pepsi Co. In April, 1964, after he returned from a business
trip to the Orient, Nixon addressed the American Society of
Newspaper Editors. In the question and answer period he
was asked if he had discussed politics with Ambassador Henry
Cabot Lodge when he was in South Vietnam "and would
you tell us any conclusions you have arrived at?" At the
time both Nixon and Lodge were considered potential presidential candidates and so the audience listened with particular
attentiveness. "We had a very interesting discussion and
actually we made a deal." Nixon paused for emphasis. "He
is going to put a Pepsi-Cola cooler in the embassy in Saigon."
The audience laughed. Nixon had brushed aside a sticky
question and even plugged a client at the same time!

But by far the most important legal work of Nixon's
career has been to twice argue the landmark case, Time, Inc.
v. Hill, before the United States Supreme Court in 1966. The
dispute grew out of an article in the February 28, 1955,
issue of *Life* magazine (owned by Time, Inc.), entitled, "True
Crime Inspires Tense Play, the Ordeal of a Family Trapped by
Convicts Gives Broadway a New Thriller, 'The Desperate
Hours.' " Nixon's clients, the James Hill family, had been
held prisoners in their suburban Philadelphia home by three
escaped convicts for 19 hours in September, 1952. The family
was treated courteously and released unharmed. But in a play
inspired by the events the fictional family did not get off so

easily. The *Life* story used actors to pose for scenes from the play in the house in which the Hills had been restrained. The Hills charged the magazine with violating their privacy by falsely implying that the play was a true account of their experience. *Life* replied that its article was "basically truthful." The family was awarded $30,000 in compensatory damages by the New York Court of Appeals, and Time, Inc. appealed the verdict. Thus the nation's highest tribunal was asked to decide between two powerful concepts of the law, the individual's right to privacy and the protection of a free press.

To prepare himself for the case, the first that Nixon had ever argued before the Supreme Court, he read an enormous number of law cases, several legal treatises, law journal articles dating from the year 1890 and seven current books (including Vance Packard's *The Naked Society*). Ultimately his written brief cited 37 court decisions and numerous other "authorities," each of which he had committed to memory so that he would be prepared to answer all questions that might arise.

Goldthwaite Dorr, a partner in Nixon, Mudge, who is in his nineties, commented, "He did his homework. A lot of them don't, you know. But he made it his own, digested everything. He was like my partner [Henry L.] Stimson, bound to grasp everything. Didn't care if he exposed his own ignorance to learn a thing. He had to know it."

The case was first heard in the Supreme Court on April 27. The *New York Times* reported that Nixon appeared "cool and relaxed." The proceedings were opened by *Life*'s attorney, Harold Medina, Jr., a formidable opponent with an illustrious background. When the cause shifted to Nixon he began innocently enough: "May it please the Court, I am Richard M. Nixon, Counsel for the Appellee." But before he was barely into his presentation a heavy barrage of questions came from the Justices. Nixon replied by citing precedents, comparing rulings, distinguishing cases on their facts, forcefully thrusting and parrying through the swift appellate argument. John P. MacKenzie of the Washington *Post* called it "one of the better oral arguments of the year." Nixon's partners were elated. They were sure they had witnessed a great court presentation; Nixon's performance was even beyond their high expectations.

The former Vice-President returned to New York late that night. But once back at his apartment he got out a dictaphone and began to record a memorandum for Leonard Garment, head of his firm's litigation division. When transcribed it was four and a half pages. Point by point, Nixon had reviewed the oral argument that he had given that day in court, analyzing where he might have pressed harder on a particular point or where he might have cited an additional case to substantiate his position. Garment was jolted—never before had he known anyone to take the trouble to do such an instant *post mortem.* "It gives you an insight into the man's unusual intellectual discipline," he said. Dorr described the memo as "completely objective as if he [Nixon] had not been involved in it."

After a second oral presentation in October, the Supreme Court, in a five-to-four decision, decided that the First Amendment of the Constitution grants the press broad immunity from liability in invasion of privacy suits brought by newsworthy persons. Speaking for the majority, Justice William J. Brennan, Jr., stated, "We create grave risk of serious impairment of the indispensable service of a free press in a free society if we saddle the press with the impossible burden of verifying to a certainty the facts associated in news articles with a person's name, picture or portrait, particularly as related to nondefamatory matter." Said Justice Abe Fortas in the minority opinion: "For this Court totally to immunize the press—whether forthrightly or by subtle indirection—in areas far beyond the needs of news, comment on public persons and events, discussion of public issues and the like would be no service to freedom of the press." While throwing out the Hills' award, the majority of the court concluded that the jury had been improperly instructed by the trial judge. Therefore, Nixon promptly announced that he intended to have the case retried. And in the spring of 1967 an out-of-court settlement was reached between the Hill family and Time, Inc. (By agreement, neither the amount nor terms of the settlement ever have been announced.) The importance of the case was indicated by the fact that only a year after it was officially reported, the *Columbia Law Review* published a 27-page article assessing its ramifications.

As a successful New York lawyer, Richard Nixon lives in a 12-room apartment that comprises the fifth floor of 810 Fifth Avenue, overlooking Central Park at 62nd Street. Ironically, it is the same building in which the famous Nixon-Rockefeller meeting in 1960 was held. Besides the New York Governor, Nixon's neighbors include publisher William Randolph Hearst, Jr. The purchase price of the cooperative apartment was $135,000 and it costs Nixon about $10,000 a year in maintenance. There are two wood-burning fireplaces and such remembrances of the occupant's career as paintings by Dwight Eisenhower and Madame Chiang Kai-shek. There are two in help, Fina and Manolo Sanchez, refugees from Castro's Cuba when the Nixons hired them. (After Nixon's defeat for Governor, Manolo and Fina, who spoke almost no English, assumed that their employer could no longer afford their services. So they decided they would seek day work elsewhere, but continue to live with the Nixons, clean and cook for them in the evenings, and contribute their wages to help support their closest American friends, the family of the former Vice-President of the United States. The Nixons declined this generous offer with gratitude.)

Each morning before eight, Manolo drives Nixon to 20 Broad Street, where his office on the twenty-fourth floor has a panoramic view of the East River. Besides his law work, Nixon sits on the boards of directors of important companies, such as the Harsco Corporation; Mutual of New York, one of the largest in the life and health insurance field; and Minneapolis-based Investors Diversified Services, the giant mutual fund with net assets of over 5.3 billion. He succeeded Herbert Hoover as chairman of the board of the Boys' Club of America, a post for which he was recommended by the late President.

Nixon belongs to impressive in-town clubs—Metropolitan, Links, Recess—and fashionable country clubs—Blind Brook in Westchester, Baltusrol in New Jersey. When the family moved from California the Nixon daughters were enrolled in the Chapin School and then went on to Eastern women's colleges: Tricia to Finch in New York, from which she graduated in June, 1968; and Julie to Smith in Northampton, Massachusetts. Both girls were presented to society at the International Debutante Ball and at Julie's coming-out she was escorted by David Eisenhower. The President's only grandson was a student at Amherst, only seven miles away from Julie's college, a distance that he covered often and with considerable success, judging from the fact that the Nixon-Eisenhower engagement was revealed in late November, 1967.

When Fletcher Knebel of *Look* magazine examined photostatic copies of Nixon's tax returns for the years 1963 through 1966, he found that the former Vice-President had an average gross income of about $200,000 a year, about three-quarters of it from his law firm and the remainder from royalties (his book earned him more than $200,000, spread over a five-year period for tax purposes), investments, real-estate sales, speeches and articles. He paid an average of about $60,000 annually in federal and state taxes and contributed an average of $12,000 a year to a range of more than 100 charities.

Richard M. Nixon had come a long way from Yorba Linda, California.

20 ❋ *Politics, 1963–1968*

THE resiliency of Richard Nixon has never been more apparent than in the week in which he was declared politically dead. On Tuesday, November 5, 1962, he was defeated for Governor of California. On Wednesday morning he told off the press via national TV. "Barring a miracle," *Time* declared, Nixon's public career has ended. Then on Sunday night over the ABC television network, Howard K. Smith presented a half-hour program, "The Political Obituary of Richard Nixon," and a miraculous thing happened: Like a Republican Lazarus, Nixon arose from his political grave.

TV commentator Smith accomplished this miracle by inviting Alger Hiss to give his opinion of the man who had helped send him to prison more than a decade earlier. The result, reported the Associated Press, was "a widespread public furor." Pickets appeared at the network's main studios in New York carrying signs, WHY A NATIONWIDE FORUM FOR A CONVICTED PERJURER? Switchboards were flooded with calls from angry viewers at stations that carried the broadcast. KABC in Los Angeles received calls in the thousands, including one threatening to bomb the studio and another to burn it down. The Veterans of Foreign Wars formally complained to the Federal Communications Commission. Barry Goldwater called it "one of the lowest and dirtiest blows ever struck at a great American." The Illinois State Senate demanded an apology from ABC. Newspapers editorialized. "The bars of decency are down for the enemies of Richard M. Nixon," said the San Diego *Union.* "Alger Hiss, the man who betrayed his country, was dredged up out of virtual obscurity and put on a nationwide television program to besmirch the name of a man who two years ago barely missed being President of the United States. . . ."

As Nixon left for a vacation in the Bahamas he sent a telegram to several newspapers, saying, in part:

> Looking to the future, I can only hope that my voice can help to preserve and extend the kind of opportunity for all Amercians which it has been my privilege to enjoy. What few disappointments have been my lot in the world of politics are as nothing compared to the mountain-top experiences which have been mine.
>
> There is no more striking example of this truth than the events of the past week. What does an attack by one convicted perjurer mean when weighed on the scales against thousands of wires and letters from patriotic Americans?

He did not sound like a man who had been so recently buried.[1]

[1] This is the Alger Hiss interview that was aired by ABC:

"My impression of him as an investigator [said Hiss] was that he was less interested in developing the facts objectively than in seeking ways of making a preconceived plan appear plausible. More interested, in other words, in molding appearances to a point of view that he began with, than in objectively developing the facts of the situation.

"This feeling grew increasingly throughout the hearings. I sensed it fairly early, and then became more and more convinced of it as the hearings progressed.

"I think that he was politically carried along. Whether the initial motivation was political, I certainly don't think that he was unaware of the political boost, the political soaring up into outer space that the hearings and the subsequent trial provided for him.

"He has called the whole situation his first crisis, by which I assume he means his first vaulting into a major political position, so I can't but feel that political motivation played a very real part."

Question: "Do you have any feelings of hostility toward Mr. Nixon?"

HISS (slowly searching for words): "I don't think I have any feelings of great personal warmth or affection. I regard his actions as motivated by ambition, by personal self-serving, which were not directed at me in a hostile sense, so that I feel that what he was engaged in was something beyond his own scope and size.

"He was responding to a situation in this country, an ugly period, an ugly time, and riding it rather than actually creating it. I think if it hadn't been Mr. Nixon, perhaps someone else would have tried to jump into the same situation and benefit by it."

In March Nixon appeared on the Jack Paar show. Should the former Vice-President be addressed as "Dick" or "Mr. Nixon," the host wondered. "I wouldn't worry about that," he replied. "I've been called everything." "Can Kennedy be defeated in '64?" Parr asked. "Which one?" countered Nixon. "Boy," muttered Parr, "I hate a smart-aleck Vice-President." Later Nixon sat down at the piano to play a simple little opus of his own composition backed by a lush violin arrangement. "If last November didn't finish him," Paar noted, "this will." Now that Nixon was no longer a serious candidate for anything, many people thought that he was more relaxed and claimed that they saw a lighter side to his personality.

In June Nixon left with his family for a long summer in Europe. During the next two months his photograph appeared regularly in American newspapers posing with flamenco dancers in Madrid, at the Aswan Dam, having an audience with the Pope, lunch with de Gaulle, conferring with Adenauer, touring Budapest, Venice, Cairo. The cover of the *Saturday Evening Post* showed the Nixons staring through barbed wire at the Berlin Wall. Inside the magazine was an article by the former Vice-President in which he outlined a detailed program for dealing with the Communist bloc of Eastern Europe.

Almost incredibly, less than a year after his defeat in California, Richard Nixon was being discussed as a potential presidential nominee by national columnists. (Arthur Krock, NOTHING PERMANENT ABOUT DEATH IN POLITICS; Marquis Childs, MR. NIXON AGAIN? IT JUST COULD BE; Roscoe Drummond, NIXON'S NAME PERSISTS IN A RUNDOWN OF LIKELIES; Joseph Alsop, THE NIXON CANDIDACY.) On the morning that John F. Kennedy was assassinated in Dallas, James Reston was saying in the *New York Times*:

> The argument for Nixon is that he would have ready-made strategy against the President. He lost to Kennedy by only 113,000 votes, and he could argue with considerable force that Kennedy's performance has fallen far short of all the promises he made about leadership, economic growth, unemployment, education, Latin America and the Atlantic alliance.
>
> The Kennedy emphasis in the last election that the Re-

publicans had allowed the defenses of the nation to fall into a dangerous state is particularly vulnerable to attack. For the so-called "missile gap" vanished miraculously almost as soon as Kennedy entered the White House, and Nixon feels that this alone is sufficient to assert that he lost the election of 1960 on a deception.

By a strange coincidence, Nixon had law business in Dallas on November 22, 1963. The day before he held a press conference in which the Texas newsmen were chiefly concerned with the President's impending visit. One question was about a possible demonstration against Kennedy and Nixon replied that "disagreement with his views is no excuse for discourtesy to the office of President of the United States." Nixon's flight back to New York on the twenty-second was uneventful. He landed shortly before one P.M. and hailed a cab. While stopped at a light in Queens a man called out that the President had been shot. When Nixon reached his apartment he was told by the doorman that the President was dead. He was badly shaken. Later he told reporter Jules Witcover, "I thought, This is a supreme tragedy. When a man is old and dies, that's one thing, but a young man—the death of a man in his youth, so idealistic, so spirited . . . We had been friends, as Senators are friends. I was as friendly with him as he was with any Senator on the Republican side. To some people he was President, to some a friend, to some a young man. To me he was all that, and on top of that, a man of history struck down in the tragic panorama of history."

The columnists had activated Nixon as a potential candidate by summer, 1963, not because of any new luster or achievement on his part, but because the two Republican front runners were viewed as fatally flawed—Nelson Rockefeller because of his personal life and Barry Goldwater because his political views were considered too far right for a centrist electorate. Now, with the death of Kennedy, Goldwater was thought of as even less viable by the pundits. For a Southerner had been elevated to the White House and this would undermine the Arizona Senator's so-called "Southern Strategy." (On the evening of November 22 Nixon felt there would be a bloodletting between Lyndon Johnson and Robert Kennedy for the Democratic nomination with the possibility of Adlai Stevenson emerging as a compromise choice, but by the next day he had concluded that the party would rally behind the new President.)

As Nixon threaded his way through Republican presidential nominating politics in 1964, three factors shaped his behavior. First, he was always aware that under some circumstances he might emerge as the G.O.P.'s nominee. He never fooled himself into believing that this was anything more than a "lightning-can-strike" proposition. It might happen if the convention was hopelessly deadlocked. It could not happen if he actively sought the nomination. Second, the party itself was important and must be protected. Such a feeling is often hard for nonpoliticians to comprehend. He had made great sacrifices for his party in the past, such as campaigning in years that he knew would be disastrous and for which he would be blamed; he had received the greatest honor that a political party had to give. Thus Nixon believed that he must be in a position to help heal the wounds that would be inflicted by a bruising intra-party ruckus. Third, as a public man, Nixon wished to maximize his influence in government and party affairs. Once in November, 1963, a friend asked him if his strategy was "to keep that big stick out there?" Nixon replied, "That's exactly it. People say to come out for somebody and then continue talking. You know very well that whether you are on page one or page 30 depends on whether they fear you. It is just as simple as that." Nixon had things to say, particularly about the conduct of American foreign policy, and "people" would listen—or listen more attentively—if they thought him a possible G.O.P. standard-bearer. He knew—and any editor knew he was right—that it was the possibility of his candidacy that moved his views from page 30 to page one.

All these factors spelled a single course of action: Nixon must stay neutral. In March he left on a round-the-world business trip (which, incidentally, would be newsworthy, would emphasize his foreign affairs experience, yet would keep him out of the daily political haggling). On his return in April his close associates, such as former Young Republicans president Charles McWhorter, informed him that according to private delegate counts Goldwater was virtually assured of the nomination. From May through the convention in July Nixon was assisted by Sherman Unger, who took leave from his Cincinnati law firm. Recalling this period, Unger wrote us, "RN was under terrific strain, and unbelievable pressure was applied from both sides to get him to assist a candidate, particularly after [William] Scranton announced. He had substantial support from both wings of the party and as the party split, his 'old friends' began to take sides and used every trick in the book to get RN to assist their 'cause.' It was both a frightening and enlightening exercise to observe. . . . RN was sacrificing and certainly alienating friends and contacts in both wings of the party in order to remain neutral. He had, as a political realist, determined that his role was to help the party heal its obvious wounds [after Goldwater was nominated]."

In late June Nixon met with Unger and his chief 1960 aide, Robert Finch, at Montauk, on the tip of Long Island, to reassess the situation. Goldwater's victory in the California primary, they concluded, had effectively eliminated Factor One (a deadlocked convention might turn to Nixon) and made predominant Factor Two (Nixon must heal party wounds). It was therefore decided that Nixon would introduce nominee Goldwater to the Republican convention, rather than speak before the balloting as previously planned.

The convention speech was one of the finest of Nixon's career, a masterful effort to blur the differences that divided the party and to provide a bridge on which Goldwater and his critics could meet. "Before this convention," he said, "we were Goldwater Republicans, Rockefeller Republicans, Scranton Republicans, Lodge Republicans, but now that this convention has met and made its decision, we are Republicans, period, working for Barry Goldwater for President of the United States."

Both before and after the National Governors' Conference in June, Goldwater's finance chairman, jewelry manufacturer Daniel C. Gainey of Owatonna, Minnesota, had sounded out Nixon on his availability to run for Vice-President on the Arizona Senator's ticket. Nixon believed the overtures to be at least semiofficial. He turned them down. For he never believed that Goldwater could beat President Johnson and he had no desire to be part of the losing ticket.

However, Nixon did campaign intensely for Goldwater, traveling more than 50,000 miles in 36 states in the six weeks before the election; working harder for Goldwater—because of his remarkable stamina—than Goldwater was able to do for himself. His efforts, moreover, may have buoyed Republican candidates for lesser offices and stood in sharp contrast to the inactivity of many other party leaders who found it expedient to stay in their home states.

Nineteen sixty-five, in political terms, was an off-off year. Yet wherever there was action, Nixon was right in the middle of it. Virginia was one of the two states that had a gubernatorial election. Although Republicans had not captured the statehouse in the Old Dominion since Reconstruction; the party put up a very attractive candidate, A. Linwood Holton, Jr., a young Roanoke attorney. And, hopeless as the cause may have been, Nixon made a whirlwind 1,100-mile tour of the state, which for two days rivaled in intensity anything that he had ever done on his own behalf. In summary, this was Nixon's schedule:

Tuesday, October 5, 1965
Arlington: Press conference and dinner speech (450–500 attended at $25 a plate).[2]
Norfolk: Press conference on arrival at midnight; then filmed TV interview.

Wednesday, October 6, 1965
Norfolk: Breakfast speech (400 attended at $7.50 a plate).
Harrisonburg: Mid-morning rally at Rockingham County courthouse (4,000–5,000).
Lynchburg: Luncheon speech (over 300).
Lonesome Pine Airport, Wise County: Rally (2,000–2,500, including five high-school bands—waited 90 minutes in chilly weather).
Roanoke: Dinner speech (600).
Returned to New York after midnight.

[2] All crowd estimates are from local newspapers.

This itinerary, traced along a map of Virginia, graphically shows the incredible amount of territory that Nixon covered —from the populous suburbs of Washington in the north, to the Tidewater in the south, to the apple-picking country of the Shenandoah Valley, to the extreme western tip, deep in the Appalachians, where the state joins Tennessee. Party leaders were described in the press as "jubilant." Yet a month later, as expected, the entire Republican slate of statewide candidates was defeated, although the size of the loss was not stunning. (It was hardly surprising that when a Nixon for President committee was announced in March, 1967, Lin Holton was a charter member.)

From his move to New York in 1963 through the end of 1965, Nixon functioned without a staff other than his longtime secretary Rose Mary Woods; he did not distribute copies of his speeches to the press; and friends made his trip arrangements on a voluteer basis. But as the 1966 congressional elections approached, Nixon's operation took on a more professional look with the hiring of Patrick J. Buchanan, a 27-year-old editorial writer for the St. Louis *Globe-Democrat*.

The North American Newspaper Alliance, a syndicate service, contracted with Nixon for a monthly column, two of which he devoted to the Republican party's role in the South. Wrote the former Vice-President on May 8 (and he repeated the same message on October 30):

> The Republican opportunity in the South is a golden one; but Republicans must not go prospecting for the fool's gold of racist votes. Southern Republicans must not climb aboard the sinking ship of racial injustice. They should let Southern Democrats sink with it, as they have sailed with it.
>
> Any Republican victory that would come of courting racists, black or white, would be a defeat for our future in the South, and our party in the nation. It would be a battle won in a lost cause.
>
> The Democratic party in the South has ridden to power for a century on an annual tide of racist oratory. The Democratic party is the party which runs with the hounds in the North and the hares in South.
>
> The Republicans, as the South's party of the future, should reject this hypocritical policy of the past.

On this issue it is time for both Republicans and Democrats to stop talking of what is smart politically, and start talking of what is right morally.

In the fall Nixon again took to the hustings. This time he appeared in 35 states for 86 Republican nominees. Although he never flattered himself with the belief that he actually elected any local candidates, Nixon rightly stated his contribution as threefold: First, he helped them raise money (some five to six million dollars between 1964 and 1967, he estimated); second, he got them publicity (101 column inches in the Salt Lake City newspapers for a stop of three hours in 1966) and third, he brought an air of enthusiasm and a sense of importance to local races. "Any national figure has a certain mystique," Nixon said. "He can stir up the enthusiasm of the workers, make them think that this particular election has a national importance beyond the local."

Nixon aimed his attack directly at the President—"Every time a housewife goes into a supermarket today, she is faced with the High Cost of Johnson. . . . Every time a businessman tries to make a loan that would produce more jobs, he runs into interest rates that are really the High Cost of Johnson. . . . Every time a young couple tries to buy a home these days, the door is slammed in their faces by the High Cost of Johnson."

But when the President left for Manila in late October to confer with the country's Vietnam allies, Nixon promptly announced he would not discuss the war issue until Johnson's return. Then on November 3, with the President safely back in this country, Nixon issued a lengthy analysis of the Manila communiqué in which he asked a series of pointed questions, such as "How many more American troops—in addition to this latest 46,000—do we currently plan to send to fight in Vietnam in 1967? Will the draft quota, which reached a 15-year high in October have to be raised again to meet our troop requirements?" At his press conference that day the President lashed out at Nixon, calling him "a chronic campaigner," who "never did really recognize and realize what was going on when he had an official position in the government," and even in private life "doesn't serve his country well." The attack, coming from Johnson, was particularly unjust because Nixon, unlike many members of the Democratic party, had endorsed the President's statement of America's purpose in Vietnam. In fact, at a March, 1966, Johnson-Nixon meeting in the White House (held in the President's bedroom because he was in bed with a cold), Johnson thanked Nixon in unmistakable terms for endorsing the American commitment in Vietnam. The next day Nixon told a friend that he, in turn, had told Johnson, "I am following a role very similar to yours. You gave us [the Eisenhower administration] strong support on foreign policy and in both '54 and '58 you went out and campaigned for Senators and congressmen on domestic issues and hit us hard and you were successful. I said, 'I am trying to do exactly the same thing and I hope you'll understand.' He said, 'I understand completely.'" After Johnson's November 3 outburst, some loyal White House aides suggested that the President had spoken against Nixon in order "to set him up as the 1968 opponent." However, the President's anger was so genuine and his language so intemperate that even Mrs. Johnson, sitting nearby, was heard to say quietly, "Stop." As the headline in the Washington Star put it, NIXON IS JUBILANT AT JOHNSON ATTACK. In marked contrast to the President, Nixon publicly kept his cool. Columnists and editorial writers rushed to his defense and he even received kind words from some unlikely quarters. The liberal New Republic's T. R. B. wrote, "We aren't accustomed to defending Dick Nixon, but we don't like any argument that impugns an opponent's patriotism." Overnight Lyndon Johnson had transformed Nixon from a Republican leader into the Republican leader.

The President's peevishness may have been aggravated by foreknowledge that the 1966 election returns would be gratifying to Nixon and painful to him. Furthermore, when the votes were counted it turned out that Nixon had predicted the outcome with uncanny accuracy. Throughout the fall he had said that the Republicans would win a minimum of 40 seats in the House of Representatives, three in the Senate, six governorships, and 700 seats in the state legislatures. As things turned out they won 47 seats in the House, three in the Senate, eight governorships, and 540 seats in the legislatures (although their gross gain was 728 legislative seats and the Democrats' net loss was 726, reapportionment having reduced the size of several legislatures).

The 1966 elections produced a number of big winners— Romney, Rockefeller, Reagan, Percy; but Nixon, without having run for anything, may have been the biggest winner of all. As Warren Weaver, Jr., noted in the *New York Times,* "Hard statistics show that a G.O.P. House candidate for whom Nixon did not campaign stood only a 45 percent chance of winning, while a man he embraced stood a 67 percent chance. It is hard to knock a coach who raises the team average that much."

On Sunday, November 6, on the TV interview program "Issues and Answers," Bill Lawrence of ABC asked: "Mr. Nixon, now that you have toured 35 states, 70 districts, renewed all your political due bills, when are you going to start running for President yourself?" Nixon's reply was surprising. "After this election," he said, "I am going to take a holiday from politics for at least six months with no political speeches scheduled whatever." Despite considerable pressure from his political friends, who contended that Governor Romney of Michigan would be too far ahead to be overtaken by the time Nixon returned to the arena, the former Vice-President remained true to his own timetable. This did not mean, of course, that Nixon was inactive. In 1967, as in years past, a major portion of his time was taken up with foreign travel. But Nixon the grand tourist was hardly a casual sightseer. Robert Ellsworth, a former Kansas congressman, went with him on a trip to Europe and the Soviet Union in March. On April 11 Ellsworth wrote us about their experiences and his letter tells a good deal about the usefulness of these travels to the Republican leader:

. . . In England, Nixon conferred with Prime Minister Wilson, Deputy Foreign Minister Thomson and former Prime Minister Macmillan; in France, with Foreign Minister Couve de Murville; in West Germany, with Chancellor Kiesinger, Vice Chancellor and Foreign Minister Brandt, Defense Minister Schroeder, Finance Minister Strauss and former Chancellor Adenauer; in Italy, with President Saragat, Premier Moro and Foreign Minister

Fanfani; in Romania, with Foreign Minister Manescu and Secretary-General Ceausescu of the Romanian Communist party, as well as Deputy Foreign Trade Minister Nicolae; and in Czechoslovakia, with Antonin Snejdarek, Director of the Institute for International Politics and Economics, and Foreign Trade Officer Babacek. He had a lengthy and valuable audience with His Holiness Pope Paul VI. As you know, the Soviet officials declined to meet with Nixon during his visit; he therefore took the opportunity to visit with many of the Russian people in Moscow and in Soviet Central Asia, and was received warmly everywhere he went.

The meetings were informal: the talks frank and far-ranging; there were no formal agenda and neither Nixon nor the conferees utilized prepared memoranda or notes.

In these discussions Nixon sought to assess the dramatic changes and developments on the continent in recent years.

1. How have internal Soviet economic dislocations, Chinese hostility, and the ferment in Eastern Europe affected the Soviet posture toward the West?

2. How do the Europeans on the scene assess Soviet intentions in pursuing a *détente* with the West? Do they view the Soviets as taking the first steps toward a genuine rapprochement with the West, or do they suspect that Soviet goals are to divide Europe from the United States and expunge American presence from the continent?

3. What is the current state of NATO, and what is the European estimation of its on-going value and necessity?

4. What is the European view of the nonproliferation treaty, trade with the East, the American effort in Vietnam and the prospects of a German settlement.

It was agreed, as the basis for the meetings, that there would be no attribution of remarks. Consistent with this ground rule, however, I can summarize certain basic impressions drawn from the round of conferences.

1. There is a strong desire on the part of Europeans to continue the trend toward a relaxation of tensions between East and West. However, there remain varying degrees of skepticism in Western Europe about Soviet motives. Among

the Germans there is a good measure of caution with respect to Soviet intentions. In Italy and France, there is less skepticism and more enthusiasm for getting on with the business of building bridges, while England seems to be in the forefront of the movement toward *détente*. . . .

2. There is great concern in Western Europe with regard to the proposed nonproliferation treaty. Some States fear such a treaty from the standpoint of their future national security. Others fear that the treaty would inhibit their peaceful development of atomic energy. Many Western European leaders brought up the subject of the technological superiority of the United States, and to some this treaty seemed to freeze America in the position of perpetual dominance in the nuclear field. . . .

3. While most Europeans seem willing to take the first move in testing Soviet intentions in achieving *détente,* the majority were in solid agreement that large American troop withdrawals, without corresponding concessions in the East, would be dangerous folly.

4. The majority of Western Europeans favor the current efforts being made by their governments to enlarge trade with the East. However, there seems to be a wide recognition that trade and cultural exchanges have little impact upon fundamental political differences that remain.

5. Among the European leadership, however, a number of caveats were expressed about growing trade with the East and the Soviets. Several of the statesmen with whom we spoke are concerned that the Soviet courting in Western Europe is designed to replace American influence rather than to coexist with the American presence.

6. While some Western leaders display an understanding of the American position in Vietnam, among the people the war remains unpopular and unsupported. Paradoxically, in the Soviet Union Nixon was able to discuss Vietnam in frank terms with large groups of Soviet citizens without a single hostile incident. . . .

Later in the year Nixon traveled to the Far East accompanied by Raymond Price, a former editorial writer for the New York *Herald Tribune,* who subsequently helped him with the research for a thoughtful article, "Asia After Viet Nam," which appeared in the October issue of *Foreign Affairs.*

"The war in Viet Nam has for so long dominated our field of vision that it has distorted our picture of Asia," Nixon wrote. "A small country on the rim of the continent has filled the screen of our minds; but it does not fill the map. Sometimes dramatically, but more often quietly, the rest of Asia has been undergoing a profound, an exciting and on balance an extraordinarily promising transformation. One key to this transformation is the emergence of Asian regionalism. . . ." Nixon went on to propose the development of regional defense pacts as one way to reduce the chances of direct confrontations between nuclear powers.

Clearly Nixon was using his years out of office to good advantage. Washington had been action years; now he had time for reflections. As Ray Price said, "You're in the caldron and then you step back and it's good for you."

Moreover, Nixon was benefiting from the teeter-totter effect of politics—when someone's up, someone else goes down. George Romney had not been able to capitalize on the clear track that Nixon had given him; he had repeatedly tripped over his own rhetoric and, most fatally, had publicly admitted being "brainwashed" by the Johnson administration on Vietnam policy. The Gallup Poll throughout 1967 showed Nixon as the favorite candidate for the Republican presidential nomination of the party's rank-and-file and he even pulled ahead among independents. His activities as a party loyalist in 1964 had won him the support of Barry Goldwater and many of his conservative followers without forcing him to endorse the Goldwater positions that had distressed moderates; his activities in 1966 had won him the gratitude of many young, pragmatic Republicans who had been elected to Congress with his help; and his repeated efforts to build a viable Republican party in the South had earned him wide support in that region without in any way getting him tagged as a racist. Thus on January 31, 1968, Richard Nixon sent a letter "To the Citizens of New Hampshire," where the first-in-the-nation presidential primary is held, saying:

. . . The Nation is in grave difficulties, around the world and here at home. The choices we face are larger than any differences among Republicans or among Democrats, larger even than the differences between the parties. They are beyond politics. Peace and freedom in the world, and peace and progress here at home, will depend on the decisions of the next President of the United States.

For these critical years, America needs new leadership.

During fourteen years in Washington, I learned the awesome nature of the great decisions a President faces. During the past eight years I have had a chance to reflect on the lessons of public office, to measure the nation's tasks and its problems from a fresh perspective. I have sought to apply those lessons to the needs of the present, and to the entire sweep of this final third of the 20th century.

And I believe I have found some answers.

I have decided, therefore, to enter the Republican Presidential primary in New Hampshire.

But before the citizens were able to cast their ballots, Nixon's opponent, George Romney, had withdrawn from the race, stating "my candidacy has not won the wide acceptance . . . that I had hoped to achieve." A Roper survey showed that the Michigan Governor, after weeks of intensive campaigning, was only favored by 9 percent of Granite State Republicans. Suddenly and unexpectedly, Nixon had the field to himself. It was, as someone said, "the first T.K.O. in American politics." The former Vice-President went on to get 80,666 votes, the largest number ever received by one candidate in a New Hampshire primary. All eyes now turned to Nelson Rockefeller, who was being urged to enter the race. But again unexpectedly, the New York Governor called a press conference to announce that he was not a candidate. "Quite frankly," he told newsmen on March 21, "I find it clear at this time that a considerable majority of the party's leaders want the candidacy of former Vice-President Richard Nixon. And it appears equally clear that they are keenly concerned and anxious to avoid any such divisive challenge within the party as marked the 1964 campaign." In the next presidential primary, Wisconsin's on April 2, Nixon, California Governor Reagan and Harold Stassen were listed on the ballot. Nixon received over 80 percent. Indiana produced a record vote for Nixon, nearly 100,000 in excess of his primary vote there in 1960. In Nebraska, despite a drive by Reagan's supporters and Rockefeller's re-entry into the race, Nixon won over 70 percent of the vote. And on May 27, in the final contested primary of the campaign, Oregon's Republicans gave the former Vice-President 73 percent of their vote.

Traveling this tortuous primary route, Richard Nixon boarded a chartered plane at Madison, Wisconsin, and was greeted by the voice of the stewardess over the intercom:

"On behalf of your crew and North Central Airlines, I would like to welcome you to the next portion of your flight to the White House."

Appendix: Nixon Speaks, 1968

These statements were made by Richard Nixon in private conversations with the authors on May 1 and May 5, 1968.

Q. Mr. Vice-President, what do you think are the lessons of the Vietnam war?

R.N. One of the primary lessons in Vietnam is that the United States ended up in the unenviable position of furnishing not only most of the arms and most of the money, but *most of the men* to help another nation defend itself against Communist aggression.

The United States is a very rich and a very strong country. But we have only two hundred million people and there are two billion people who live in the free world. We simply cannot continue—whether it's in Asia, Africa, or Latin America—to carry this immense burden of helping small nations who come under attack, either externally or internally, without more assistance from other nations who have an equal stake in freedom.

We need a new type of collective security arrangement in which the nations in an area would assume the primary responsibility of coming to the aid of a neighboring nation rather than calling upon the United States in each instance for that assistance.

The reason for this goes beyond the fact that the United States should not carry this immense burden by itself. It goes to the fact that whenever the United States becomes militarily involved in helping another nation defend itself against Communist aggression the possibility of a confrontation with the Soviet Union or Communist China is immensely escalated. Whenever we can assist with our arms and our money but not with our men, then the possibility of that confrontation is reduced. And if we're going to avoid World War III we must reduce to the minimum those instances around the world where the United States does risk a confrontation with the Soviet Union or with Communist China.

Now this is a change in direction for American policy. We must move away from the old concept of military alliances with the weak nations and move toward a new concept in which we aid economically and even with military assistance, but where we reduce those cases where the United States becomes involved with its armed forces. In terms of Asia, being quite specific, we have got to put additional emphasis on developing around the perimeter of Communist China a new collective security arrangement in which all the nations in that area including Japan will play a major role, in which they will assume more responsibility than presently in dealing with Vietnam-type insurrections.

One last point: Because of the terrible American disillusionment with Vietnam, the likelihood that the American people would support another American intervention—even in Latin America, our closest friends—is quite unlikely, I think. Therefore we have to face the fact now and help these countries develop the resources so that they will be able to defend themselves if they come under attack.

Q. Mr. Nixon, you have declared a moratorium on discussing Vietnam while the negotiations are in progress, but could you tell us what you would consider the elements of an acceptable settlement?

R.N. You have to remember that a presidential candidate —a potential President—is in a very different position from an editor or a Congressman. Once he makes a statement indicating what he would settle for he pulls the rug out from under the negotiators. At this time President Johnson is attempting to negotiate a settlement with the North Vietnamese. If I or any other candidate were to indicate what we would settle for, and if that position were different from and possibly more attractive to the North Vietnamese than what the President was offering, this immediately would torpedo the negotiations. So I will not discuss that under any circumstances. It would be inappropriate and highly irresponsible to do so. I think Senators McCarthy and Kennedy rendered a great disservice to the country by indicating, for example, that they would recommend at this time that the South Vietnamese be forced into a coalition government with the Communists. By doing so, they are giving the enemy the hope that by delaying a settlement with the Johnson Administration they have a good chance of getting a better deal from another administration.

Q. Looking farther down the road, where do you see the potential Vietnams in the future?

R.N. One area of potential explosiveness is the Middle East. That is probably the major tinderbox of the world at the present time. It is an area where the United States may not be able to avoid a major commitment because the Middle East involves not simply the small nations in that area but also the future of Europe. It is a part of the "blue chip," as we call it. What we have to do is move diplomatically to support the moderate Arab states and attempt thereby to defuse the situation; while, in the long term, moving much more aggressively on programs like the Eisenhower-Strauss Plan to develop the resources of the Middle East so as to reduce the pressures for expansion from the Arab extremists—the pressures that led to the Arab-Israeli war of June, 1967.

Q. Have Communism and the Communist threat changed since 1960, or since 1950?

R.N. It's infinitely different. As we enter the 70's the time has come to recognize that all our old alliances must be reappraised in the light of the change.

NATO can't be put together again and shouldn't be put together again on the same basis on which it was founded. The NATO of 20 years ago was completely adequate for Europe as it was then. Europe was then weak economically and drawn together by a common fear of the Soviet Union. Europe today is strong economically, and the various nations are feeling their independence because of this economic strength. It's just impossible for the United States to still have the same relationship that it had with Europe when it was a rather weak collection of states.

Another thing we have to bear in mind is the change in the military power balance. Even six years ago the American advantage over the Soviet Union was 7:1. Now it's equal. And by the time the next President is inaugurated the Soviet Union may be ahead of us in missiles. What this means is that the

United States will not be able to move as aggressively as it did, for example, in the Cuban confrontation [of October, 1962]. What made the Cuban confrontation possible was the strength that President Eisenhower left with President Kennedy. Lebanon [in 1958] was possible because of the strength we then had in being. But now as we see the Soviet Union with virtual parity, at least as far as missiles are concerned, we must recognize that any kind of confrontation runs the greater risk of a world war.

There has also been a change within the Communist world. Unlike 20 years ago, it is no longer a monolithic empire. The Eastern European countries can be referred to as satellites and nothing more. Whether it's Rumanian foreign policy or Czech economic policy or Polish student rebellions, we must recognize that the Eastern European countries are beginning to develop independent nationalistic policies. We must encourage this trend. However, we must be very careful to recognize that the differences the Soviet Union has with the countries of Eastern Europe cause it infinitely less difficulty than the differences in Western Europe cause us.

Policy toward China becomes immensely important since the split between Communist China and the Soviet Union. I am not among those who believe that the United States would be served by our joining in a grand coalition with the Soviet Union in order to contain Communist China. This is something that you hear talked about. I think the fear that the Soviet Union has of Communist China might bring it into a coalition with the West—a shotgun marriage with the West, just like the Hitler-Stalin pact. The Communists are a very pragmatic people. But my point is this: this would be very dangerous as long-range U.S. policy because ten years from now the greatest threat to peace is going to be from Asia, not the Soviet Union. That's why during the course of the next President's term of office we must develop the conditions that will bring the leaders of Communist China to the same conclusion that the leaders of the Soviet Union now seem to have reached about the dangers of a world conflict. When we look at the Soviet leaders we must recognize that they have changed not because of their hearts but because of their heads. They have changed because of NATO, because they looked down the nuclear gun barrel during the Cuban confrontation, because of the power of the United States. Communist China has not yet been convinced that their interests would be very badly injured or threatened by continued expansionism and that their interests would be better served by turning inward rather than outward.

When we look at Japan and South Korea and Thailand and South Vietnam we see a group of nations that produce twice as much as Communist China does today. As this group gets assistance from the United States and Europe it will become even stronger and less susceptible to Communist infiltration. Eventually these nations can and should develop the military potential to make them at least a buffer between Communist China and the U.S. When that happens and only then will the Chinese Communists begin to think as the Soviet leaders began to think five years ago. Then the dialogue can and should be opened. I think this can come to pass in the 70's and I think it must come to pass. Unless our policies are directed toward this end we would be leaving Communist China isolated, growing increasingly apart from the rest of the world, developing its nuclear power and eventually exporting not only revolution to the smaller countries but the nuclear capabilities that could trigger a nuclear war.

Q. Do you think you could get along with De Gaulle?

R.N. He's a man of immense pride. He's a man who doesn't talk to ambassadors. But he will talk to the President of the United States and we must try. Looking to the future of Europe it's ridiculous to suggest that there can be a NATO without France. It's ridiculous to suggest that Britain's future can be viable outside of Europe. I know there are well-intentioned people who say that a kind of British-American arrangement might be the alternative to letting Britain into Europe. But that's only a temporary expedient. That's only a lever that might get Britain into Europe. Britain belongs in Europe. Europe needs Britain and Britain needs Europe.

American policy must be directed at developing some kind of *détente* with De Gaulle, and this involves personal diplomacy at the highest level. I'm not so presumptuous as to say I could do it. But it must be tried and I think it could succeed, because De Gaulle is a man with a great sense of history and he does not want to be remembered as the man who not only destroyed Europe but destroyed France in the process. And I think that's where his present policies will lead.

Q. Mr. Nixon, you are finally living in the lap of luxury, you have it made—so why did you resume politics?

R.N. Whether I have it made or not has no reference to what I do. It gets back to my conviction that men at the highest level in politics do not choose their path. They can try all they want, but if it isn't the right time and the right place they're not going to get very far. In my case a series of events that nobody could have anticipated when I left California in 1963 has brought me back into politics. Those events were the terrible defeat of the Republican party in 1964, the emergence again of a grave foreign policy issue—the Vietnam war—and the feeling on the part of many Republicans that I could unite the party and that I could provide national leadership, particularly in foreign policy. I wouldn't say that these events created a draft, but they did create an attitude that made it inevitable that I would return to politics.

Once a man has been in politics, once that's been in his life, he will always return if the people want him. He cannot return unless they do. That's why I had no hesitancy about entering all the primaries. That decision was quite a risk at the time. All the polls showed Romney was going to win. But I felt that unless I could demonstrate that people wanted me the nomination would not mean anything.

Q. You have seen the Presidency in action. How would you operate as President?

R.N. For one thing, I would disperse power, spread it among able people. Men operate best only if they are given the chance to operate at full capacity.

I would operate differently from President Johnson. Instead of taking all power to myself, I'd select cabinet members who could do their jobs, and each of them would have the stature and the power to function effectively. Publicity would not center at the White House alone. Every key official would have the opportunity to be a big man in his field. On the other hand, when a President takes all the real power himself, those around him become puppets. They shrivel up and become less and less creative.

Actually, my belief in dispersal of power relates to the fundamental proposition of how to make a country move forward. Progress demands that you develop your most creative people to their fullest. And your most creative people can't develop in a monolithic, centralized power set-up.

Q. How would you label yourself?

R.N. Labels mean different things to different people. The nineteenth-century liberal is the twentieth-century conservative and the nineteenth-century conservative (with a small c) is the twentieth-century liberal. For example, in the conservative-liberal dialogue, which began in eighteenth-century America, probably the major difference was that the conservatives then were for strong central government. Hamilton was a strong central government man, whereas the liberals like Jefferson were for individual liberties, for decentralization of power.

In the twentieth century the liberals became the strong central government people—all power should be consolidated in Washington—and the conservatives became the people who were for decentralization.

Well, basically I'm a strong advocate of individual liberties. I'm very skeptical about centralized power. I believe in strong local government.

Now let's take this conservative-liberal dialogue as it relates to foreign policy. The conservatives have been considered the isolationists and the internationalists were considered to be the liberals. So looking at my record you would have to say I'm a liberal on foreign policy. Because I recognize America's role in the world I am not an isolationist. I have supported foreign aid, for instance.

But the old liberals who were internationalists 20 years ago now are turning inward. They are telling us to get out of Asia and Latin America, that we're overcommitted. My view, however, hasn't changed. While I make it very clear that we have to get other nations to assume their share of the responsibility, I also believe that we cannot withdraw from the world. Am I a conservative or a liberal? My answer is that I'm an internationalist.

By another foreign policy standard it is said that a conservative is basically anti-Communist and a liberal does not believe that Communism is a particular threat. By this test

I've been called a conservative. But I don't see the Communist world as one world. I see the shades of gray. I see it as a multicolor thing. So rather than say I'm a conservative, I say I'm a firm opponent of totalitarianism of any kind and a strong proponent of freedom. If you want to describe me, you might say I'm a "whole-worlder." Too many people have been "half-worlders." Some have been able to see the danger in Asia but not in Europe and others have been able to see the danger in Europe but not in Asia. What we've got to see is the whole world.

On the race issue I'm a liberal. On economics I'm a conservative. Domestically, you could say I'm a centrist. But really I don't go for labels. You can't classify me. I'm a pragmatist, but not a pragmatist in the sense that I'm for anything merely because it works. I'm a pragmatist with some deep principles that never change. I'm just not doctrinaire. If there is one thing that classifies me it is that I'm a non-extremist.

Index

Acción Democratica Party, Venezuela, 182
Acheson, Dean, 7, 104
Adams, Earl C., 252
Adams, Sherman, 101, 105, 110, 112–114, 136, 138, 146, 156, 157, 160–162
Adams, Duque & Hazeltine, 252
Adelson, William, 21
Adenauer, Konrad, 200, 201, 295, 303
Adoula, Cyrille, 255
Aiken, George D., 107
Akalovsky, Alexander, 191
Albania, 195
Alhambra *Post-Advocate*, 41
Alsop, Joseph, 284, 295
Alsop, Stewart, 5
American Broadcasting Co., 2, 293, 303
American Civil Liberties Union, 271–272, 284
American Express Co., 252
American Jewish Committee, 215
American National Exhibition, Moscow, 188
American Society of Newspaper Editors, 288
Americans for Democratic Action, 107
Amherst College, 292
Andrews, Bert, 50, 51
Anti-Poll Tax Bill, 213
Arab-Israeli war of June, 1967, 311
Army-McCarthy hearings, 134–136
Arvey, Jake, 88, 89
"Asia After Viet Nam" (Nixon), 305
Associated Press, 99, 221, 293
Austria, 197

Babacek, Vladimir, 304
Bailey, John, 233, 243
Bailey-Sorensen Report, 233, 243
Baldwin, Roger, 284
Baltimore *Sun*, 235
Baltusrol Country Club, 291
Baltzell, E. Digby, 6
Barkley, Alben, 88

Barnes, Stanley, 36
Bassett, James, 97, 101, 115, 121, 136, 261–262
Batista, Fulgencio, 209
Batten, Barton, Durstine and Osborn, 111
Bay of Pigs landing, 252
Becky Sharp (film), 28
Behrens, Earl, 86
Belden Associates, 268
Bellow, Saul, 5
Bentley, Elizabeth, 44, 48, 54
Berle, A. A., Jr., 45
Berle, Milton, 111
Berlin, 254–255, 265–266
Betancourt, Romulo, 182
Bewley, Thomas, 25, 26
Bird in Hand (Drinkwater), 19
Blair and Co., 287
Blind Brook Country Club, 291
Blough, Roger, 218
Bobst, Elmer H., 285
Boddy, Manchester, 67, 68, 69, 70
Bohlen, Charles E., 133
Boston *Globe*, 31
Botein, Bernard, 286
Boys' Club of America, 291
Braden, Tom, 272
Brandeis, Louis D., 22
Brandt, Willy, 303
Breasher, Ernest, 97
Breckinridge, John C., 3, 126
Brennan, Bernard, 92, 94, 96
Brennan, William J., Jr., 290
Bricker, John, 60
Bridges, Styles, 146
Briggs, Dean, 13
Brock, William, 20
Broder, David S., 8, 261
Brown, Edmund G. (Pat), 2, 70, 259–261, 264–274, 278, 280, 284
Brown, Joe E., 1
Brownell, Herbert, Jr., 22, 76, 80, 84–87, 105, 152
Bryce, Lord, 258
Buchanan, Patrick J., 300
Bulgaria, 195
Burns, Arthur F., 215
Butler, Paul M., 130
Byrnes, James F., 92

317

Cabinet Committee on Price Stability for Economic Growth, 208, 215, 217 n.

Caldera, Rafael, 182

California, 34–43, 64–75, 256, 258–263, 264–282

California Democratic Women's League, 68

"California Democrats for Nixon," 71

California Department of Health, 258

California Dynasty of Communism (Prussion), 271, 272

California Republican Assembly, 265

California Republican Central Committee, 89

California 12th Congressional District, 34–36, 38

"California Volunteers for Good Government," 65

Campaigns
  1940: 34
  1944: 113
  1948: 34–43, 46, 64
  1950: 64–75, 76, 128
  1952: 1, 7, 22, 59–60, 76–125, 131
  1954: 6, 126, 132, 139–143
  1956: 144–157
  1960: 1–2, 3, 220–250, 307
  1962: 2
  1964: 2, 307
  1968: 2, 306, 307

Canada, 212

Captive Nations Resolution, 189, 190, 191

Caracas, 166–187

Caracas *Tribuna Popular*, 167, 168, 170

Cardozo, Benjamin N., 22

Cargill, 287

Carnegie Endowment for International Peace, 46, 50, 55, 56 n., 61, 62

Case, Clifford P., 140

Castro, Fidel, 209–213, 237, 253

Catholic vote, 3, 232–234, 243–244

Ceausescu, Nicolae, 304

Celler, Emanuel, 58

Central Intelligence Agency, 50, 134, 210, 237

"Challenge of 1952, The," 77

Chambers, Whittaker, 1, 43–63, 69

Chambers, Mrs. Whittaker, 57

Chapin School, 292

"Chapman, Mr.," 115–116

Chase Manhattan, 283

Checkers (dog), 123, 257

"Checkers speech," 7, 111–125, 276; *see also* "Nixon fund"

Chiang Kai-shek, Madame, 291

Chicago *Daily News*, 84

Chicken Luncheon, 135–136

Childs, Marquis, 295

China, 133, 193, 237, 255, 309–313

Chotiner, Murray M., 36, 38, 66, 67, 69, 71, 74, 75, 84–86, 89, 92, 94, 99, 101, 104, 106, 109, 113–117, 120–122, 129, 142, 260

Christian Socialist party, Venezuela, 182

Christopher, George, 260

Cincinnati *Enquirer*, 234

Citizens for Eisenhower, 104, 126

Citra-Frost Company, 25, 26

Civil Rights Act, 1957, 213

Civil Service Commission, 142

Clay, Lucius D., 104, 105

Clement, Frank G., 155

Cleveland, Grover, 162

Cleveland *Plain Dealer*, 234

Collins, Thomas E. Jr., 185

Columbia Broadcasting System, 111, 137, 241

Columbia Law Review, 291

Commission on Government Contracts, 208, 213

Communism, issue of, 7, 35, 39, 41 n., 43, 44–63, 68, 70–72, 78, 88, 102–103, 105, 120, 126–143, 212, 228, 256, 265–266, 311, 315, 316

"Compact of Fifth Avenue," 221–227

Conant, James, 133

Congo, 255, 256

Congress of Industrial Organizations, 107
  Political Action Committee, 39, 40, 88, 89

Congressional Quarterly, 42

Considine, Robert, 264

Coolidge, Calvin, 207
Costello, William, 257
Coudert Brothers, 22
Council on Foreign Relations, 265
Couve de Murville, Maurice, 303
Cox, Lewis, 15
Creel, George, 71
Cronin, John F., 44
Crosley, George, 52, 55
Crossman, R. H. S., 5
Crusade for Political Purity, 61, 62, 91, 98, 104
Cuba, 31, 209–213, 237, 253, 255, 265–266, 270, 276, 277, 312, 313
Cushing, Richard Cardinal, 244
Czechoslovakia, 198, 312

Daley, Richard, 245
Dannenhauer, Jane, 275
Davies, Lawrence E., 73
Davis, John W., 22
Davis, Polk, Wardwell, Gardiner and Reid, 22
Dawes, Charles G., 207
Day, Roy O., 37, 38, 65
"Declaration of Conscience," 130
Defense Department, 213
De Gaulle, 295, 313–314
Delaware State College, 214
Democratic National Committee, 102, 231 n., 242
Democratic National Conventions, 88, 155, 242
Democrats for Nixon for United States Senator, 70
Denver Post, 124, 134
Desperate Hours, The (play), 288–291
Detroit News, 277
Dewey, Thomas E., 1, 22, 46, 50, 77, 80, 81, 86, 109, 113, 115–116, 122, 138, 141, 154
Dewey, Ballantine, Bushby, Palmer, and Wood, 22
Dexter, Walter F., 21, 37
Dillon, C. Douglas, 50
Dixon-Yates issue, 139
Dodson, Leonidas, 19
Dollard, Charles, 55
Donovan, Richard, 97

Donovan, Robert J., 285
Donovan, Leisure, Newton and Lombard, 22
Dorn, Evelyn, 24
Dorr, Goldthwaite, 289, 290
Douglas, Helen Gahagan, 63, 64–75
Downey, Sheridan, 64, 67, 68
Drown, Helene, 31, 111
Drown, Jack, 31
Drummond, Roscoe, 295
Duke, James Buchanan, 20–21
Duke Bar Association, 23
Duke University, 21, 26, 127
Dulles, Allen, 50, 51, 237
Dulles, John Foster, 22, 46, 50, 51, 56, 60–62, 133, 137, 139, 145, 162–164, 166, 169, 180, 181, 199, 208
Dumbarton Oaks Conference, 1944, 46
"Dump Nixon" Movement, 144–157

East Whittier, California, 11 n., 17
East Whittier Friends Meeting House, 17
Edson, Peter, 96–97, 99
Ehrlichmann, John, 275
Eightieth Congress, 41, 46
Eisenhower, David, 292
Eisenhower, Dwight D., 2–3, 19, 59–62, 127, 134–140, 144, 147–156, 166, 167 n., 169, 180, 181, 184, 187, 188, 194, 203, 205, 207, 215, 217, 251, 261, 263, 291, 312
in campaign of 1952, 76–126
in campaign of 1956, 220–250
illnesses, 1955–57, 158–164
Eisenhower, Mrs. Dwight, 87, 115, 120, 241, 251
Eisenhower, Milton, 138, 158, 191, 194, 198, 200
Eisenhower-Strauss Plan, 311
Ellsworth, Robert, 303
Emerson, Thomas I., 31
"End Poverty in California" program, 35
Estrada, Pedro, 169
Eversharp-Schick, 287
Executives' Club of Chicago, 254
Export-Import Bank, 209

Fair Campaign Practices Committee, 233, 238 n.
"Fair Deal," 91
Fair Employment Practices Act, 213
"Fair Play Amendment," 83
Fala (dog), 113
Fanfani, Amintore, 304
Federal Bureau of Investigation, 23, 45
Federal Communications Commission, 293
Felknor, Bruce L., 238 n.
Ferman, Irving, 214
Finch, Robert H., 161, 220 n., 233 n., 243, 276, 298
Finch College, 292
Fine, John S., 87
Finletter, Thomas K., 22
Fisher, Joel M., 287
Flemming, Arthur S., 163
Folger, J. Clifford, 220
Foreign Affairs, 305
Fortas, Abe, 290
Francis Amendment, 265
Frankfurter, Felix, 48
Franklins, The, 18
Freedom Forces (Cuba), 253
Freedoms Foundation, 215
Fulbright, J. William, 7
Fullerton High School, 11

Gainey, Daniel C., 298
Gallup Polls, 4, 89, 155, 220, 229, 234, 243, 306
Garment, Leonard, 290
Gaunt, Loie, 275
General Cigar, 287
General Precision Equipment Corporation, 287
General Services Administration, 213
Geneva Conference, 1955, 158, 199, 205
Germany, 199, 200, 201, 202, 205
Gibbons, Boyd, 37
Gibson, Dunn and Crutcher, 105
Gizenga, 255
Goddard, Henry W., 58
Goldwater, Barry, 226, 261, 271, 293, 296–299, 306
"Great Crusade," 83, 87

Greece, 195
Greek-Turkish Aid Bill (Truman Doctrine), 68, 69
Green Island, 32
Greenberg, Carl, 279
Greenfield, Meg, 4
Gromyko, Andrei, 200, 266
Guantánamo, Cuba, 253
Guylay, L. Richard, 161

Hagerty, James C., 100, 101, 115, 136, 147–149, 152, 157, 159, 160, 163
Hague, Gabriel, 221
Haldeman, Robert, 276
Hall, Leonard W., 127–128, 136, 146, 148–154, 156, 161, 162, 220, 233 n., 239–241, 243, 261
Halleck, Charles E., 141, 149
Hamilton, Alexander, 283, 315
Harding, Warren G., 11
Harriman, Averell, 193
Harris, John, 31
Harsco Corporation, 291
Harvard Club of California Prize, 13
Healey, Dorothy R., 266
Heard, Alexander, 258
Hearst, William Randolph, Jr., 291
Hébert, F. Edward, 47, 48
Herter, Christian A., 50, 148–155, 180, 199
Herter Committee, 42
Hess, Stephen, 221
Hill, James, 288, 289, 290
Hillings, Pat, 113, 115, 116, 154–155
Hillman, Sidney, 39
Hiss, Alger, 1, 6, 7, 43–64, 69, 78, 119, 131, 138, 139, 265, 293–294
Hiss, Mrs. Alger, 49
Hitler-Stalin pact, 312
Hoffman, Paul G., 81, 86, 105, 112, 138
Holmes, Oliver Wendell, 46
Holton, A. Linwood, Jr., 299, 300
"Honest Deal," 91
Hoover, Herbert C., 58, 65, 76, 107, 145, 291
Hoover, J. Edgar, 23

Horack, H. Claude, 23
Hornblower & Weeks, 287
"Hound's tooth," 108
House Committee on Un-American Activities, 6, 42-49, 58, 69
House of Morgan, 283
Hughes, Charles Evans, 22
Hughes, James D., 173, 179, 185, 186
Hughes Tool Co., 272, 273, 274
Humphreys, Robert, 100, 110, 114, 115
Hungary, 199

"I Love Lucy," 111
Illinois State Senate, 293
In the Court of Public Opinion (Hiss), 53
International Debutante Ball, 292
International Latex Corporation, 214
Investors Diversified Services, 287, 291
Iran, 197
Iraq, 198
Irving Trust Co., 287
Israeli-Arab war of June, 1967, 311
"Issues and Answers," 303
Italy, 195

Japan, 313
Jefferson, Thomas, 315
Jessup, Philip, 78
Jiménez, Pérez, 166, 168, 169, 174, 179, 182, 184, 186
John Birch Society, 5, 256, 265
Johnson, Hiram, 259
Johnson, Lyndon B., 5, 7, 187, 217 n., 230 n., 245, 248-251, 296, 299, 301, 302, 310, 315
Johnson, Mrs. Lyndon, 251, 302
Johnston, Victor, 146
Jones, Doris, 275
Jorgensen, Frank E., 36, 37, 65
Justice Department, 45, 237

KABC, Los Angeles, 293
Katcher, Leo, 97
Kaufman, Samuel H., 58

Kaye, Peter, 266
Kelley, Stanley, Jr., 230
Kendall, Donald M., 285
Kennedy, John F., 5, 42, 206, 229-237, 242, 244-248, 252-255, 262, 268, 269, 273, 276, 295, 296, 312
Kennedy, Robert, 8, 234, 237, 296, 310
Kersten, Charles J., 50
Khrushchev, Nikita, 188-206, 228, 235, 253, 255, 266, 272
Khrushchev, Mrs. Nikita, 202
Kiesinger, Kurt Georg, 303
Kihss, Peter, 284
King, Martin Luther, Sr., 238
King, Martin Luther, Jr., 237-238, 272
King, Mrs. Martin Luther, Jr., 237
"Kitchen Debate," 191, 235
Klein, Herbert G., 229, 236, 276, 278
Knebel, Fletcher, 292
Knight, Goodwin J., 151, 155, 161, 259, 260
Knight, John S., 84
Knowland, William F., 19, 38, 64, 74, 81-85, 87, 89, 96, 105, 123, 136, 154, 259, 260
Knowland, Mrs. William, 84-85
Kohler, Foy D., 191
Korean War, 70, 73, 77, 98, 130, 222, 223, 313
Kozlov, Frol R., 191, 193
Kozlov, Mrs. Frol, 202
Krehbiel, John, 267
Krock, Arthur, 295
Kroll, Jack, 88-89
Kuchel, Thomas H., 259, 260
Kuest, Frank, 123
Kuznetsov, Vaily V., 191

La Habra, California, 25
Laird, Melvin, 221
Lang, Walter, 252
Laos, 255
Larrazabal, Wolfgang, 166, 183, 184, 185-186
Lasky, Victor, 275
Latty, E. R., 21
Lawrence, William, 2, 303
Lazarus, Fred, Jr., 213

Leathers, Harlan, 22
Lebanon, 277, 312
Lewis, Ted, 241 n.
Life, 288–290
Lincoln, Abraham, 3, 19, 113, 228, 229
Links Club, 291
Lippmann, Walter, 124
Lodge, Henry Cabot, 84, 152, 228, 230 n., 253, 288
Logue, Robert, 12
London *Spectator*, 258
Look, 246, 292
Look Ahead, Neighbor Special, 100, 105
Lord, Day and Lord, 22
Los Angeles *Daily News*, 67, 97, 112
Los Angeles *Mirror*, 97
Los Angeles *Times*, 261, 279, 281, 285
Los Angeles Times-Mirror Syndicate, 254
Louis Harris and Associates, 269–271
Luce, Clare Boothe, 87

McCarthy, Eugene, 8, 310
McCarthy, Joseph, 6, 69, 126–143, 190
McClellen, John L., 133
McDonald, David, 217, 218
McDowell, John, 48, 54, 55
McElroy, Neil, 180
McKay, Douglas, 104
McKeesport, Pennsylvania, debate, 42
McKeldin, Ted, 151
MacKenzie, John P., 289
Macmillan, Harold, 303
McVey, Betty, 275
McWhorter, Charles, 297
Manescu, Corneliu, 304
Marcantonio, Vito, 68, 72, 73, 74 n.
Marín, Luis Muñoz, 185, 212
Market Opinion Research, 277 n.
Marshall Plan, 42
Martin, Joseph W., Jr., 37, 60
Matsu, 237, 277
Matsui of Japan, 287
Mazo, Earl, 247 n., 248–249
Meany, George, 213

Medina, Harold, Jr., 289
"Meet the Press," 57, 97, 210, 232, 272
Mendoza, Eugenio, 185
Merriam, Robert, 221
Mikoyan, Anastas I., 191, 192, 194, 195, 204, 205
Mikoyan, Mrs. Anastas, 202
Metropolitan Club, New York, 291
Metropolitan Life Insurance, 252
Middle East, 256, 311
Milhous, Elmira, 10, 15–16, 23
Millbank, Tweed, Hope and Webb, 22
Mitchell, James, 215, 218
Mitchell, John, 287
Mitchell, Stephen, 100, 104, 107
Molotov, Vyacheslav, 197
Montgomery *Advertiser*, 124
Morgan, Gerald D., 161
Moro, Aldo, 303
Morocco, King of, 208
Moscow, Alvin, 257
Mosk, Stanley, 264
Mudge, Stern, Baldwin & Todd, 283–287
Mundt, Karl E., 47, 100
Mundt-Nixon Communist Registration Bill, 140 n.
Mutual Broadcasting System, 111
Mutual of New York, 287, 291
Mutual Security Agency, 133

Nabrit, James, Jr., 213
Naked Society, The (Packard), 289
National Association for the Advancement of Colored People, 238
National Broadcasting Company, 111, 115, 206, 229
National Bulk Carriers, 287
National Conference of Christians and Jews, 215
National Governors' Conference, 1964, 298
National Newspaper Publishers Association, 215
National Security Council, 161, 162, 163, 165, 207–208
National Young Republican Convention, Boston, 1951, 77

Naval Air Transport (SCAT), 32
Navasky, Vitor S., 4
Nelson, Rockwood, 37
New Caledonia, 32
New Deal, 20, 32, 41, 58
New Hampshire primary, 1956, 146, 147; 1968, 2, 306–307
"New Nixon, The," 124
New Republic, 41 n., 257, 302
New York Court of Appeals, 289
New York *Daily News,* 241 n.
New York *Herald Tribune,* 50, 106, 115, 124, 246–247, 248, 305
New York *Journal-American,* 124
New York *Post,* 97, 99, 100
New York Times, 73, 209–210, 217, 229, 242, 246, 257, 284, 289, 303
Newhouse Newspapers, 4
Newsome, Roy, 12
Newspaper Enterprise Association, 96–97
Newsweek, 279
Nicolae, Nicolae, 304
Nidecker, John, 275
Nixon, Arthur, 15, 17
Nixon, Donald, 11, 13, 15, 16, 18
Nixon, Edward, 15, 16
Nixon, Francis A. (Frank), 9, 11, 13–14, 15, 16, 37, 98, 127
Nixon, Mrs. Francis, 10, 11, 13, 14, 15, 16, 17, 23, 37, 98, 109
Nixon, Harold, 9, 15, 16, 17
Nixon, James, 13–14
Nixon, Julie, 88, 184, 252, 262, 291–292
Nixon, Patricia (Tricia), 38, 88, 119, 184, 252, 262, 291–292
Nixon, Richard Milhous
    ancestry of, 13–15
    Asia trip, 1967, 305–306
    and Castro, Fidel, 209–213, 253
    character and personality, 2, 5, 6
    Checkers speech, 111–125
    Congressional campaign of 1948, 34–43
    Congressional record, 42, 213
    and Douglas, Helen Gahagan, 64–75
    at Duke University, 2, 21–23, 26

"Dump Nixon" movement, 144–157
    early life of, 9–13, 15–18
    visits Eisenhower in Europe, 1952, 79
    as Eisenhower's running mate
        1952 campaign, 76–126
        1956 campaign, 220–250
    and Eisenhower's illnesses, 158–164, 257
    European trip, 1967, 303
    in gubernatorial campaign, 1962, 264–283
    and Hiss, Alger, 44–63, 257
    income of, 292
    "Kitchen Debate," 191, 235, 257
    and Khrushchev, Nikita, 188–206
    Latin American trip, 1958, 165–187, 257
    as lawyer
        in Whittier, 24–26, 31
        in New York, 283–292
    and McCarthy, Joseph, 126–143
    marriage to Pat Ryan, 30
    Moscow trip, 1959, 188–206
    Moscow trip, 1967, 303
    in Navy, 32–33, 37
    and New York Bar admission, 6, 285–287
    and "Nixon fund," 91–125, 257
    in Office of Price Administration, 31–32
    in Presidential campaign of 1960, 220–250, 257
    public style of, 7
    in senatorial campaign, 1950, 64–75
    and *Six Crises,* 257–258
    at Whittier College, 18–20
Nixon, Mrs. Richard (Pat), 3, 7, 34, 38, 85, 97, 102, 103, 106, 108, 111, 114, 115, 118–120, 123, 125, 127, 159, 165, 170–187, 191, 192, 194, 195, 202, 241, 251, 262
    childhood and early life, 27–31
    marriage, 30
Nixon for President committee, 2
"Nixon fund," 1, 7, 19, 22–23, 83 n., 90, 91–110, 131
Nixon, Mudge, Rose, Guthrie, Alexander & Mitchell, 287

Nixon's Hamburger Stand, 33
North American Newspaper Alliance, 300
North Atlantic Treaty Organization, 164, 196, 202, 304, 312–313

Oakland *Tribune*, 65, 259
O'Brien, Robert W., 121
Oceanside *Blade Tribune*, 272
Of Thee I Sing, 219
O'Neill, Thomas, 235
"Operation Poor Richard," 180
Order of Coif, 21
"Order of the Hound's Tooth, The," 123
Oregon primary, 1956, 146
Orthagonians, The, 18, 20
Otten, Alan, 254

Palmer, Kyle, 263
Parr, Jack, 295
Paul VI, Pope, 295, 304
Peale, Norman Vincent, 232
Pearl Harbor, 31
Pearson, Drew, 129
Peachman, Joseph, 215
Peirce, Neil R., 246
People's President, The (Peirce), 246
People's World, 275 n.
Pepper, Claude, 71
Pepsi Co., 285, 288
Percy, Charles, 221, 226, 303
Perdue, William, 22
Peress, Irving, 135
Perkins, Roswell, 221
Perry, Herman L., 37, 65
Persons, Wilton B. (Jerry), 114, 132, 134, 146, 147, 160, 161
Pfleiderer, Stephen D., 244
Phillips, John, 37
"Pink sheets," 74
Poland, 197, 199, 205
Political Science Quarterly, 258
Porter, Charles O., 106–107
Potsdam agreement, 200
Powell, Adam Clayton, 42, 234
Powers, Gary, 206
Pravda, 196
Prendergast, William, 221
Price, Raymond, 305, 306

Price, Waterhouse and Co., 105
"Programs for a Greater California," 268
Progressive Party, 67
Prudential Insurance Co., 252
Prussion, Karl, 271, 272
Public opinion polls, *see* Belden Associates, Gallup Polls, Louis Harris and Associates, Market Opinion Research, Roper surveys, *and* University of Michigan, Survey Research Center
Puerto Rico, 212
"Pumpkin Papers," 57

Quakers and Quakerism, 13, 14, 15, 17, 24, 31, 33, 49
Quemoy, 193, 237, 277

Rankin, John, 42, 47
Raskin, A. H., 217
Rayburn, Sam, 6, 141, 250
Reagan, Ronald, 303, 307, 308
Recess Club, 291
Rees, David, 258
Reporter, 97, 274
Republican Citizens League of Illinois, 253
Republican Finance Committee, 95
Republican National Committee, 82, 88, 102, 109, 117, 119–123, 158, 244
Republican National Convention, 1952, 59–60, 77, 96, 102
Republican Party, in California, 34, 36–43, 64–75, 264–282
in the South, 300
Republican Platform Committee, 221, 226
Republican Senate Campaign Committee, 146
Republicans for Eisenhower, 81
Reston, James, 219, 263, 295
Reuther, Walter, 213, 236
Rexall Drug, 252
Rhodes, James, 279
Richard M. Nixon Chair of Public Affairs, 19
Robinson, Claude, 236
Robinson, O. Preston, 273
Robinson, William, 115

Rockefeller, Nelson, 158, 220–221, 226, 227, 271, 279, 291, 296, 303, 307, 308
Rodham, Wade, 173, 176, 177
Rogers, Ted, 111, 115, 120
Rogers, Will, Jr., 69, 74
Rogers, William P., 50, 98, 99, 109, 111, 113, 132, 134, 136, 138, 152, 159–161, 163, 164
Rogers, Mrs. William, 160
Romney, George, 8, 271, 277 n., 279, 303, 306, 307, 314
Roosevelt, Eleanor, 215
Roosevelt, Franklin D., 35, 46, 113, 126, 131, 138, 207
Roosevelt, James, 71, 75
Root, Clark, Buckner and Ballantine, 22
Roper surveys, 243, 307
Rovere, Richard, 3–4
Rubottom, Roy R., Jr., 181
Rumania, 312
Russia, 46, 57, 256, 309–313
Ruwe, Nick, 275

St. John, Adela Rogers, 256
St. Louis Globe-Democrat, 300
Salinger, Pierre, 243
Salt Lake City Deseret News & Telegram, 273
San Diego Union, 266, 276, 293
San Francisco Chronicle, 86
San Marcos University, 209
Sanchez, Fina and Manolo, 291
Santa Fe Railroad, 10
Santa Fe Springs, California, 11 n.
Saragat, Giuseppe, 303
Saturday Evening Post, 295
Schroeder, Gerhard, 303
Scott, Hugh, 261
Scranton, William, 279, 298
Seaton, Fred A., 101, 104, 241
Shell, Joseph, 264, 265
Sherwood, John, 173, 176, 177
Shockney, Henrietta, 9, 10
Shroyer, Tom, 79
Shultz, George, 215
Sinclair, Upton, 35
Six Crises (Nixon), 257–258
Small Town Girl (film), 28
Smathers, George A., 71
Smith, Dana C., 91–97, 106, 109, 112, 123

Smith, Grant, 14
Smith, Howard K., 293–294
Smith, Margaret Chase, 87, 130, 151
Smith, Paul S., 19, 113
Smith College, 292
Snejdarek, Antonin, 304
Snyder, Howard McC., 241
Society of Friends, see Quakers
Sorensen, Theodore, 233, 234, 243
Sparkman, John, 88, 100 n., 113
Sparks, Edward J., 167, 181
Square Shooters, The, 18
Stassen, Harold E., 4, 65, 79, 83, 84, 108, 122, 128, 133, 138, 141, 144, 145, 147–157, 307
State Department, 128, 131, 180, 181, 184, 210, 213
Stein, Herbert, 215
Stevens, Robert, 135, 136
Stevenson, Adlai E., 5, 7, 60–63, 78, 88, 91–92, 98, 100, 104, 112, 119, 125, 127, 128, 131, 136, 137, 143, 297
"Stevenson Fund," 100, 112, 119, 125
Stimson, Henry L., 289
Stone & Webster Engineering, 287
Strauss, Joseph, 303
Stripling, Robert, 47, 48
Studebaker-Worthington, 287
Student exchange program, 209
Subversive Activities Control Act of 1951, 266
Sullivan and Cromwell, 22
Summerfield, Arthur, 100, 102, 105, 110, 114, 115, 120–122, 215
Supreme Court, 22, 217, 272, 288–290
Symington, Stuart, 133

Taft, Robert A., 60, 76, 79–84, 86, 96, 104, 147
Taft-Hartley Labor Law, 42, 70, 79, 217
Taylor, Robert, 175
Teapot Dome Scandal, 11
Temple Beth Israel Men's Club, 109
Texas Board of Canvassers, 245–246

Thailand, 313
Thomas, J. Parnell, 55
Thompson, Lewellyn, Jr., 191, 192, 203
Thomson, George, 303
Thornton, Dan, 151
Tillman, "Pitchfork Ben," 283
Time, 2, 44, 293
Time, Inc. v Hill, 288–291
Tipton, Harold, 73
"Tractors for Cubans," 253
Treadwell, William M., 287
Trinity College, 20–21
Truman, Harry S., 6, 7, 46, 47, 58, 63, 68, 69, 71, 76, 77, 88, 101, 135, 138, 140, 207
Truman Doctrine, 68, 69
Trysting Place, The (play), 18
Tshombe, Moise, 255
Tupolev, Andrei N., 193
Turkey, 68, 69, 195
"Twelve Goals for Californians," 265
Twining, Nathan, 180
Tydings, Millard, 131
Tydings Committee, 138

Un-American Activities Committee, see House Committee on Un-American Activities
Unger, Sherman, 298
United Nations, 46, 228, 255, 256
United Press, 99, 272
United Republican Finance Committee of Los Angeles County, 94
United Steelworkers of America, 217
University of Michigan, Survey Research Center, 244
University of Oregon, 107
Upton, Albert, 17, 19, 26, 113

Variety, 124
Venezuela, see Caracas, Venezuela
Ventuni, Oscar Garcia, 173 ff.
Vershinin, Konstantin A., 196, 197
Veterans of Foreign Wars, 293
Vietnam, 200, 201, 265–266, 301–302, 305, 306, 309–314

Volunteers for Eisenhower, 92
Voorhis, Jerry, 34–42

Wadmond, Lowell C., 286
Waldron, Agnes, 276
Wall Street Journal, 254
Wallace, Henry, 40, 67, 68, 146
Wallis, W. Allen, 215, 216
Walters, Vernon, 171, 173, 177
Warren, Earl, 36, 66, 74, 75, 79, 81–84, 89, 96, 98, 259
Washington, George, 283
Washington Post, 8, 289
Washington Star, 159, 261, 302
Waugh, Samuel C., 176
Weaver, Warren, Jr., 303
Welch, Robert, 256, 265
Wheeling, West Virginia, 121–123, 128, 129
White, Harry Dexter, 54, 55
White, Theodore H., 235, 239
Whitener, Basil, 21–22
Whittier, California, 14, 24, 34, 41, 89, 98
Whittier Alumni Association, 26
Whittier Chamber of Commerce, 24
Whittier College, 17, 18, 19, 20, 26, 89, 121 n., 127
Whittier High School, 11
Wicker, Tom, 242, 246, 257
Willkie, Wendell, 34
Wilson, Glen, 102
Wilson, Harold, 303
Wilson, Richard, 246
Wilson, Woodrow, 71, 162
Win With Nixon Special, 276
Wingert and Bewley, 24
Witcover, Jules, 4, 296
Woods, Rose Mary, 98, 121–122, 140, 275, 300
Wray, Merton G., 17, 18
Wroble, Lester, 32–33

Yalta Conference, 46
Yorba Linda, California, 9, 10, 13, 14, 292
Young Democrats, 102
Young Republicans, 77, 110, 297

Zanuck, Darryl, 120
Zwicker, Ralph W., 135

E 7
651. MARY'S COLLEGE OF MARYLAND LIBRARY
ST. MARY'S CITY, MARYLAND